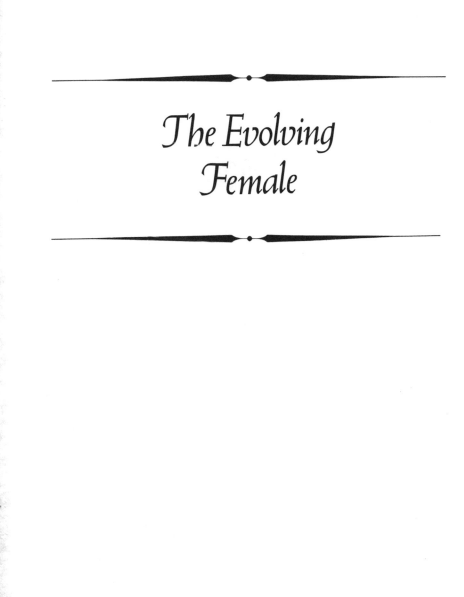

The Evolving Female

The Evolving Female

Women in Psychosocial Context

Carol Landau Heckerman, Ph.D.

Brown University
Providence, Rhode Island

 **HUMAN SCIENCES PRESS**

72 Fifth Avenue   3 Henrietta Street
NEW YORK, NY 10011 ● LONDON, WC2E 8LU

Printed in the United States of America
9 987654321

Library of Congress Cataloging in Publication Data

Main entry under title:

The Evolving female.

   Bibliography: p.
   Includes index.
   1. Women—Psychology—Addresses, essays, lectures.
   2. Women's rights—United States—Addresses, essays,
lectures.   3. Mental health—United States—Addresses,
essays, lectures.   4. Psychoanalysis—United States—
Addresses, essays, lectures.   5. Psychotherapy—United
States—Addresses, essays lectures.   6. Women—
Physiology—Addresses, essays, lectures.   I. Heckerman,
Carol Landau. [DNLM: 1. Women—Essays.
Psychotherapy—Essays.   3. Psychology, Social—Essays.
WM420.3 E93]
HQ1206.E96   301.41'2   LC 79–4240
ISBN 0–87705–392–8
      0–87705–411–8 pbk

Preface

$\mathcal{T}$his book is based on the 1977 Fall Grand Rounds at Butler Hospital, a Brown University-affiliated psychiatric hospital. Each year, the hospital sponsors lecture series in order to provide new outlooks on current mental health problems.

In organizing the lecture series and this book, I hoped to provide a wide range of perspectives on issues related to women and psychotherapy. I invited not only mental health professionals, but also authors from the disciplines of epidemiology, journalism, literary criticism, and education to contribute their theoretical understanding and data in this area. Several of the authors did not present papers at the lecture series, but agreed to write chapters for this book.

Many people donated their time and talent in preparing the lecture series and the book. The administration of Butler Hospital, Frank Delmonico and Robert Westlake, urged me to present the lecture series. The Fall Grand Rounds Committee, which included Carol Carroll, Mary

Hostetler, Sheila Josephson, Jeanne Moore, and Wilma Rosen, worked creatively to organize the lecture series. Several colleagues, Dorothy Bianco, Betty Fielder, Edward Fink, Jane Kuppe, Sharlene Wolchik, and Paul Zazow, were generous with their encouragement and suggestions. I am particularly grateful for the energetic assistance of my friend and colleague Jeanne Parr Lemkau, who wrote one of the chapters in the book and was also actively involved in every step of its preparation. I also thank my husband, David Heckerman, who contributed his editorial advice, his perspective, and his emotional support.

Carol Landau Heckerman

Contributors

DEBORAH BELLE, ED. D. is Director of the Stress and Families Project and Research Associate and Lecturer at the Harvard Graduate School of Education.

TAMARA E. BELOVITCH is a student at the University of Rhode Island.

GARY R. BOND, PH.D. is Assistant Professor in the Department of Psychiatry at Northwestern University Medical School.

BONNIE DONADY is Coordinator of the Wesleyan Math Clinic.

EILEEN D. GAMBRILL, PH D. is Associate Professor in the School of Social Welfare at the University of California at Berkeley.

STANLEY KOGELMAN has his Ph.D. in mathematics and M. S. W. in clinical social work. He is co-founder

7

and director of "Mind Over Math," a consulting service in Bayside, New York.

JEANNE PARR LEMKAU, PH.D. is Assistant Professor of Psychology at Auburn University.

MORTON A. LIEBERMAN, PHD. is Professor and Chairman of the Committee on Human Development in the Departments of Behavioral Sciences and Psychiatry at the University of Chicago.

SOPHIE FREUD LOEWENSTEIN, PH.D. is Professor of Social Work and Chairperson of the Human Behavior Sequence at Simmons College School of Social Work.

CHERYL A. RICHEY, D.S.W. is Assistant Professor in the School of Social Work at the University of Washington at Seattle.

LEON SALZMAN, M. D. is Professor of Clinical Psychiatry at Georgetown University Medical School.

WILLIAM A. SHUEY, III is a teacher and writer and lives in Providence, Rhode Island.

SHEILA TOBIAS is an educator and was Associate Provost of Wesleyan University from 1970–78. She is presently a partner in "Overcoming Math Anxiety," in Washington, D.C.

MYRNA M. WEISSMAN, PH.D. is Associate Professor of Psychiatry and Epidemiology at the Yale University School of Medicine, and Director of the Depression Research Unit at the Connecticut Mental Health Center.

Contents

9

I

Introduction

An Historical View
of Psychotherapy
and Women's Rights

Psychotherapy and women's rights. At first glance they may seem unrelated—a psychological process and a political issue. Yet in this introduction I examine the relationship between the two, the impact that psychotherapy as an institution has had on women's rights, and vice versa. The relationship has been a stormy one—beginning with Freud and continuing to the present.

PSYCHOANALYSIS VERSUS WOMEN'S RIGHTS: THE BEGINNING

Women's rights and psychotherapy have been tied together from the beginning. Freud (1925) himself was moved to comment, "I cannot evade the notion (though I hesitate to give it expression) that for women the level of what is ethically normal is different from what it is in men. Their superego is never so inexorable, so impersonal, so independent of its emotional origins as we require it to be in men. . . . We must not allow ourselves to be deflected from such conclusions by the denials of the feminists who are anxious to force us to regard the two sexes as completely equal in position and worth" (p. 257). All psychotherapies—from psychoanalysis to behavior therapy—are based on theories of human development and psychopathology that are the basis for the therapeutic techniques applied in psychotherapy. The psychological theories of development underlying psychotherapeutic practice also impact more directly on the culture. This can be seen clearly in the case of Freud's psychoanalytic theory, which has had a major impact on Western civilization. Thus, not only are women in psychotherapy affected by psychoanalytic theory, but all women in American society are affected by the influence of psychoanalytic theory on education and on cultural values. There have been numerous discussions of Freud's prejudicial view of women; several books containing his early papers and critiques of these papers have also been published (Miller, 1973; Strouse, 1974). The specific problems for women, however, can be briefly outlined.

Psychoanalytic theory of personality is intrapsychic in nature. One must look inward to find the causes of psychological problems. The premise is that psychological dysfunction is produced as a result of internal or intrapsychic conflict. The person's sexual and aggressive impulses are repressed due to anxiety, and this leads to the development of symptomatology. Although it is clear in psychoanalytic theory that parents are powerful determinants of personality development, the impact of the larger environment is neglected. Problems are seen as the result of individual psychopathology, and the environmental pressures on an individual that lead to stress are not emphasized. Thus, one issue that is important for women is the psychoanalytic view that psychopathology is a result of internal conflict. This issue has been debated for decades and poses particular problems for women (Weisstein, 1971).

The two most important areas in which psychoanalytic theory has hurt the cause of women's rights are the emphasis on biology and the generalization of a developmental theory based on little data. Freud's work with neurotic clients was the basis for his theory of development. With respect to the emphasis on biology, it should be noted that Freud's theory of development places heavy emphasis on biological needs and impulses during every developmental stage. Of most concern to women, of course, is the issue of penis envy. During the Oedipal stage, according to Freud, a male child becomes aware of his penis and becomes sexually aroused by his mother. Castration anxiety follows, manifested by the terror that his father will become angry and deprive him of his penis. Intense conflict follows; the boy's only option is to identify with his father, incorporating his father's psychological characteristics, which allows the resolution of the Oedipal conflict. Girls, on the other hand, become aware that they do not have a penis, which leads to inevitable horror and envy. The only possible resolution of this stage for them is ultimately to replace the penis with a child. Freud concluded that since the female did not experience the terrible fear of castration and the resulting internalization of paternal values and a strong superego, the girl's superego was doomed to be inferior to that of the male (Freud, 1925).

A second biological issue related to the concept of penis envy is that of masochism. Deutsch (1924) tied female biology to masochism when she wrote:

> The girl on the other hand has in addition to this (feelings of guilt around the Oedipus complex) a two-fold task to perform: (1) she has to renounce the masculinity attached to the clitoris; (2) in her transition from the "phallic" to the "vaginal" phase, she has to discover a new genital organal.... The man attains his final stage of development when he discovers the vagina in the world outside him and possesses himself of it sadistically. In this his guide is his own genital organ with which he is already familiar and which impels him to the act of possession. The woman has to discover this new sexual organ *in her own person,* a discovery which she makes through being masochistically subjugated by the penis, the latter thus becoming the guide to this fresh source of pleasure. (p. 405)

Somehow, in this illogical progression, masochism is closely related to sexual pleasure for all women. Similarly, the only healthy stage of development is to "give up" the "masculine clitoral orgasm" for the "feminine vaginal orgasm." All this just because the woman does not have a penis to begin with!

We can now see that three of the most problematic concepts that have been instilled in the culture through psychoanalytic theory are penis envy, masochism, and the importance of the vaginal orgasm. Interestingly, the debate over these issues began almost immediately within psychoanalytic circles. Two of the major debaters, Deutsch and Horney, were women. We have already examined some of Deutsch's writing and, in several critical articles, Horney attacked these concepts as early as 1926. Some extensive direct quotation from Horney is in order, because nonpsychoanalytic critics often neglect to mention that these debates have been going on for almost 50 years.

In some of his latest works Freud has drawn attention with increasing urgency to a certain one-sidedness in our analytical researches. I refer to the fact that until quite recently the minds of boys and men only were taken as objects of investigation. The reason for this is obvious. Psychoanalysis is the creation of a male genius, and almost all those who have developed his ideas have been men. It is only right and reasonable that they should evolve more easily a masculine psychology and understand more of the development of men than of women. (1926, p. 324)

In psychoanalytic literature—taking the views of Rado and Deutsch as representative in this connection—the problem has been tackled only from the viewpoint of regarding feminine masochism as one psychic consequence of anatomical sex differences. Psychoanalysis thus has lent its scientific tools to support the theory of a given kinship between masochism and female biology. The possibility of social conditioning has as yet not been considered from the psychoanalytical side. . . . There is no need to question the fact that women may seek and find masochistic satisfaction in masturbation, menstruation, intercourse, and childbirth. Beyond doubt this occurs. What remains for discussion is the genesis and frequency of occurrence. Both Deutsch and Rado, in dealing with the problem, completely ignore discussion of frequency, because they maintain that the psychologic-genetic factors are so forceful and ubiquitous that a consideration of frequency becomes superfluous. . . . When it is claimed, moreover, that the desire for masculinity is not only a dynamic factor of primary order in neurotic females, but in every human female, independent of individual or cultural conditions, one cannot but remark that there are no data to substantiate this claim. (1935, pp. 241–242)

It is clear that a vigorous argument occurred over the emphasis on biology, the faulty logic in Freud's developmental theory, and the lack of data supporting it. Why does the debate continue? Why must these issues be addressed and refuted over and over again? It seems that it was necessary to have an active political women's movement along with these published discussions in order, finally, to challenge strongly psychoanalytic theory. Indeed, psychoanalytic theory is a formidable opponent. There is no doubt that Freud's work was truly revolutionary—it brought the issues of sexuality and aggression into the forefront of cultural discussion. It is ironic, therefore, that the rights of women were restricted by a revolutionary scholar. Freud believed that the primary role for women was that of mother and that women were destined to be passive, masochistic, and morally inferior to men. Women who did not accept this role were considered psychopathological or masculine in their development.

THE DEBATE DIES: DEPRESSION AND THE WAR

As noted, the feminist movement and the struggle for women's rights within the psychoanalytic movement were quite active during the 1920s and 1930s. This paralleled the social and political activism occurring at the same time, when feminists were active, when women were demanding their rights. As Filene (1974) describes, however, during the Depression and World War II, the social energy of the country was absorbed in solving the economic crises at home and later in fighting a war. He writes:

The organized feminist movement went moribund soon after the first world war. Now its principles lay beneath the Crash apparently dead, apparently unmourned even by female public leaders. "Today there is no time for feminism," said Mrs. Chase Going Woodhouse, director of the Institute for Women's Professional Relations in 1940. "The problems (women) consider are not feministic but economic" (p. 158).

Women and men rose to the challenge and concentrated on economic redevelopment. Later during World War II women again served their country by occupying most of the traditionally male work roles. But in the 1950s the return to normalcy brought back the traditional patterns. Women were no longer needed to support the economy, and so America greeted the postwar baby boom with mother at home, father at work.

The 1950s was a general time of quiet acceptance of traditional values, and traditional sex roles were no exception. Men were to take care of their families by earning money, and women were to tend to the needs of their husbands and children. These sex roles had Freud's psychological seal of approval; as if that were not enough, Dr. Spock (1968) agreed. His best-selling book on child rearing emphasized the "appropriate" sex roles for boys and girls. During the same period (1940 to 1960), articles discussing biological and cultural effects on feminine psychology were published (Thompson, 1943; Zilboorg, 1944), but the zeal was missing from the debate.

THE WOMEN'S MOVEMENT TRIES AGAIN

The late 1950s and 1960s brought a time of intense and rapid social change, rebellion, and questioning of traditional values. Through television, the civil rights movement vividly brought the nation's attention to the discriminations suffered by a minority group.

1st factor

The civil rights movement was only the beginning of a large social movement for human rights. The women's movement is one aspect of the social changes of the 1960s, where almost all traditional values were challenged—professionalism, capitalism, racism. When the traditional standards of sexual behavior and marriage were criticized, so were traditional sex roles; thus the word "sexism" entered our vocabulary.

A second factor leading to the women's movement was the concept of self-help and self-interest. As the turbulent 1960s continued, the political unit of the coalition was replaced by the self-interest group. Each specific group had its own needs and interests, which only members of that group would support in a crisis. Outsiders were not to be trusted. Thus blacks, Chicanos, Native Americans and, finally, women all formed their own groups.

The need for a specific women's movement can be seen when we read about the experiences of women in the New Left movement who realized that their male colleagues were often the speakers and leaders while women did much of the difficult but invisible work. White men were fighting for the liberation of the Vietnamese or for the rights of black people, yet they were at times insensitive to women's rights. Many women of the New Left became disillusioned and bitter as they realized that they also suffered discrimination and needed their own self-interest group (Piercy, 1970).

When women organized as a political force, it was the natural extension of the human rights movement. Most writers point to the publication of Friedan's *The Feminine Mystique* (1963) as the document that spearheaded the women's movement. Even reading this book 15 years later, it remains an impressive document. Notably, much of Friedan's attention is given to psychoanalytic theory, the psychological theory of the status quo, and the oppressive force it had on women. Thus, by the late 1960s, when the women's movement gained momentum, there did indeed exist the combination of an active political group of women with the scholarly documentation of the logical fallacies and lack of support for orthodox psychoanalytic theories of development.

As the women's movement continued, even more attention was given to the institution of psychotherapy instead of to psychoanalytic theory and treatment in particular. Chesler's *Women and Madness* (1972) attacks psychotherapy in the strongest terms. Chesler rekindles the debate over whether psychopathology is a result of internal conflicts or of environmental pressures, and she draws attention to the thin line between psychopathology and "feminine" role behavior in our culture. She describes women as being oppressed by the mental health system. She writes that women who desire happiness and greater growth, perhaps at the expense of their marital or family relationships, are perceived as deviant. Chesler argues that these women's husbands, psychotherapists, and the economic system all collude in the oppression of women. Her book was a timely challenge to the mental health system, although many of the issues had been raised decades earlier.

Friedan and Chesler brought attention to the relationship between psychotherapy and women's rights, just as Horney had 40 years before, only now the time was right.

New books on the psychology of women were written, and the debate became heated once again. By the late 1960s, even leading male psychoanalysts were criticizing Freud's view of women (Marmor, 1968; Salzman, 1967), and the arguments continue into the 1970s (Bardwick, 1971; Miller, 1973; Strouse, 1974). In addition, by now Freud's heavy emphasis on instincts had been challenged seriously by ego psychologists who emphasized cognitive functions in the personality (Hartmann, 1958; White, 1966).

Nonetheless, the orthodox psychoanalysts do not give up easily. The psychoanalytic viewpoint continued to dominate psychiatric, psychological, and social work training programs in the 1960s. And the biased views of women persisted. We read even in recent books comments such as the following from a chapter by Meissner (1978) in a new book on marital therapy.

> Too often women become mothers who fundamentally deny and devalue their feminity, who are caught in the unfortunate torment of penis envy, who do not value their mothering and nurturing functions, and who tend to relate to their children either as narcissistically compensating or as intolerably burdensome reinforcers of their own sense of self hate and worthlessness. It will be of great interest to see what changes in the patterning of maternal responsiveness are wrought by the currently changing status of women in society. One would hope that meaningful changes could be achieved without severe psychic cost, but the evidence of the bitterness, competitiveness and hostility of the liberated woman does not seem optimistic. (p. 64)

In a recent journal supplement devoted to female psychology, Ritvo (1977) presents his views on the female adolescent.

> On the regressive side, the menarche tends to stir up old anal and castration conflicts. The girl just perceives and experiences the onset of menstruation as an excretory phenomenon on the model of the old familiar anal and urinary functions. Girls predisposed by earlier neurotic conflicts also perceive it as a damage or mutilation and link it to old concerns about genital injury and castration and dissatisfaction with the body image. The memories of puberty in the analysis of some women show that the experience of the menstrual flow, which, in contrast to the experience with urine and feces, cannot be controlled by voluntary sphincters, contributes to the character traits of helplessness and passivity. (p. 128)

Thus, penis envy is alive and well in 1979, and the emphasis on the restriction of a woman's role because of her biology persists in psychoanalytic articles, despite the fact that logical and theoretical refutations of these concepts have existed since the 1920s. More sophisticated psychoanalytic writers sidestep the criticisms of Freud's emphasis on biological urges and declare that feminist writers deny the existence of the unconscious—the "aspect of mental life (expressed in its own language) that is different from conscious thought processes" (Mitchell, 1974, p. 8). Barglow and Schaefer (1977) criticize feminists for taking an "adultomorphic view of Freud's theories" (p. 307) and write that feminists therefore miss the whole point. This is a substantive point. The issue of unconscious motivation is critical to an understanding of psychoanalytic theory. Erikson (1974) discusses this point in some detail; see his discussion of the feminine unconscious and his response to the feminist criticism of his work.

In fact, most feminist psychotherapists do not accept the notion that behavior is strongly influenced by unconscious motivation, and they challenge the belief that it should be the focus of psychotherapy. Similarly, many psychotherapists challenge the required regressive aspects of psychoanalysis. Perhaps adult psychotherapy clients should be treated from an adult-centered rather than an infantile perspective. It is possible that feminist psychotherapists are not ignorant of Freud's work, but merely do not accept his basic assumptions. Although some psychoanalysts have attempted to discuss unconscious motivation with new concepts that are not sexist (Mitchell, 1974), most feminist therapists accept the premises of humanistic and social learning theory and not those of psychoanalytic theory.

Humanistic psychologists have disagreed with Freud's emphasis on the infantile and regressive forces of human nature (Maslow, 1968). Behaviorists have pointed out that by focusing on unconscious motivation in psychotherapy, at least two problems arise (Eysenck, 1960; Skinner, 1963).

First, it is difficult if not impossible to measure and evaluate treatment. Second and perhaps more important is that unconscious motivation can be used to explain anything and, in fact, the way in which it has been used has restricted the rights of women.

By the 1970s, Freud and orthodox psychoanalysis had been challenged by the behaviorists, the humanists, and the ego analysts as well as by the feminists. Thus, contrary to the views of Chesler, not all psychotherapists are male psychoanalysts. As detailed in a later section, behavioral and humanistic views of women are more egalitarian. Feminist therapy, then, is only one of many antipsychoanalytic psychotherapies.

WHAT DO WOMEN NEED FROM PSYCHOTHERAPY?

We can see that orthodox psychoanalytic psychotherapy has been a formidable opponent for feminists, but what should new nonsexist psychotherapies provide?

On one level, it is simple. Women who enter psychotherapy want relief from their pain. Most people, men and women, go to psychotherapy for the same reasons. They are in conflict; they want to make changes in their lives; they are lonely; they want to grow. But, in the past, psychotherapists were not able to deal with these issues for women as well as they could for men. The Broverman studies suggested that therapists have had different concepts of mental health for female than for male clients (Broverman, Broverman, Clarkson, Rosenkrantz, & Vogel, 1970; Broverman, Vogel, Broverman, Clarkson, & Rosenkrantz, 1972). The psychologically healthy woman was seen as different from the psychologically healthy man *and* different from the psychologically healthy person. Although the results of these studies have often been misquoted, similar feelings have been reported by the American Psychological Association Task Force on Sex

Bias and Sex Role Stereotyping in Psychotherapeutic Practice (1975). The report states, "That psychologists expect women to be more passive and dependent than men while acknowledging that these traits are not ideal for mental health has been empirically demonstrated (Broverman et al.; 1970; Broverman et al., 1972; Fabrikant, 1974)." Most psychological theories of development have been male-centered, since they reflect the larger culture with its stereotypes. Yet the goal of psychotherapy should clearly not be only the relief of pain, but growth and greater choice for all clients.

Women need freedom of choice in the selection of psychotherapists. As late as 1970, most clinical psychologists and psychiatrists were men, and most clients were women (Gove & Tudor, 1973). Not only did the therapists lack a firsthand understanding of women's issues, but their training had often been male-centered. It should be noted that many female clients had requested male therapists in the past. We can also view this as a belief in the higher status of male professionals. Today, however, women are requesting female therapists and therapists without sexist views, and also therapists of different mental health disciplines.

Women need freedom from sexual exploitation. As Loewenstein describes in Chapter 1, psychotherapy can be a romantic situation, an intimate relationship behind closed doors with the woman client often depending on the male therapist for advice. As Chesler (1972) wrote, this situation can easily lead to a socially sanctioned "love affair" in which the woman can escape her marriage without having to confront the problems there. Similarly psychotherapy, because of its intense emotional nature, can lead to mutual attraction. Women clients are sexually exploited by approximately 6% of the therapists polled in a recent American Psychological Association study (Holroyd & Brodsky, 1977). Since this study is based on the self-report of the therapist, it is undoubtedly an underestimate. A more recent study (Butler & Zelen, 1977) also revealed that in the case of most therapists who engaged in sexual intercourse with their clients, they admitted that they were meeting their own needs and not the needs of the clients. So much for the "love cure."

Women need freedom from prolonged dependency on a therapist. The emotional dependency that can be fostered by a therapist over a long period of time is less blatant than sexual exploitation, but it is equally dangerous. The financial and emotional rewards for therapists with clients of the opposite sex who idolize him or her can be dangerously appealing. At times the therapist's needs can be confused with the client's needs, and a long-term dependent but nontherapeutic relationship can develop. As Loewenstein describes in Chapter 1, many women enter therapy because of an unhappy passionate relationship only to have the therapeutic relationship become as passionate, as dependent and, ultimately, as destructive.

Women need to be treated as intelligent human beings who are consulting a professional for his or her service. Thus the client, instead of being seen as a person who must develop a dependent relationship on the therapist (based on earlier conflicts with parents), should be treated as a person with a specific problem that requires assistance. A mutual specific therapeutic contract with specific goals should be established (American Psychological Association, 1975).

Women need therapists who resist the temptation to engage in "either-or" thinking. Women's problems may be the result of environmental and/or internal conflicts. One of the most useless debates is the view that psychological problems are only a result of the oppressive environment as opposed to the view that psychological problems are only a result of internal conflicts. These arguments appear too often in psychoanalytic and feminist articles. The disagreements may have polarized the opponents to unreasonable positions (Barglow & Schaefer, 1977; Chesler,

1972). Each individual woman has a personal history that exists in the context of our society. Personality theories and developmental theories of the past have tended to be male-oriented and have neglected women's issues. Each stage of development presents certain internal conflicts as well as certain problems with the external environment. The sensitive therapist must try to address not only the problems that are a result of environmental stresses, but also those that are a reflection of some internal conflicts or earlier family problems.

Finally, women not only need therapists who are non-sexist, but also therapists who have expertise in the area of women's issues. There is a difference between nonsexist and feminist therapists. Nonsexist therapists believe in equality between the sexes. Feminist therapists have non-sexist values and also know the literature on issues relevant to women's lives—abortion, birth control, rape, work, menopause, and so on. Feminist therapy should be available to those women who request it, but nonsexist therapy must be demanded.

REFERENCES

Bardwick, J. *Psychology of women: A study of biocultural conflicts.* New York: Harper & Row, 1971.

Barglow, P., & Schaefer, M. A new female psychology? Supplement—female psychology. *Journal of the American Psychoanalytic Association,* 1977, **24**, 305–350.

Broverman, I. K., Broverman, D. M., Clarkson, F. E., Rosenkrantz, P. S., & Vogel, S. R. Sex-role stereotypes and clinical judgments of mental health. *Journal of Consulting and Clinical Psychology,* 1970, **39**, 1–7.

Broverman, I. K., Vogel, S. R., Broverman, D. M., Clarkson, F. E., & Rosenkrantz, P. S. Sex role stereotypes: A current appraisal. *Journal of Social Issues,* 1972, **28**, 58–78.

Butler, S., & Zelen, S. L. Sexual intimacies between therapists and patients. *Psychotherapy: Theory, Research and Practice,* 1977, **14**, 139–145.

Chesler, P. *Women and madness.* New York: Doubleday, 1972.

Deutsch, H. The psychology of women in relation to the functions of reproduction. *International Journal of Psychoanalysis,* 1924, **6**, 405–418.

Erikson, E. Womanhood and the inner space. In *Identity, youth and crisis.* New York: W. W. Norton, 1968.

Erikson, E. Once more the inner space: Letter to a former student. In J. Strouse (Ed.), *Women and analysis: Dialogues on psychoanalytic views of feminity.* New York: Dell, 1974.

Eysenck, H. J. (Ed.) *Behavior therapy and the neuroses.* Oxford: Pergamon Press, 1960.

Fabrikant, B. The psychotherapist and the female patient. In V. Franks and V. Burtle (Eds.) *Women in therapy: New psychotherapies for a changing society.* New York: Brunner/Mazel, 1974.

Filene, P. G. *Him/her self: Sex roles in modern America.* New York: Harcourt Brace Jovanovich, 1974.

Freud, S. Some psychical consequences of the anatomical distinctions between the sexes. In J. Strachey (Ed.), *Collected papers.* London: Hogarth Press, 1950. (Originally published 1925.)

Freud, S. Female sexuality. In J. Strachey (Ed.), *The complete psychological works of Sigmund Freud.* Vol. 21. London: Hogarth Press, 1974. (Originally published 1931.)

Friedan, B. *The feminine mystique.* New York: W. W. Norton, 1963.

Gove, W. R., & Tudor, J. F. Adult sex roles and mental illness. *American Journal of Sociology,* 1973, **78**, 812–835.

Hartmann, H. *Ego psychology and the problem of adaptation.* New York: International University Press, 1958.

Holroyd, J. C., & Brodsky, A. M. Psychologists attitudes and practices regarding erotic and nonerotic physical contact with patients. *American Psychologist,* 1977, **32**, 843–849.

Horney, K. The flight from womanhood. *International Journal of Psychoanalysis,* 1926, **7**, 324–339.

Horney, K. The problem of feminine masochism. *The Psychoanalytic Review,* 1935, **22**(3), 241–257.

Marmor, J. Changing patterns of feminity: Psychoanalytic implications. In S. Rosenbaum and I. Alger (Eds.), *The marriage relationship.* New York: Basic Books, 1968.

Maslow, A. H. *Toward a psychology of being.* New York: Van Nostrand, 1968.

Meissner, W. Marriage from a psychoanalytic perspective. In T. J. Paolino, Jr. and B. S. McCrady (Eds.), *Marriage and marital therapy: Psychoanalytic, behavioral and systems theory perspectives.* New York: Brunner/Mazel, 1978.

Miller, J. B. (Ed.) *Psychoanalysis and women: Contributions to new theory and therapy.* New York: Brunner/Mazel, 1973.

Mitchell, J. *Psychoanalysis and feminism.* New York: Pantheon, 1974.

Piercy, M. The grand coolie dam. In M. Morgan (Ed.), *Sisterhood is powerful.* New York: Random House, 1970.

Report of the Task Force on sex bias and sex role stereotyping in psychotherapeutic practice. *American Psychologist,* 1975, **30,** 1169–1175.

Ritvo, S. Adolescent to woman: Supplement on female psychology. *Journal of the American Psychoanalytic Association,* 1977, **24,** 127–137.

Salzman, L. Psychology of the female: A new look. *Archives of General Psychiatry,* 1967, **17,** 195–203.

Skinner, B. F. Behaviorism at fifty. *Science,* 1963, **140,** 951–958.

Spock, B. *Baby and child care.* New York: Meredith, 1968.

Strouse, J. *Women and analysis: Dialogues on psychoanalytic views of femininity.* New York: Dell, 1974.

Thompson, C. Penis envy in women. *Psychiatry,* 1943, **6,** 123–125.

Weisstein, N. Psychology constructs the female. In V. Gornich & B. K. Moran (Eds.), *Women in sexist society: Studies in power and powerlessness.* New York: Basic Books, 1971.

White, R. W. *Lives in progress.* New York: Holt, Rinehart and Winston, 1966.

Zilboorg, G. Masculine and feminine: Some biological and cultural aspects. *Psychiatry,* 1944, **7,** 257–296.

II

The Mental Health Problems of Women

Social Roles and the Individual

Comprehensive assessment of women's mental health problems must include an examination of both internal conflicts and external stresses. The chapters in this section examine several specific problems of women within the context of the social environment. In order to delineate these specific problems, it is important to discuss the concept of social roles. A role is defined as socially expected behavior or behavior pattern determined by an individual's status or function in society. Each individual occupies many different roles. On any given day a woman may be a friend, worker, mother, child, and wife. Each role requires a specific behavior pattern.

At one time in American society a woman's gender in and of itself would define her role. As Chambliss and Rhyther (1975) note, "Male-female role relations in the United States have many of the characteristics of feudal role relations. The restrictions of each sex to certain kinds of tasks and cultural techniques is a caste relationship" (p. 138). They go on to define a caste as "a collection of people who all have the same relationship to the tools and mode of production. In a caste structure, people are bound to a specific economic role (and perhaps some noneconomic roles as well) for life" (p. 174). Both women and men were restricted to specific economic and social roles, with women at home and men at work.

It is necessary to examine the effects of these roles on the individual. In the past, the concept of a role has been discussed primarily in terms of efficiency—does the role serve its function in attaining the goals of the society? Friedan (1963) suggests that the functionalist school of sociology, with its emphasis on the necessity of roles to promote the operation of the society, has had a negative effect on women by neglecting their needs for those of the society. Any role can be oppressive if the social function alone instead of the whole person is valued. We are a role-oriented society, however, and the psychological hazards of our social structure are well known. Prior to the 1960s, when sociologists did examine the negative effects of roles and bureaucracy, they tended to discuss the problems of men at work (Reisman, 1950; Whyte, 1958). Once again it was left to Friedan to bring attention to the pressures on women that resulted from the role of housewife. Today, 15 years later, sex roles and sex differences are being studied intensively by psychologists and sociologists.

How do roles affect the individual woman? Women have commitments to other people and to certain functions in society. Our roles help us to structure these commitments. Roles provide structures for us in society; they also provide us with some sense of order, a consistent set of rules and expectations. Each role has gratifications as well as restrictions. There are many benefits to being a person who works or who mothers. Yet many scholars in the area of socialization note that women are conditioned to attend to their roles as caretakers and supporters of others and to neglect roles involving self-development (Bernard, 1971; Douvan & Bardwick, 1971). This problem was expressed by Angelina Alioto, the wife of a prominent politician, when she said, "You know I've been my mother's daughter, my father's daughter, the wife of my husband, the mother of my six children and grandmother to my 11 grandchildren, but I have never been me" (Clark, 1977, p. 16).

During the past 10 years, however, the restrictions on women's behavior have been challenged. No longer does gender determine an individual's roles, and women are occupying an increasing number of roles in society. This greater freedom to choose different roles is one of the benefits of the women's movement.

Yet the present time of social change has placed us in a

difficult situation. Since the old order is clearly under attack, women too often find themselves trying to play all the possible roles they can, such as wife, mother, daughter, worker, and friend, but with the same expectations as they had in the past. Herman and Kuczynski (1974) discuss intrarole and interrole conflict. Intrarole conflict occurs when there are incompatible demands for behavior within a given role. For example, a professor may feel the demand to complete a research project, whereas the chairman of her department may see the need for her to teach an additional section of a course. Interrole conflict occurs when an individual is torn between two roles, when the role demands of one situation are incompatible with those of another. The female student who has a final exam the next day may be torn between her desire to study and her commitment to a friend who may need emotional support.

These role conflicts occur when there are incompatibilities *within* a given role or *between* two different roles that the same individual may have. An additional problem is the ability to shift roles. It is often difficult to remember the norms of one situation as compared to another and to understand the varied demands that correspond to an individual's different functions. For example, a woman may enjoy the assertive, active qualities she needs at work, but may find it difficult to shift when she wants to relax.

The large number of roles has led also to the problem of overload. As Herman and Kuczynski (1974) conclude, the expectations for each individual role taken alone may be reasonable but, when the total sum of the different behaviors required is considered, the woman suffers because too many demands are placed on her. This may cause problems in organizing time as well as the necessity to set priorities and make choices.

The chapters in this section discuss the problems of women that result from our many roles in society. Each chapter examines a particular role and the related stresses.

WOMEN AS LOVERS

A woman's ability to love and her dependence on others for affirmation are reinforced from an early age (Douvan & Adelson, 1966). The ability to engage in a love relationship is a crucial developmental task, as described by Freud (1914), Erikson (1950), Maslow (1968), and others. Feminists have emphasized the value in retaining and developing these strengths, such as the ability to love, instead of abandoning these values for those of power and status (Harrison, 1973).

Mature love involves mutual respect and sharing. Nin (1975) describes such an ideal, mature love.

> I met many couples who fitted this description. Neither one dominated. Each one worked at what he did best, shared labors, unobtrusively, without need to establish roles or boundaries. The characteristic trait was gentleness. There was no head of the house. There was no need to assert which was the supplier of income. They had learned the subtle art of oscillation, which is human. Neither strength nor weakness is a fixed quality. We all have our days of strength and our days of weakness. They had learned rhythm, suppleness, relativity. Each had knowledge and special intuitions to contribute. (p. 47)

Yet for women, mature love can be confused with passion or romance. In her chapter, "Passion as a Mental Health Hazard," Loewenstein distinguishes passion from mature love. She defines passion as "an intense and obsessive emotion of constant yearning for an intense preoccupation with a love object, with or without sexual aspects." Passion, then, involves the loss of self for another. Although the positive aspects of passion are well known, Loewenstein is concerned here with the irrational, regressive aspects of passion.

In her survey of almost 700 women in the Boston area, Loewenstein follows their lives with respect to the results of passionate relationships. Many women expressed feelings of rage, despair, confusion, and anguish, usually after the passionate experience. Almost 20% of her sample had sought psychotherapy because of a passionate experience. Some of the women then became passionately and destructively involved with their psychotherapists. Loewenstein also discusses the potential difficulties in the psychotherapeutic environment, which has many of the same qualities as a romance.

One problem with women as lovers is that too often in the past women sacrificed themselves for their relationships. Instead of developing first as individuals and then sharing their lives with another person, they became obsessed and preoccupied with their lovers. Thus, a woman's role as lover can encompass her entire person to the neglect of other aspects of her life. As Gould (1978) recently noted (and contrary to the "total woman" philosophy), before a person can improve a relationship, he or she must first develop as an individual. Thus, of Freud's two tasks or roles of lover and worker, women sometimes let love dominate their lives. Similarly, many men become overinvolved with work, and this can be another source of conflict for women.

WOMEN AS WORKERS AND WORKING WIVES

The increase of women in the labor force is well documented (U.S. Bureau of the Census, 1972). Indeed, the freedom to work in a meaningful job is one of the goals of the women's movement. Work brings financial rewards and increased feelings of competence, more diverse interests, and the ability to interact with a greater number of people.

In her chapter on the emotional hazards of work, Lemkau discusses the particular stresses that affect women in different jobs. For example, women who are secretaries face a completely different set of problems than women who are accountants. Lemkau discusses these differences in terms of status, power, income, and the utilization of one's abilities.

Occupational segregation still exists, despite the trends in greater freedom for women in the area of employment. Many women who have diverse qualifications are asked if they can type and are channeled into lower-paying secretarial jobs. Lemkau notes that the average female secretary earns 65% what the average male secretary earns. Women who are in male-dominated fields such as medicine, accounting, or law may find themselves outcasts. For example, a woman working in a large corporation may be performing her job well, but may be left out of office politics because they take place at private male clubs. At the same time, she may feel a lack of support, since there are few other women around in the same situation.

The number of married women working outside of the home is also increasing (U.S. Bureau of the Census, 1972). We see that many women must fulfill multiple work and family roles. Lemkau discusses this issue with respect to role overload and role discontinuity, which occur in the two-career family, where both individuals have commitments to one another, to their jobs, and perhaps to their homes and children. Thus, new flexibilities must be developed in order to shift and divide responsibilities and provide balance in one's life. Lemkau notes that couples must adjust to these new changes without any institutionalized social support for new life-styles and proliferation of roles. She adds that mental health professionals should be aware of the effects of these work-related stresses and role conflicts on the mental health of men and women.

WOMEN AS CHILDBEARERS

The next two chapters deal with the issue of bearing and raising children. The role of mother or potential mother was synonymous with the role of women for many years. In Belle's paper on low-income mothers and their chil-

dren, she describes a group of single-parent families—
women who were originally studied by the research team
at Harvard under the leadership of the late Marcia Guttentag. Belle describes the financial, emotional, and social
stresses on a single woman. She emphasizes the environmental issue of financial support. Although raising a child
alone may not be stressful in and of itself, for women,
being a single parent is highly correlated with poverty.
The financial limitations on single women with children
often dominate their lives. At the same time, single
women may have little social support. Frequently divorce
has been a traumatic situation in which the husband and
father has been alienated from his wife and children.
Thus, support is sometimes lacking in this area.

Some of the women have been torn between their economic needs to work and their lack of social outlets and
support. Thus, their lives become long hours of working
during the day and taking care of their children at night.
Once again the stresses of different roles all take their toll
on the individual woman. The need to be the breadwinner
and the caretaker of the children may occupy all of the
single mother's time and energy, leaving little of either for
herself.

This role overload, according to Belle, can be buffered by
friends, coping strategies, or social agencies. If these buffers do not exist, the result can be depression or other emotional problems for the mother and her children.

Belle concludes that necessary social changes include
greater enforcement of financial support agreements,
more employment and education opportunities, and more
child-care facilities for single parents. She adds that preventive mental health programs can lessen the stresses on
these women and their children.

Birth control has given women greater freedom of
choice, but unwanted pregnancies still occur. In her chapter on abortion, Belovitch describes the conflicts that
women have over an unwanted pregnancy. Once again, it

can be seen that some of these conflicts are internal, whereas others are a function of the environment. Women often have ambivalent feelings about having a child. Many women who are of childbearing age have been brought up to value, perhaps overvalue, their roles as bearers of children. Yet for a myriad of reasons, some women may not want children at a particular point in their lives. However, unwanted pregnancy may occur. Sometimes a woman decides to have an abortion. This decision is often a difficult one, and internal conflicts may develop.

What about the external pressures on women who seek abortions? In addition to internal conflicts, a woman must also face social sanctions on abortion. For many years abortion was illegal, and rich and poor women alike had few options. Affluent women could escape to another country or to a private physician who would perform an illegal abortion. Poor women had to endure gruesome situations that endangered their lives. At one time there were legal sanctions on abortion that limited women's choices.

Women who were brought up as Catholics were taught that abortion is murder. These women may have internalized this belief; if not, they may still come into conflict with members of their family who hold these beliefs and with the church.

Finally, although most people in the United States now believe in freedom of choice regarding abortion, a battle is going on to rescind the Supreme Court decision and to make abortions illegal once again. The recent Health, Education, and Welfare guidelines that prohibit abortions for women on welfare are an unfortunate step in this becoming a reality.

Belovitch then presents interviews with women who experienced conflicts about abortion because of internal or external pressures. She also talked with women who made a definite choice, obtained a safe abortion, and experienced no conflict. Once again, we see the importance of assessing both the individual's conflicts and the environmental issues.

We have seen that the roles of lover, worker, and potential mother all cause different stresses. The next two chapters offer different perspectives: an historical view of women in fiction, and a humanistic view of new choices for women in midlife. These chapters remind us that women have more freedom today than ever before. Adler (1927) wrote that "So long as we cannot guarantee every woman absolute equality with men we cannot demand her complete reconciliation with life, with the facts of our civilization and the forms of our social life. . . . The pressure exerted on women and the inhibitions to which she must submit today are not to be borne by any human being; they always give rise to revolt" (p. 123). In this case Adler was referring to the general limitations of social roles for women of his time. These historical restrictions have existed for centuries, and some of them still remain. But we have seen progress.

Shuey's chapter on renunciation and rebellion in fiction points out that the social roles of women were much more restrictive in the past. He traces the way in which women's responses to their social roles has been portrayed. His descriptions of Dickens' Little Dorrit and of the characters of Henry James and D. H. Lawrence show the tradition of renunciation. Women renounced their "worldly" needs for the needs of others. Instead of coming into the intense role conflicts just described, women "rose above them." Instead of struggling with her role as an individual who needs love and support, Little Dorrit supported her entire family, both emotionally and financially. The renunciatory female was glorified; she was a character to be admired. As Shuey traces the renunciatory woman, she seemed to bloom and thrive in the eighteenth and nineteenth centuries. Renunciation as a coping style is dying in the twentieth century. Characters such as Lessing's Martha Quest represent the new tradition of rebellion against limited roles. Instead of accepting role restrictions, Martha Quest actively fought against oppression. In the modern novel women would rather fight than renounce their needs. Martha Quest's rebellion involved the active rejection of social role restrictions. She left two unhappy marriages and became active in the struggle for her own freedom and for the freedom of black people. Martha Quest can be regarded as the prototype for later feminist fictional characters.

But the question of how to cope remains for women who are neither renunciatory and therefore abandoning the conflict, nor rebellious and actively fighting role restriction. What about those who are in the middle?

THE CHANCE FOR NEW ROLES IN MIDLIFE

The increase of role possibilities and the necessity to choose and make decisions are not all negative. This is discussed by Loewenstein in her chapter entitled "Toward Choice and Differentiation in the Midlife Crises of Women." She writes that midlife, with its changing roles, offers the possibility for an identity crisis—a reevaluation of the sense of oneself and one's purpose. Although Loewenstein discusses these changes with respect to different commitments (to one's body image, to relationships, and to work), we can see that they also involve choices in life roles. For every loss, one can see new choices. For example, although aging can be seen as a loss of youth, at the same time it can be seen as a gain in life experiences. Similarly, when a woman's children have grown and left home, women may miss their children, but may also feel relief from some of the responsibilities to them. The role of mother can be replaced by a new role such as worker, student, or wife.

Relationships, too, change in midlife. Divorce, which is one possibility in midlife, offers the freedom to develop new relationships. Thus the role of wife might be shifted to that of friend. There is often a reevaluation of one's occupational role in midlife; the question "Is that all there is?" occurs. Loewenstein explains that a woman physicist can lose faith in science; a woman psychiatrist can lose faith in psychotherapy; and a mother can lose faith in her family. But these crises can lead to changing roles and possibilities for new choices. With that choice, however, comes not only the opportunity for personal growth, but also a confrontation with responsibility and freedom. Loewenstein points out, however, that for midlife women, the emphasis has been on the loss of the role of child-bearer, not on the possibilities of new roles.

The ability to shift roles and make new choices requires flexibility, and most women and men today have been socialized to accept traditional sex roles. It seems that there is no easy answer. As Bem (1975), Spence, Helmreich, and Stapp (1975), and others have described, the concept of androgyny (where women and men can have different types of personality characteristics that can be used in different roles) can be adaptive. Thus, if one can be both nurturant and assertive, both active and passive, one can more easily adjust to the different role expectations. This adaptability allows greater freedom and choice. Such flexibility or behavior could make the conflicts between and within roles less difficult.

Thus, we see that renunciation has been replaced by rebellion; in addition, greater flexibility to perform in different roles can lead to greater freedom. Once again, however, there is a danger of attempting to meet all role expectations by becoming "superwoman," which would lead to greater stress. This is discussed by Lemkau in her chapter and by Hall (1972). Some combination of individual and social action is necessary. Women are attempting to confront and define their own role expectations and not accept blindly the limitations of society. These new roles also affect a woman's immediate social environment, so family and work situations may change. Finally, larger social institutions must be considered. Several of the chapters in this section mention that social changes such as equal pay for equal work and increased day-care facilities can support women and men who are experiencing stress. As Gould (1978) noted, if society's institutions, such as government, religion, or traditional marriage, foster a restricted notion of what men and women should be, it is incumbent on mental health professionals to fight against these restrictions.

REFERENCES

Adler, A. *Understanding human nature.* New York: Greenburg, 1927.

Bem, S. L. Sex role adaptability: One consequence of psychological androgyny. *Journal of Consulting and Clinical Psychology,* 1975, **31,** 634–643.

Bernard, J. The paradox of the happy marriage. In V. Gornick and B. K. Moran (Eds.), *Women in sexist society.* New York: Basic Books, 1971.

Chambliss, W. J., & Rhyther, T. E. *Sociology: The discipline and its direction.* New York: McGraw-Hill, 1975.

Clark, L. W. *Women women women: Quips, quotes and commentary,* New York: Drake Publishers, 1977.

Douvan, E., & Adelson, J. *The adolescent experience.* New York: John Wiley, 1966.

Douvan, E., & Bardwick, J. Ambivalence: The socialization of women. In V. Gornick and B. K. Moran (Eds.), *Women in sexist society.* New York: Basic Books, 1971.

Erikson, E. *Childhood and society.* New York: W. W. Norton, 1950.

Freud, S. On narcissism. In J. Strachey (Ed.), *The complete psychological works of Sigmund Freud.* Vol. 14. London: Hogarth Press, 1974. (Originally published 1914.)

Friedan, B. *The feminine mystique.* New York: W. W. Norton, 1963.

Gould, R. E. Sexual changes and difficulties of mid-life. Paper presented at Symposium on midlife: Issues and clinical implications, Butler Hospital, May 26, 1978, Provindence, R.I.

Hall, D. T. A model for coping with role conflict: The role behavior of college educated women. *Administrative Science Quarterly,* 1972, **17,** 471–486.

Harrison, B. Bestial until victory—winning hearts and minds. *The Nation,* 1973, **216,** 117–119.

Herman, J. B., & Kuczynski, K. A. The professional woman: Inter and intra role conflict. Paper presented at the annual convention of the American Psychological Association, September 1974, New Orleans, La.

Maslow, A. H. *Toward a psychology of being.* New York: Van Nostrand, 1968.

Nin, A. *Notes and lectures.* New York: Harcourt Brace Jovanovich, 1975.

Riesman, D. *The lonely crowd.* New York: Yale University Press, 1950.

Spence, J. T., Helmreich, R., & Stapp, J. Ratings of self and peers on sex role attributes and their relations to self-esteem and conceptions of masculinity and femininity. *Journal of Personality and Social Psychology,* 1975, **32,** 29–39.

U.S. Bureau of the Census. Census of the population: General social and economic characteristics, 1970 final report. Washington, D.C.: U.S. Government Printing Office, 1972.

Whyte, W. H., Jr. *The organization man.* New York: Doubleday, 1958.

1

Passion as a
Mental Health Hazard

Sophie Freud Loewenstein

*A*nyone who has ever been possessed by passionate love for another human being keeps this experience imprinted in her or his soul. That powerful mysterious experience attests perhaps more than any other psychic phenomenon to the irrational aspects of the human mind. It is thus no wonder that much of the world's literature and art deals with passion, and somewhat surprising that psychologists and psychiatrists have not devoted more concentrated attention to this subject. A few social scientists of various disciplines periodically have tried to understand the nature of love and passion, but they have produced few empirical research studies in this area (Rubin, 1973). While researchers have felt comfortable penetrating the intimacy of our sexual lives, they have not shown equal interest in the emotions that give meaning and transcendence to the sexual act.

This chapter reports a part of a large-scale study on the role of passionate love in women's lives. In the course of

I thank Jerold Harmatz for his statistical assistance.

this research I became aware of two reasons why mental health professionals should have a special concern with the passionate love experience. First, an astonishing number of women seek therapeutic help in connection with an upsetting passion, and we must understand the meaning of that experience in order to meet their needs. Second, the therapeutic experience itself sometimes becomes a form of passion, with the same potential for producing creative growth or having a destructuve impact as any other passion experience. I will present some data and reflections on these two ways in which the passion experience becomes a mental health concern.

SOME PRELIMINARY CONSIDERATIONS

Most social scientists, beginning with Freud, seem to agree that the potential for passion is created in infancy, in the intense but ambivalent tie of the infant to his or her mother (Freud, 1914; Reik, 1944; Reich, 1954; Benedek, 1976), a form of regression in the service of the ego. Moller (1960) has demonstrated that even the *minnesongs* of courtly love from which our current romantic love ideals have evolved celebrate infantile rather than sexual love. Kernberg (1976) thinks that the pathological, irrational manifestations of passion constitute a regression to that earliest period of infancy, while manifestations of mature love "the normal integration of genitality with the capacity for tenderness and a stable deep object relation," trace back to a successful resolution of the Oedipal conflict.

Current psychoanalytic literature, following Reik's (1944) and Sullivan's (in Carson, 1969) thinking on this subject, is also unanimous in separating sexual desire and passionate love (Benedek, 1976; Christie, 1972) as two different emotions that frequently but not necessarily coincide. For some women passion is intimately bound up with their sexuality, and they could not imagine one without the other. "Passions for people" writes one of my research respondents ". . . ultimately get down to a desire to experience that sense of total combination with the object's body that one can sometimes experience in successful sexual union."[1] Other women in my study emphasized the difference between sexual love and passionate feelings: "love gets you through times of no sex better than sex gets you through times of no love." It is, however, agreed that obstacles to sexual consummation seem to heighten and maintain the yearning quality of the passion (Christie, 1972).

The Latin root of passion refers to suffering and the German word *Leidenschaft* can be literally translated as sufferingship. Passion thus involves inevitable anguish, doubts, and uncertainty, even when there is mutuality, while these emotions turn into dejection and despair when love is not reciprocated. In Freud's (1914) words, "A person who loves has, so to speak, forfeited a part of his narcissim, and it can only be replaced by being loved" (p. 98). Although my larger study investigates both positive and negative aspects of the passion experience, this chapter will focus on the narcissistic injuries resulting from unhappy passions.

Psychoanalysts and social scientists (Bak, 1973; DeBeauvoir, 1953; Freud, 1914; Kernberg, 1976; Rougemont, 1956) have emphasized two aspects of the passion experience, the fusion of self with another and the overevaluation of the love object, thus involving a loss of ego boundaries and reality distortion, both symptoms of serious mental illness. In addition, a striking feature of passionate love is its obsessive nature, along with a frightening and exhilarating loss of control and loosening of inhibitions. Salzman (1973) suggests that the ever present obsession with the

---

[1] All quotations from respondents' questionnaires in this chapter are verbatim transcripts, except that several statements from different parts of the questionnaire are sometimes combined and, for brevity, statements are not always given in their complete form.

love object usually displaces other obsessive defenses formerly marshaled to protect the ego against experiences of weakness. One falls ill, one falls in love, fate has taken over one's destiny and, as in other forms of madness, the outcome may be uncertain.

Passion in this study was defined as "an intense and obsessive emotion of constant yearning for and intense preoccupation with a love object, with or without sexual aspects." Respondents were directed not to "include affectionate loving experiences that did not include passion." Thus, an attempt was made to capture the irrational projective aspects of love, instead of mature love, tenderness, and affection. It is for this reason that the word passion rather than love is used throughout the study. Of course, we might presume that most respondents do not read definitions very carefully, but answer with their own images of passion in mind. Their comments suggest that my subjects knew exactly what I hoped to study and that there is considerable intuitive agreement, at least among women, as to the nature of passion. Here is what one respondent writes: "It feels like souls touched and doors to other worlds opened through someone else's eyes. It seemed like living double-time, to be so very close to someone else. Like two lives that can be enjoyed and experienced beyond the range of your own imagination and comprehension"; another writes: "It never occurred to me to give a name to the exquisite confusion, the total breakdown of reason that I've experienced with some men. At such times nothing but feelings matter, nothing else."

METHOD

The data to be presented are derived from 700 questionnaires that I assembled over 2 years in the greater Boston area. Although questionnaires are not the traditional research tools for collecting intimate personal information, this method allowed me to collect a large sample, and it gave anonymity to the respondents who wanted it. I used and abused my role as classroom teacher and public lecturer to beg, cajole, charm, bribe, and blackmail my students and audiences to return the questionnaires I distributed to them in order to assure a high rate of return from at least certain groups. Bonds of respect and affection that many respondents had formed with me resulted in questionnaires that are for the most part intensely personal expressive documents.

Table 1-1 briefly labels the different groups that make up my total sample and the number of women in each sample.

Some of the samples, such as samples 3 and 11, are made up of upper-middle-class women, while samples 4, 6, 10, 12, and 14 were quite heterogeneous in social class. Samples 2, 5, and 7 were made up primarily of mental health professionals. Apart from classes and lecture audiences, there were a number of friendship networks.

Of course, no claim is made as to the representative nature of the total sample. An attempt to obtain cross-population representation by distributing questionnaires to all female employees and "wives" of the staff of an electronics plant failed miserably, and we concluded that a personal contact was needed as a motivational factor in this intimate research.

The age range of the total sample was from 17 to 84 years, with a mean age of 35 years and a median age of 33 years. Only 10% of the total sample reported experiencing no passions. The rest of the women experienced anywhere from one to nine or more passions, the mode, median, and mean all being around two passions, regardless of the age of the respondent.

The questionnaires asked women to describe the four most important passion experiences in their lives. In addition, a few demographic data were collected on each woman. Questions were asked about her marriage and

Table 1-1

Women Ever in Therapy for All Reasons and for Passion Reasons Only in Different Samples

Types of Samples	Women in Sample, Number	Women in Therapy for All Reasons		Women in Therapy for Passion Reasons		
		Number	Percent of Women in Sample	Number	Percent of Women in Therapy	Percent of Women in Sample
1. College extension class	126	53	42.1	32	60.3	25.3
2. Social work school	87	54	62.1	19	35.2	21.8
3. University continuing education class	67	42	62.1	11	26.1	16.4
4. College extension class	55	34	58.1	16	47.0	29.0
5. Social workers	53	35	66.0	13	37.1	24.5
6. Catholic college lecture	46	10	21.7	1	1.0	2.1
7. Hospital mental health workers	44	30	68.2	11	36.6	25.0
8. Professional friends network	44	25	56.8	13	52.0	29.5
9. Divorced women	36	25	69.4	12	48.0	33.3
10. Community college adult education class	31	6	19.4	3	50.0	9.6
11. Suburban, middle-class women	27	12	44.4	3	25.0	11.1
12. Community college freshmen	25	13	52.0	0	0	0
13. Feminist friends' network	22	18	81.8	9	50.0	40.9
14. Older women	17	2	11.8	1	50.0	5.8
15. High school graduates	14	3	21.4	0	0	0
Total	694	362	52.1	144	39.7	20.7

children and, if relevant, her relationship to her parents as well as other general questions related to love and friendship. Both precoded and open-ended questions were used throughout the questionnaire. Additional depth of understanding was gained through 30 individual interviews with volunteer respondents. I do not claim to have collected objective facts; I simply examined how women view, interpret, and construct their own lives, both currently and in retrospect. The study is limited to women, but there is much evidence from world literature, the arts, and clinical observations that passion is a very similar experience for women and men.

Among other questions, respondents were asked whether they had ever been in therapy, whether they had "had a passion for their therapist," and whether they had "sought psychiatric help" in connection with their passion experience. It is with the implications of the answers to these specific questions that we will be dealing.

SEEKING HELP FOR PASSION EXPERIENCES

We can see from Table 1–1 that half of the respondents of this study had at one time been in psychotherapeutic treatment. There is, however, a considerable difference among samples; the range varies from 81.8% of the feminist friendship network to 11.8% of the older women. As one might expect, the percentage of divorced women and of mental health workers who were in therapy are also quite high, while the Catholic group, the community college class, and the high-school graduates were among the lower percentages. This distribution suggests once more the association between social class and the use of psychotherapeutic mental health services (Miller & Mishler, 1959). It is interesting, however, that in 9 out of the 15 groups, 52% or more of the women have sought help, suggesting that our average of 50% may be valid for other middle-class urban women. Ryan (1969), in a survey of Boston, found that women college graduates or college students of middle- or upper-middle-class background between the ages of 22 to 36 constitute the highest help-seeking group in the population; these attributes match those of our high help-seeking groups.

If we now consider what percentage of women ever in therapy had sought help for passion-connected difficulties (Table 1–1), we find an average of 39.7%, close to one-half, with a range of 0% from the groups who had made little use of therapy in general, to a high of 60.3% in one of the evening college classes. We notice that in 10 of the 15 groups, 35% or more of women were in therapy for passion-connected reasons. Another way of considering the data is to examine what percentage of our respondents were ever in therapy for passion-connected reasons, and we notice a 20.7% for the total sample, roughly one-fifth of all women, with eight groups of higher percentages. In addition, 19 women had sought therapy two or more times around passion experiences, so that the actual "passion therapies" are even more frequent. On the other hand, about 20 respondents counted marital counseling or divorce counseling subsequent to a passion-preceded marriage as help-seeking around a passion experience, substituting long-range for short-range consequences. These should not be included in the total count, since they cancel each other.

Thus, we cannot escape the striking and little recognized fact that passion experiences may be a major mental health hazard for certain populations of women. It is comforting that we can compare our data to those of Saghir, Walbran, Robins, & Gentry (1970), who studied 57 homosexual women and 43 heterosexual controls in Chicago and San Francisco. Thirty-seven percent of the homosexual women in his sample had psychotherapy, while 25% of the heterosexual controls had had such an experience. The actual prevalence of psychiatric disorders among these women was quite high, with 75% of the homosexual women and 44% of the heterosexual women being diagnosed as having one or more psychiatric disorders. In addition, Saghir et al. related these women's depressive episodes to their passion experiences. They found that 68% of the depressed homosexual women and 60% of the control depressed women gave the breakup of a romantic relationship as having been the immediate cause for their seeking help. Incidentally, the lesbian women in my research sought help at about the same rate as other women, 14 out of 33.

Along with asking about psychiatric treatment as a short-range consequence of their passion, respondents were also asked to check the presence or absence of both joyful and depressive emotions.

The first row of numbers in Table 1–2 represents the negative emotions checked by the 144 women who had sought therapy for one or more passion experiences. We notice that the most frequently checked emotions were rage, despair, confusion or identity crisis, and lowered self-esteem, all of them experienced by more than half of these women with at least one of their passions. Even physical illness, the least frequently checked short-term consequence of passion, was checked by about one-quarter of all women who had sought passion-connected help. This is not to deny that there were not also many joyful emotions connected with passions; it simply highlights that a great deal of distress is frequently associated with passion experiences. A vignette quoting one respondent who had checked every single negative emotion will express the pain more vividly than numbers.

Ms. A[2] Ms. is a 27-year-old divorced medical secretary who is describing her 2-year-long passion for a man whom

[2]Anonymous respondents will be referred to by alphabetical letters. Respondents who had personal interviews will be called by fictitious first names. Occupations that might be identifying have been changed to others of similar status.

Table 1–2
Comparison of Negative Emotional Reactions to Passions of Women Who Went into Therapy with Women Who Did Not Go into Therapy for Different Groups

	Despair		Rage		Physical Illness		Emotional Illness		Suicide Thoughts		Damaged Self-Esteem		Confusion or Identity Crisis		Total	
	Num-ber	Per-cent	Num-ber	Per-cent	Num-ber	Per-cent	Num-ber	Per-cent	Num-ber	Per-cent	Num-ber	Per-cent	Num-ber	Per-cent	Num-ber	Per-cent
Groups of women who went into therapy																
Total women in therapy	113	18.9	88	14.7	41	6.8	77	12.9	54	9.0	111	18.5	115	19.2	599	100
College extension class 2	12	19.7	8	13.1	3	4.9	7	11.5	5	8.2	12	19.7	14	22.9	61	100
University continuing education class	9	22.5	5	12.5	2	5.0	6	15.0	3	7.5	7	17.5	8	20.0	40	100
Catholic college evening lecture	Not applicable—only 1 woman in therapy															
Groups of women who did not go into therapy																
College extension class 2	33	21.8	25	15.8	6	3.8	7	4.4	11	6.9	35	22.0	41	25.9	166	100
University continuing education class	31	21.6	15	11.2	5	3.5	4	2.8	9	6.3	41	25.3	41	28.7	142	100
Catholic college evening lecture	13	28.5	5	10.2	2	4.1	1	2.0	4	8.2	13	26.5	11	22.4	49	100

she eventually married and divorced: ". . . my love for him was destroying me. There was a gradual loss of identity. At times I thought I was crazy through my despair. I lost all of myself and was ready for the nuthouse. I realized I had to get out. I had to grow up and learn to love me. A lot of anger had to be dealt with towards him."

The question arises whether women who seek therapeutic help are more troubled than those who do not. Although we cannot measure subjective feelings of depression and turmoil, we can compare the kinds and numbers of negative emotions checked by women who did or did not seek help. Table 1–2 presents a comparison of the total sample and of three of the subsamples of women along these dimensions. Only in one category, emotional illness, do we find appreciable differences between help-seekers and nonhelp-seekers, the percent of those seeking help being about three times as great as those who did not. The remarkable consistency of percentages for each negative emotion across diverse groups as well as across the total sample gives us extra confidence in the validity of our data.

Thus, only a sense of having an emotional illness differentiated help-seekers from nonhelp-seekers to some extent, while other feelings of unhappiness were not determining factors in the help-seeking decision. The following is an example of a help-seeker who seems to have suffered intensely.

Ms. B is a married 55-year-old elementary school teacher who had a sexually nonconsummated first and only passion of her life at age 25, while still single. She checked despair, suicidal thoughts, and damaged self-esteem. "I became engaged to this person but he started to get indifferent and I left the service to go home. I think I had the symptoms of an emotional illness but did not seek psychiatric help and was able to get through it on my own strength. It was an extremely unhappy time in my life. Wouldn't want to repeat the experience, very painful, but eventually I got over it with considerable effort. . . . I often wonder if I had married my passion, would life have been any different. My present husband has hurt me as well so I feel generally that I have not been lucky in my love experience."

To gain additional understanding of the processes that impel women to seek help, I scanned the questionnaires for information on the circumstances surrounding the fateful passion, including respondents' demographic data and written expressions of feelings.

A major factor that was associated with help-seeking was sexual consummation of the passion, as shown by answers to the questionnaire. This association held for the first three passions in a woman's life, but reversed itself for the fourth passion. For the first two passions three times as many sexually consummated passions were associated with help-seeking than nonconsummated passions, and for the third passion the numbers were double. In addition, one-half of all women and more than three-quarters of help-seekers had sexual intercourse with their first passion objects. These differences were in the same direction for the second and third passions. Sexual consummation lifts a passion out of the realm of fantasy, and rejection and disappointment may have a special poignancy after sexual consummation has taken place.

When either the love object or the respondent was married at the beginning of a passion, signifying an extramarital passion for either one or both partners, there was an association with help-seeking for all but the third passion, no doubt because it created extra reality obstacles and guilt. For the first passion, for example, of the 66 women with married lovers, 9 women (13.6%) sought help, while out of the 567 women with unmarried lovers, only 45 (7.9%) sought help. Of course, in view of the relatively small group of women with married lovers as compared to the others, we can only offer these figures as suggestive. The associations between marital status of the respondent at the beginning of a passion and help-seeking are similar. The strongest association here is for the first passion, in that 26.7% of married women with a first passion sought help compared to 7% of never-married women.[3] Further analysis of the data indicated that women who experience their first passion after they are already married are profoundly upset by that experience and perhaps feel cheated, since they had gotten married without knowing that these feelings existed.

Ms. C is a 31-year-old accountant, married since age 19, who describes an extramarital passion that has lasted off and on for almost 7 years; it is her first and only passion, one that includes sexual consummation. "I terminated the relationship for two years because of our marital partners and children, but it began again as intensely. It resulted in a question of Who-what am I? I entered therapy to evaluate myself. I do feel the relationship has had a profound effect on my future. I am now emerging from a severe identity crisis and have no idea if the crisis invited the rekindling flame or vice versa. My marriage may end because of the ramifications of the last eight months."

However, it is the divorced status that is by far the most strongly associated with help-seeking, probably because divorced women are particularly vulnerable to yet another experience of disappointment or betrayal. The following vignette is a striking example of this situation.

Ann is a 37-year-old architect who met her fourth passion object 4 months after separation from her husband, at age 35. The relationship lasted for 2 years, after which time the man left for another country. When she visited him during her vacations, she found that he was involved with another woman. She checks every single negative emotion except rage. "My passion for him has not yet

[3]In all these examples, chi-squares proved to be highly significant, $p < 0.001$ but, since cell sizes were affected by the low number of help-seekers relative to the total sample, the chi-squares appear to be artificially high.

ended. I am trying very hard to forget him. This most recent experience has had a very great impact on my life. It helped me for awhile to cope with the loss of my husband (who was never the object of my passion, by the way) but now I find myself doubly rejected. I'm trying very hard to fall out of love, to de-escalate the feeling from one of passion to friendship. It is extremely difficult. I miss him terribly. I feel very lonely and particularly lacking in self-esteem. I have a terrible fear of facing a possibly passionless future."

In general, conditions of loss, transition, or unhappiness at the time of falling in love were associated with help-seeking, suggesting that the decision to seek treatment is a complex one and that the disappointing passion experience may only be the final catalyst toward that step.

In examining whether a particular passion is associated with help-seeking, we found the association highest for the second passion and lowest for the first passion. Since the great majority of first passions occur in adolescence, when there is a general expectation of an active and possibly upsetting passion life, it is perhaps postadolescent passion disappointment that is a more severe narcissistic injury. We also notice with interest that the women in our sample needed more help with passions as they increased in age; women in their thirties were seeking help more often than women in their twenties, while the lowest percentage of help-seekers was among adolescents. Some of these differences may simply be due to increased knowledge about the availability of therapeutic resources and increased ability to pay for them. In addition, as already suggested, first or even second passions at a relatively mature age are apt to be particularly unsettling. However, as these women get into their forties, they are no longer likely to seek "passion therapy," regardless of the level of distress. Only four women in their forties did so, and two of them had sought such help before. Among the five women who had their first passions in their forties, the level of turmoil was very high, but none of them sought help.

As one would expect, feelings about long-range consequences of a particular passion are associated with help-seeking, in that passions associated with long-range consequent unhappiness led to help-seeking twice as often as other more benign passions (22.9% versus 9.4%). The next vignette illustrates both vulnerability during periods of transition and the nature of long-term negative consequences leading to help-seeking.

Jane is a 33-year-old divorced nursery school teacher. Her sexual passion with a married man occurred at age 25, while still never married. She checked all negative emotions except physical illness. "I was working at my first job. He was my boss. I was in an emotionally vulnerable position, not knowing where I was going. After eight years I still feel unresolved. The ending was extremely abrupt involving another woman. I developed a kind of shell and bitterness which is probably still with me. The experience still hurts. I am still discovering things which grew out of it, like a fear of involving myself totally with anyone. Also a constant battle with depression and feelings of worthlessness and inadequacy."

In summary, if we were to imagine a composite woman most likely to seek psychiatric help in relation to a passion, she would be in her thirties, married or divorced, or single and in love with a married man, suffering from the consequences of a sexually consummated passion that had occurred at a time of transition in her life.

Although circumstances surrounding help-seeking for passions were frequently ambiguous and complex, some major constellations of "causes" for help-seeking emerged.

1. Most frequently mentioned was *pain over separation.* Ms. D is a 25-year-old nursing student. Her sexual passion occurred at age 20, during her prolonged stay in a foreign

country; it lasted for 3 years, after which time she had to return to this country to finish her education. She checked every single negative emotion. "My second passion is still the core of my emotional life. I don't understand it. Why won't it end with him and start with someone who is near? I haven't seen him for years and still I compare everyone to him. Even as I write this I cry for him. . . . I died when I left him and I haven't come alive yet."

2. The pain over the loss is often aggravated by an acute narcissistic injury caused by feeling rejected, abandoned, or betrayed. Unlike Ms. D, some respondents just state the facts and let the readers imagine the rest.

Ms. E. is a single 25-year-old secretary who checks every single negative emotion. Her sexual passion occurred at age 20 and lasted 2 years. "I had a serious auto accident in August and he moved to New York in October." Sudden unexplained rejections seem to be particularly hard to accept.

Ms. F is a 37-year-old married counselor. She refers to a sexual passion when she was single and 27 years old. "He couldn't find a way to live in New York City. One day he moved away without telling me."

3. Guilt or acute conflict when either the woman or her love object were married formed another major cluster around her help-seeking. Ms. G was one example of such a situation, and there were many others.

Ms. G is a 34-year-old housewife, married since age 18 and involved in a sexual passion with a married man that causes her to feel intense guilt. "I am constantly feeling passionate towards different men in my life but this is the first passion in which sex is consummated. I love my husband as a person and friend but I don't feel passion towards him that I do towards these other men. It is an extremely frustrating situation."

This theme often overlaps with pain over separation or rejection, for example, when a single woman falls in love with a married man, as in the previous example of Jane.

4. For some women the violent feelings unleashed by passion were extremely unsettling, and they experienced much *confusion and anxiety* for which they sought help.

Francis, a 33-year-old married housewife describes her nonsexual passion for a woman that lasted 6 months. "We were very good friends and one day I realized how passionately I felt towards this person. Since my love for her was not reciprocated I had to seek help to end an unrealistic and unrealizable relationship. Life is quite fickle and you never can seem to get what your heart most desires. There was pain and agony but perhaps growth only comes after some painful development. I don't regret experiencing the six months for it was important for me to know that I can feel so intensely for a person. I don't want to go through it again unless the feelings are returned."

5. Some women found themselves repeatedly in destructive or disappointing relationships and sought help primarily to *seek understanding* or *combat their destructive tendencies.*

Ms. H is a 25-year-old married laboratory technician. Her first sexual passion, lasting 18 months, was experienced at age 18 when she was single and in college. "I was self-destructive in that I lived with a male who hated women. He rejected me as a woman and as myself. It led to self-doubt and fear of being alone and led me into seeking psychiatric help."

Ms. I, a 31-year-old married college instructor, describes her third 2-year sexual passion for a married man at age 25. "He showed little or no interest in me. In therapy I began to examine the myths I attached to some types of men and I began to rid myself of these myths. We examined my feelings, wants, desires, needs in regard to men. I began to choose men who did reciprocate my passion and also began to feel more realistic in my expectations of men. Also felt more whole myself, less in need of men."

6. Finally, a small group of women whose lovers committed suicide or had serious accidents or physical or

mental illnesses needed help with these *reality traumas.* Feelings of loss, mourning, and narcissistic injuries were, of course, present in such cases, as in most of the others.

So far we have emphasized the suffering of women who had sought passion-connected treatment, which is the focus of this chapter. The overall creative or destructive impact of passion on women must be evaluated. For many women the intensity and heightened sense of aliveness of a passion experience is worth the suffering involved. The women were asked about their overall reaction to their passion experiences and their importance in their lives. Of the 144 women who sought treatment, only 16 women (11%) felt that their passions had been unimportant, as compared to 23.9% of the total sample. More than half of the help-seeking women felt positively about their passion experiences. Thirty-one percent thought that their passions had been wonderful, growth-producing events, and an additional 34% felt that they had been worth the pain. This compared very closely to similar percentages in the general sample.

PASSION FOR A PSYCHOTHERAPIST

An appreciable number of women thus enter therapy to seek help with the loss, narcissistic injury, turmoil, or confusion felt in connection with a passion experience. How will the therapeutic encounter help them? This brings us to the second factor that makes the passion experience intimately relevant to mental health professionals.

Kremen and Kremen (1971) have suggested that romantic love has four main elements: a partial knowledge of the love object, which leads to idealization; obstacles to attaining the love object; a period of discontent with self; and an objective value attributed to the love object. These four factors fit the therapeutic encounter very well. Respondents were asked in the questionnaire whether they had "had a passion for a psychotherapist during treatment." Of the 362 women ever in treatment, 91 women, exactly one-quarter, responded in the affirmative. This included all five women who were or had been in psychoanalysis, as well as passion for four women therapists. In addition, 15 women (4% of the total sample) spontaneously mentioned their therapist as one of their major life passions, two of those being former psychoanalytic patients. Freud (1915) was well aware of the similarity between love in the therapeutic situation and other forms of romantic love feelings and, in writing about transference-love, he debates the authenticity of such feelings and concludes convincingly that the differences are small. "It is true that the love consists of new editions of old traits and that it repeats infantile reactions. But this is an essential character of every state of being in love" (p. 170). Freud (1920) changed his mind on this later, but Schafer (1977) thinks that this was mostly for political reasons. Freud felt that passion was an integral part of psychoanalytic treatment, and he called it a transference neurosis. It is the paradox of psychoanalysis that a patient can only be touched at the core of her being if she passionately falls in love with her analyst, but there is a risk that her passion will become a case of unrequited love, narcissistic injury, and/or bitter loss. The same problems can be said to exist for psychotherapy. Freud (1914) did not minimize that risk: "The psychoanalyst knows that he is working with highly explosive forces and that he needs to proceed with as much caution and conscientiousness as a chemist."

Women who seek treatment for a passion experience might thus shift from one distressing passion experience to one that hopefully has a healing effect, and my data show that this does indeed happen. This is similar to Haley's (1963) suggestion that schizophrenia, which he thinks is caused by paradoxical double-bind communication, can only be cured by exposure to similar communication, but this time in a benevolent context.

Several books (Chesler, 1972; Ferguson, 1973; Freeman, 1972; Freeman & Roy, 1976; Mitchell, 1973,) have dealt with the potential betrayal experience in the therapeutic encounter from very different viewpoints. I do not want to dwell here on the increasingly popular subject of sexual seduction in therapy (Davidson, 1977; Kardener, 1974; Marmor, 1976; Stone, 1976; Voth, 1972), because there were only four cases of sexual activity and two more of proposed sexual activity in my sample. I have come to feel that some of the anger that women have expressed against psychiatric sexual seduction (Freud, 1920; Schafer, 1977) is really anger about emotional seduction displaced into the sexual arena.

The most poignant recent book on the subject, a truly remarkable human document is Ferguson's (1973) love letter to her dead psychiatrist, portraying the hazards of the therapeutic experience even with a devoted therapist who would have expressed contempt for sexual seduction. Ferguson appears to have been in a Laingian type of psychoanalysis where deep regression and total dependency is tolerated and even encouraged. Barnes, in *Two Accounts of a Journey through Madness* (1971), describes a similar therapeutic approach with propitious results, but Ferguson's psychiatrist suddenly died of a heart attack, terminating the analysis prematurely. In the course of her analysis the patient's entire affective life came to revolve around her analyst. Nothing and nobody else came to hold any real meaning for her, the very way in which people in love suddenly lost interest in other aspects of their lives. His death emptied her life of meaning, and she nearly died as well. Ferguson started treatment after a divorce, at a time of loss. She appears to be a borderline personality and thus particularly susceptible to fusion and vulnerable to subsequent loss. However, one senses that she becomes more and more withdrawn and poorly functioning in the course of treatment.

Among the 91 women who checked that they had had a passion for their therapist, 15 mention considerable pain, often in a muted way. "I found it very difficult to give him up," "I finally had to leave since I couldn't do anything about it," "I became totally involved in therapy; finally had the strength to sever the dependency."

Ms. J is a 32-year-old single social work student. "I saw him for three years and I left him one day." Ms. J lists this therapist as her only passion at age 23. She checks despair, emotional illness, confusion or identity crisis, and suicidal thoughts as a result of her psychiatric nonsexual passion.

I have learned from a suicide hotline volunteer (Hilt, 1977) that a number of calls come from women patients who feel suicidal about their unhappy passions for their therapist.

Ms. K is a 27-year-old single social worker who describes her 4-year long passion for her therapist at age 20. "We had a reciprocal identification and feelings for each other. We kept our friendship after therapy but he broke it up and left the country. My passion continued for three years when he said he could not continue relating to me." She checks despair, rage, damaged self-esteem, and confusion and identity crisis as consequences.

Ten of the 15 women who considered the therapist as an object of one of their major passions had experienced considerable hurt. There were among them six checks for despair, six for rage, three for emotional illness, one for physical illness, two for suicidal thoughts, two for damaged self-esteem, and seven for confusion or identity crisis. Each of these women checked at least two or more of these negative emotions.

Two respondents had an intense passion experience when they consulted a psychiatrist again after an interval of some years. Their passion, which had been present but subdued in their initial treatment, seemed to have developed in their fantasy during the interval, perhaps even motivating the later consultation.

Sarah, a 47-year-old pediatrician, visited her psychiatrist 6 years after a 3-year long treatment had terminated, wanting help with feelings of alienation and futility. She made a plea for symmetry, and the therapist apparently also saw her at this point more as a colleague than as a patient and responded by confiding he had also recently fought with similar feelings. This self-disclosure unleashed in Sarah intense fantasies of a possible mutual love relationship that she had formerly kept under control. She started pursuing the startled doctor in socially inappropriate ways, very unusual actions for this inhibited woman, and the experience ended with eventual feelings of rejection, narcissistic injuries, and despair.

Finney (1975) discusses the ambiguous nature of these "after therapy" relationships from the therapist's point of view, admitting that there are no precise guidelines for such situations. From an ideal human standpoint, a creative therapeutic encounter might result in a beautiful in-depth friendship; this is not an unusual situation in same gender therapeutic experiences, but it seems to be exceptional in cross-gender therapies.

Weiss (1975), in his divorce research, has similarly found that human bonds, once established, are tenaciously preserved. Such feelings can be easily revived under propitious circumstances, attesting to a healthy human capacity to sustain relationships over a long period of time. A small number of women in my sample sought out their late adolescent lovers whose images had been maintained in fantasy, uncontaminated by daily living; one of these encounters actually resulted in a marriage.

Two contrasting vignettes of women that I interviewed will convey in yet a different way some of the potential dangers inherent in therapy and perhaps especially in cross-gender therapy.

Nancy is a 34-year-old divorced librarian who finds it difficult to relate intimately to others. Her warm and trusting 4-year relationship with her psychiatrist, a married man of about her age, is currently her major significant relationship. She feels that she has made great progress in treatment and expresses respect and admiration for her doctor. They have "an exquisite understanding about the nuances of communication." After 2 years of no touching, they had a particularly hard and successful session, and he shook her hand and then started to shake hands regularly. A year later he started to grab her hand in both of his to show appreciation and empathy, and half a year later he started to give her bear hugs on special occasions. "I am proud of you, thank you" was the message that she read. Then the bear hugs started to feel differently, more like tender holding, and one day he made an erotic noise while he held her and then kissed both her hands. Meanwhile, they have discussed these happenings and they both agree that they want to avoid sexual involvement. Nancy feels happy and appreciated and loved in this relationship. The eventual outcome of this therapy experience remains uncertain. We wonder uneasily how termination will be handled, if it ever becomes a goal in the far future.

Kathy, aged 46 and now divorced, went into therapy for help with an unhappy marriage after a stillbirth at age 34. She, too, experienced exceptional and unique communication with her psychiatrist. For the first time someone taught her to verbalize her feelings, which was a liberating experience. She was communicating and understanding on a level that had never been possible with her husband. She had graduated from the same high-status college as her doctor at about the same time, and Kathy saw him somewhat as a peer. Sometimes they had violent arguments about money, and she experienced these symmetrical engagements as highly involving. They teased each other and had private jokes, and she felt that he was also attracted to her. It was, however, only when his wife died, after 3 years of therapy, something they never discussed in therapy, that her passion for him became unmanageable. He reassured her, explaining that this was normal and expected transference, but she felt she was losing her sanity and, on her insistence, they both saw a consultant, who advised an immediate change of therapist. Kathy, however, was desperately in love, and there was no way she could turn this off. She could not relate to her new woman psychiatrist or to the subsequent man psychiatrist, neither of whom apparently understood the reason for her desperation. She made four suicide attempts in 18 months, two in her love object's car. She repeatedly invaded his waiting room, threatening to hurt herself if he did not talk to her, until he called the police one day. Kathy grabbed the policeman's gun to shoot herself and ended up in court accused of armed assault.

Kathy was labeled borderline personality with a transference psychosis. No doubt, like Ferguson, she also was particularly vulnerable to fusion and loss and started treatment at a time of loss. However, 8 years later, Kathy has divorced her husband, is entirely self-supporting as a research chemist, has successfully steered two sons through adolescence, and enjoys a network of friends. She has come to feel that her mental health depends on managing without a husband or psychiatrists.

I reported this somewhat unusual case because it gives us several useful warnings. Above all, we must beware of thinking that a sudden separation can be useful when transference "runs amok." Actually, it is distressing that some of the practices from the days when Breuer abandoned Anna O. are still in effect (Freeman, 1972). Kathy feels that a third person in the treatment situation and an opportunity to work through her violent emotions gradually would have been a solution. Even today she still longs to talk out this whole experience with her doctor, and she hopes that he will read this chapter.

The importance of the wife's death during treatment in

giving full rein to Kathy's fantasies was not sufficiently appreciated; perhaps therapists often overlook the importance that events in their private lives can have for patients. Walster (1976), in discussing the nature of passion, comments that "although psychologists tend to focus almost exclusively on the contribution of sex to love, other rewards can have an equally important impact" (p. 160). She feels that the recognition of any unsatisfied need could provide "fuel for passion" and, indeed, many women find the experience of a deep level of communication and understanding as deeply arousing as Nancy and Kathy. This is perhaps an inevitable aspect of therapy. Kathy quoted to me writing to her doctor, "You touch me emotionally constantly and wanting the other kind of touching comes from that." The fact that the therapist is a high-status, intelligent man who is probably in reality a highly suitable love object for the woman patient is yet another realistic difficulty. In comparison with a husband, a therapist undoubtedly has the upper hand. The relationship does not become corroded by the discouraging aspect of daily living.

We have thus heard that the benevolent context of the therapeutic encounter can misfire, even with therapists of goodwill and integrity. However, in case the view is too pessimistic, here is a case that fits Haley's (1963) paradoxical cure.

Ms. K is a 53-year-old professor who talks of her therapeutic experience at age 47. "He taught me to laugh at my depression and to believe in the possibility of love. During a hard time in my second marriage my relationship with him was the most important thing in my life."

Recent writings on psychoanalytically oriented psychotherapy suggest that intense transference-love is no longer considered inevitable, or even desirable. Langs (1974) thinks that a patient's excessive transference manifestations are usually due to therapeutic errors or countertransference problems and are not a repetition of a patient's past relationships. He repeatedly warns therapists not to overlook the realities of the therapeutic relationship. His valuable guide to therapists gives detailed advice on how to avoid arousing such iatrogenic reactions. However, he also recognizes the reality difficulties in the situation. "For many patients the therapist is in reality one of the few truly concerned and consistently helpful persons in their lives. The patient's response to this is usually only partly transference—that is based on past longings and relationships; it is also quite appropriate. This can also create very sticky ties to the therapist for the patient and make final resolution and termination of treatment quite difficult, especially for deprived and lonely individuals" (p. 223). The situation becomes even more complex when young therapists, and sometimes even mature ones, find an understandable need to avoid some of the sterility of the therapeutic "role" and wish to interact more "authentically" with their patients, which may include some self-disclosure, an occasional affectionate touch, or other steps outside of therapeutic boundaries, all of which may apparently arouse the patient's passionate feelings.

SUMMARY AND CONCLUSION

Although it is well known that all people, and especially women, enter therapy for help with experiences of rejection, betrayal, and disruption of attachment ties (Shainess, 1977), the frequency with which these disruptive experiences occur in connection with a disappointing love experience has not been recognized. As therapists, we must be alert to the deep narcissistic injuries that can occur by "unrequited love" experiences. There is danger that therapists might dismiss passion experiences as infantile, childlike fantasies that have little to do with "real" problems and everyday realities—especially if they have not been sexually consummated—without becoming aware of

the serious disruptions such experiences can cause in women's lives.
In view of the regressive and impulsive behavior that we have regularly observed during these episodes, there is also danger that clinicians might overestimate the seriousness of a woman's character pathology at such times, especially in cases of intense "transference-passion" for the therapist.

In cross-gender therapy the possibility exists that a woman shifts her passion feelings to her therapist and repeats the same experience with him. Certain personality characteristics and life circumstances seem to render some women more vulnerable to transference passions than others. It then becomes the therapist's difficult task not to respond to her loving overtures while still accepting, sustaining, and supporting her. Since human beings have difficulty compartmentalizing feelings and since one person's caring is another person's loving, it is perhaps no wonder that this does not always succeed. No attempt is thus being made to cast people into roles of victims or villains. The boundaries between caring about someone, liking them, loving them, and passionately loving them are fine lines that are difficult to maintain.

REFERENCES

Bak, R. Being in love and object loss. *International Journal of Psychoanalysis,* 1973, **54,** 1–7.

Barnes, M., & Berke, J. *Two accounts of a journey through madness.* New York: Harcourt Brace Jovanovich, 1971.

Benedek, T. Ambivalence, passion and love. *Journal of the American Psychoanalytic Association,* 1976, **25,** 53–79.

Carson, R. C. *Interaction concepts of personality.* Chicago: Aldine Publishing Company, 1969.

Chesler, P. *Women and madness.* New York: Doubleday, 1972.

Christie, G. The origins of falling-in-love and infatuation. *American Journal of Psychotherapy,* 1972, **26,** 244–256.

Davidson, V. Psychiatry's problem with no name: Therapist-patient sex. *American Journal of Psychoanalysis*, 1977, **37**, 45–50.

DeBeauvoir, S. *The second sex*. New York: Knopf, 1953.

Ferguson, S. *A guard within*. New York: Pantheon, 1973.

Finney, J. Therapist and patient after hours. *American Journal of Psychotherapy*, 1975, **29**, 593–602.

Freeman, L. *The story of Anna O*. New York: Walker and Co., 1972.

Freeman, L., & Roy, J. *Betrayal*. New York: Stein and Day, 1976.

Freud, S. *On narcissim*. In J. Strachey (Ed.), *Standard edition of the complete psychological works of Sigmund Freud*. Vol. 14. London: Hogarth Press, 1957. (Originally published, 1914.)

Freud, S. *Observations on transference love*. In J. Strachey (Ed.), *Standard edition of the complete psychological works of Sigmund Freud*. Vol. 12. London: Hogarth Press, 1957. (Originally published 1915.)

Freud, S. *Beyond the pleasure principle*. In J. Strachey (Ed.), *Standard edition of the complete psychological works of Sigmund Freud*. Vol. 18. London: Hogarth Press, 1955. (Originally published 1920.)

Haley, J. *Strategies of psychotherapy*. New York: Grune & Stratton, 1963.

Hilt, T. Personal Communication, 1977.

Kardener, S. Sex and the physician-patient relationship. *American Journal of Psychiatry*, 1974, **131**, 1134–1136.

Kernberg, O. Boundaries and structure in love relations. *Journal of the American Psychoanalytic Association*, 1976, **25**, 81–114.

Kremen, H., & Kremen, B. Romantic love and idealization. *American Journal of Psychoanalysis*, 1971, **31**, 134–143.

Langs, R. *The technique of psychoanalytic therapy*. Vol. II. New York: Jason Aronson, 1974.

Marmor, J. Some psychodynamic aspects of the seduction of patients in psychotherapy. *American Journal of Psychoanalysis*, 1976, **36**, 319–323.

Miller, S. M., and Mishler, E. G. Social class, mental illness and American Psychiatry: An expository review. *Millbank Memorial Fund Quarterly*, 1959, **37**, 1–26.

Mitchell, S. *My own woman*. New York: Horizon Press, 1973.

Moller, H. Meaning of courtly love. *Journal of American Folklore,* 1960, **73**, 39–52.

Reich, A. Narcisstic object choice in women. *American Journal of Psychoanalysis,* 1954, **1**, 22–44.

Reik, T. *A psychologist looks at love.* New York: Farrar and Rinehart, 1944.

Rougemont, D. *Love in the western world.* New York: Pantheon, 1956.

Rubin, Z. *Liking and loving.* New York: Holt, Rinehart and Winston, 1973.

Ryan, W. *Distress in the city.* New York: University Book Service, 1969.

Saghir, M., Walbran, B., Robins, E., & Gentry, K. Psychiatric disorders and disability in the female homosexual. *American Journal of Psychiatry,* 1970, **127**, 147–154.

Salzman, L. *The obsessive personality.* New York: Jason Aronson, 1973.

Schafer, R. The interpretation of transference and the conditions for loving. *Journal of the American Psychoanalytic Association,* 1977, **25**, 335–365.

Shainess, N. Treatment of crises in the lives of women: Object loss and identity threat. *American Journal of Psychotherapy,* 1977, **31**, 227–237.

Stone, A. The legal implications of sexual activity between psychiatrist and patient. *American Journal of Psychiatry,* 1976, **133**, 1138–1141.

Voth, H. Love affair between doctor and patient. *American Journal of Psychotherapy,* 1972, **26**, 394–400.

Walster, E. Passionate love. In Z. Rubin (Ed.), *Doing unto others.* Englewood Cliffs, N.J.: Prentice-Hall, 1976.

Weiss, R. *Marital separation.* New York: Basic Books, 1975.

2

Mothers and Their Children
A Study of
Low-Income Families

Deborah Belle

$\mathcal{J}$t seems to be easier these days than it used to be to speak of the stresses of parenthood. When Ann Landers conducted her write-in poll on the issue, more parents wrote to say they would not become parents if they had it to do over again than wrote in defense of having children. For those who decide to go ahead and have children, the books of child-rearing advice these days are typically sober in tone, if not actually frightening. Although there are obvious disadvantages to viewing the child as a bundle of

This chapter is based on research supported by grant number MH28830–02 of the Mental Health Services Branch, National Institute of Mental Health, Susan Salasin, Project Officer. Neither the Stress and Families Project nor this chapter would have been possible without the work of the other members of the Stress and Families Project staff: Bonita Allen, Polly Ashley, Kris Dever, Jacquelyn Gibson, Cynthia Longfellow, Vivian Makosky, Jacqueline Ryan, Elizabeth Saunders, and Phyllis Weinfeld, and the work and inspiration of its first director, Marcia Guttentag. I also thank Rochelle Albin for helpful criticism of an earlier draft of this chapter.

worries instead of as a bundle of joy, the current climate does allow us to be hardheaded. Evidence that will be reviewed in this chapter suggests that parental responsibility for young children, especially under adverse circumstances, is associated with depression and with psychiatric disturbance. This association is particularly important for women, who are more likely than men to bear parental responsibilities under adverse circumstances.

At the present time we know very little about the effects of stress on parents and on the parent-child relationship. We know very little about the parental behavior of depressed or highly stressed parents and little about the effect of such parental behavior on young children. This chapter will therefore be exploratory, first discussing some important trends in family life, then reviewing several recent studies that relate parental responsibilities to mental health, and finally describing an ongoing research project that attempts to elucidate some connections between stress and family life.

Although family roles are changing, mothers presently bear most of the child-care responsibilities in American families. The recent increase in single-parent families headed by women is well known and is reflected in Figure 2–1, which shows how children's family arrangements have changed in recent years. As can be seen, the percentage of children living with both parents has declined markedly from 1960 to 1975, for both whites and blacks, while the percentage of children living only with their mother has increased dramatically (U.S. Bureau of the Census, 1976). While a higher proportion of black children than white children live only with their mother, the rate of increase in single-parent living arrangements for black and white children is similar.

The increase in female-headed families is particularly significant, because these families are likely to be impoverished. According to the National Council of Organiza-

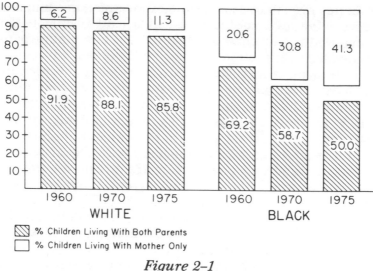

Figure 2-1
Children's Living Arrangements

tions for Children and Youth (1976), over half of all children in families headed by a woman were living below the official federal poverty line in 1974. This poverty line is drawn at an extremely low point; for instance, in 1974 it allowed about $5000 per year for a nonfarm family of four, including two parents and two children. Of all young children under 6 years of age in families headed by a woman, 60% are below the official poverty line. In 1974, almost 80% of children under 6 years in female-headed families were living on less than half of the national median income, a more reasonable measure of poverty.

Two-parent families have themselves changed in recent years. Probably the most dramatic change has been the entry of married women into the paid labor force. The labor force participation rate for married women increased from 14.7% in 1940 to 44.4% in 1970. While only 28.3% of married mothers with children aged 6 to 17 years held paid jobs in 1950, 52.4% of such mothers held paid jobs in 1975. The proportion of married mothers with children under 6 years of age who held paid jobs tripled between 1950 and 1975, from 11.9 to 36.6% (U.S. Bureau of the Census, 1976).

Despite this major change in women's roles, women still do most child care and housework in two-parent families. After an exhaustive review of research on the topic, Pleck (1976) concluded that there was no evidence for a significant change in recent years in the amount of child care and housework done by men, nor was there evidence that men with working wives did significantly more child care or housework than married men whose wives did not work outside the home.

Nye (1976) found in an interview study that a majority of both men and women believe that women should have primary responsibility for child care. When asked who should keep children clean, fed, and warm, husbands responded that these tasks should be performed by the wife more than by the husband, with majorities of 70, 69, and 52%, respectively. Still higher percentages of wives believed that each of these tasks should be primarily the wife's responsibility. Nye also found that wives' actual involvement in child-care tasks exceeded even these expressed norms. Both husbands and wives also believed that wives should take greater responsibility for child-care tasks in families with preschool children than in families with only school-age children. Thus, whether marriages with children endure or dissolve, mothers still bear most of the day-to-day responsibility for their children. To understand the mental health of women, it is necessary to understand the impact of these responsibilities.

Single-parent families have attracted concern, and there is evidence that members of such families experience mental health problems more frequently than members of husband-wife families. A recent analysis of who uses mental health facilities in this country found an alarmingly high rate of utilization by women who headed families and by children in female-headed families (Belle, 1978, in press; Guttentag, Salasin, & Belle, 1977). The goals of this study were to discover and examine sex differences in patterns of utilization, diagnosis, and treatment in mental health facilities and to pinpoint types of people of both sexes who frequently experience contact with mental health facilities. Even though using a mental health facility is not synonymous with experiencing mental illness, high rates of treatment among certain groups in the population are signs of a population "at risk."

The basic data and many of the analyses used in the study were obtained from the Biometry Branch of the National Institute of Mental Health. Analyses were based on their statistical notes and computer tapes. The most recent available data were used, generally from 1969 to 1973. All utilization rates were age-adjusted whenever possible.

As Figure 2–2 shows, women who headed families in 1970 were admitted to outpatient psychiatric services at a rate that exceeded one admission for every 100 female family heads in the population. Divorced and single female family heads had an admission rate at this level. Women who were separated from their husbands and who headed families had an admission rate of over three per 100 population. Widowed female family heads, however, appeared far less vulnerable. Their utilization rate was less than 0.3 per 100 such women in the population.

The alarming rates of utilization among women who headed families were echoed in the high rates of utilization among children in female-headed families. Children in such families were admitted to outpatient psychiatric services at a rate approaching one admission per 100 population, or more than double the admission rate of children in husband-wife families. Furthermore, the impact on children in single-parent families appears strongest among the youngest children. Children aged 6 to 17 years in female-headed families had an admission rate more

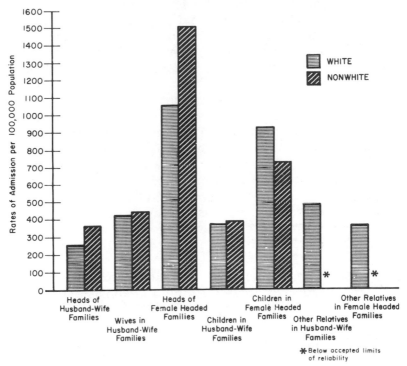

Figure 2–2

Utilization of Outpatient Psychiatric Services, 1970 by Type of Family
and Relationship to Family Head

than double that of 6 to 17-year-old children in husband-
wife families, but children under 6 years had an admission rate that was four times as large as that of children
under 6 years in husband-wife families. While children
under 6 years from all family types combined had a lower
admission rate than older children, children under 6 years
living with separated, single-parent mothers had a higher
admission rate to outpatient psychiatric services than
children 6 to 13 years old living with such mothers. This
reversal of the positive association of age and utilization
rate is cause for concern.

At state and county mental hospitals, admission rates of women who headed families and of children in female-headed families again exceeded those of parents and children in husband-wife families, although "other relatives" in husband-wife families also had high admission rates. This is shown in Figure 2–3.

The utilization of most mental health facilities was associated with low income. Thus, for instance, the men and women with the highest utilization rate at state and county mental hospitals and outpatient psychiatric services had incomes under $3000 a year, and those with the highest utilization rates at community mental health centers had weekly incomes of less than $100. These were the lowest income categories measured at each facility. Private mental hospitals, for obvious reasons, were an exception to this generalization about high utilization by the poor.

Another finding of this work was that the sex differences in diagnoses received were striking and consistent from

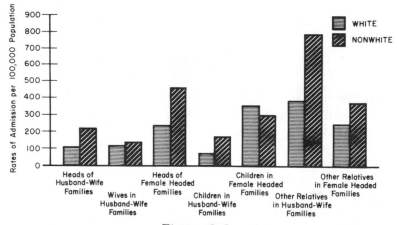

Figure 2–3
Utilization of State and County Mental Hospitals, 1970 by Type of Family and Relationship to Family Head

one type of mental health facility to the next. In each type of facility studied, men had higher age-adjusted rates of treatment for alcohol disorders, drug abuse, and mental retardation, and women exceeded men in diagnosed depressive disorders. This diagnosis was the most frequent diagnosis among female patients at community mental health centers, general hospital inpatient psychiatric units, and private mental hospitals, and it accounted for the highest percentage of female patients who were terminated from outpatient psychiatric services.

Utilization data indicate who is being treated for mental health problems, but they do not reveal the full extent of suffering, since many people who do not have contact with hospitals or clinics experience mental health problems such as depression. Surveys and interview studies of the general population can locate such people. Several recent studies of nonhospitalized populations have found that parents living with children experience high rates of depression and psychiatric disturbance. Low income, the presence of young children, and the presence of many children have also been implicated as risk factors.

Pearlin and Johnson (1975) conducted a survey using a brief self-report measure of depressive symptoms. They found that symptoms of depression were particularly common among the formerly married, especially those with children, those with inadequate financial resources, and those who were socially isolated. The rate of depression among the unmarried increased with the number of children at home and increased as the age of the youngest child in the family fell.

These findings held for both men and women, but it should be noted that women are more likely than men to experience these risk factors. In Pearlin and Johnson's (1975) sample, as in the general population, a higher proportion of women than of men are formerly married. As noted earlier, a higher proportion of children in single-parent families live with their mothers, and the financial situation of female-headed families is vastly inferior to that of male-headed families. Pearlin and Johnson (1975) also found that social isolation was more common among the unmarried than among the married.

Even under conditions of similar financial hardship and social isolation, however, the unmarried were more prone to depression than the married. Pearlin and Johnson (1975) describe a situation in which multiple stresses are more likely to impinge on the unmarried and are more likely to be reflected in an increased incidence of depression. When these hardships and burdens are absent, the incidence of depression among the unmarried is similar to its incidence among the married.

Vulnerability to depression because of parental status is not restricted to the formerly married, however. An English study (Brown, Bhrolchain, & Harris, 1975) indicates that similar dynamics can also operate among the married. In this study wives were interviewed to determine if there was emotional intimacy between the spouses. Marriages without such intimacy did not protect women from depression in the way that emotionally intimate marriages did. Brown studied a community sample of 220 London women, including working-class and middle-class women who fell into the following marital and parental status categories.

1. A group of younger women (aged less than 35 years) who were either single or married, and had no children at home.
2. Married women whose youngest child at home was aged less than 6 years.
3. Married women whose youngest child at home was aged between 6 and 14 years.
4. Married women whose youngest child was 15 years or over.
5. A group of older women (aged 35 years and over), including the divorced, widowed, and separated, who

had no children at home, who had never had children, or whose children had left home, as well as single women.

Each woman in the study was interviewed to discover whether or not she was experiencing or had recently experienced a psychiatric disturbance, particularly depression. Of the 220 women, 35 were judged to have suffered from an affective disorder of some kind. Brown et al. (1975) found that working-class women whose youngest child was under 6 years had the highest rate of disturbance; in fact, 42% of these women were considered to have experienced an affective disorder; middle-class women and working-class women without young children at home had lower rates of disturbance.

Brown et al. (1975) were able to pinpoint several factors that were associated with psychiatric disturbance and that were more common among working-class than middle-class women. Together these factors accounted for the class difference in rate of psychiatric disturbance. One such risk factor was the occurrence of recent threatening life events. Working-class women were more likely than middle-class women to have experienced such events. In fact, as Brown et al. (1975) note, many such events are essentially confined to the working class—having a husband sent to prison, a son arrested for breaking and entering, a husband losing his job, an eviction threat. Another vulnerability factor was the presence of a long-term difficulty in an area such as housing, money, or health.

For women who experienced either a threatening life event or a major difficulty, the most effective buffer against depression appeared to be an intimate, confiding relationship with the husband or, if unmarried, with a boyfriend. Working-class women with young children were less likely than their middle-class counterparts to have such a relationship. Brown et al. (1975) also found that having many children and having lost one's mother in childhood each increased the chance of depression when there were severe difficulties or threatening life events. These vulnerability factors were more common among working-class than among middle-class women. Employment was an additional buffer against depression in this study, but one that was distributed approximately equally between working-class and middle-class women.

In another community survey, Radloff (1975) found that parental status was significantly related to the number of self-reported symptoms of depression. The "empty nest" group, persons who had reared children but were no longer living with them, had significantly lower depression scores than persons who had never had children or persons currently living with children. There was also a tendency for the depression scores of parents to increase as the age of the youngest child at home decreased. Like Brown, et al. (1975) Radloff (1975) found that employment buffered women to some extent against depression in the face of life event losses such as deaths and separation.

It appears from the three studies just described that responsibility for young children is particularly associated with depression. Why should this be so? Answers to this question must be speculative, and further research and reflection on this question seem imperative. It is clear that young children are highly dependent on adults. They demand time and energy and even sacrifice. Since child-care facilities for preschool children are still rare, most children under 6 years must be cared for at home or through arrangement with relatives or friends. Such arrangements may themselves involve the child's mother in unwanted obligations. Preschool children may restrict their mothers' social and emotional support network because of their own emotional needs. A recent study of divorced mothers (Fox, 1976) found that mothers of preschool children were more likely than mothers of older children to report their children's jealousy of mothers' boyfriends. Mothers of older children were more likely to report that their children were encouraging "father shopping."

Young children have fewer cognitive resources to use in understanding the meaning of crucial family events such as divorce or ongoing conditions such as poverty. It is not uncommon for a child whose parents have separated to blame himself or herself for the father's departure. Longfellow (1978, in press) has reviewed the literature on children's response to parental divorce and concluded that the younger the child, the greater the vulnerability to disturbance. A child's emotional problems may then produce problems for the parent as well.

Children can also, of course, provide support to their parents. In the study by Fox (1976) children were often named by divorced mothers as the reason for going on, as wonderful organizing principles in a confusing, demoralizing time. Children often give parents a reason to be strong and competent and thus the satisfaction of being so. However, their needs are liable to exceed a parent's resources and lead to a sense of failure.

The Stress and Families Project currently in progress in Boston studies low-income mothers and their young children to learn more about the stresses that lead to depression and other disturbances among this group. The project studies 40 low-income mothers who have at least one child between 5 and 7 years of age. The sample includes women living with husbands, women living with lovers, and women living without men.

A team of researchers works with each family. One researcher conducts a series of interviews with the mother on topics such as daily routine, recent life events, ongoing life conditions, social networks, coping strategies, family nutrition, experiences with social service institutions, work history, experiences of discrimination, and generational change in the woman's role. Brief self-report measures of depression, self-esteem, and anxiety are also administered. The second researcher in the team conducts nonparticipant observations of family interaction and interviews the children about the parent-child relationship. This researcher also interviews the mother and the father, if present, about child-rearing beliefs and practices. Involvement with a family generally entails weekly or twice-weekly visits to the family's home extending over a 3-month period.

Researchers on the staff have spent many hours in the homes of research families. We have witnessed the daily routines and even a few crises of the research families. We have visited families when there was no money in the house, when a burglary had occurred the night before, and when a child was injured playing and had to be rushed to the hospital. We have accompanied some of the mothers on shopping trips and tours of the community garden. We have met relatives, neighbors, friends, and social workers. In addition to our formal interview and observational data, we have brought back from our families a sense of how their lives are lived: how dangerous their street feels at different times of day, how the children at a nearby playground seem to get along, and how visitors are received when they drop by unexpectedly. We hope to take advantage of such insights and perceptions as we seek to understand the connections between stress and family life.

We are presently working with the last of our research families, and we have begun to analyze data from the families with whom work is already completed. Because data collection and analysis are not yet complete, only a few conclusions can be ventured at this time.

The study began with an interest in why so many low-income mothers of young children experience depression. Using a generally accepted cutoff score for the depression measure, almost half of our respondents for whom this data has been analyzed would be classified "depressed." Our recruitment effort was merely to find low-income mothers of young children, but we have clearly found a deep vein of unhappiness. The women who reported many depressive symptoms include both married and unmarried women, both black and white women. There are also women in the study who report no or very few symptoms of depression.

Even the most seriously depressed women in the study cannot be characterized as always dispirited and passive. One of our respondents, a severely depressed woman, fought off an intruder in her apartment at night. Another woman whose son was hurt while playing took him quickly and competently to the hospital emergency room and took control of the situation as he was being treated. In another instance, one of our researchers had her tape recorder stolen; her respondent ran into the street, corralled a boy she saw with a tape recorder, and took it from him while delivering a ferocious lecture.

Yet depression does take its toll on these women. Preliminary analysis of data from a subsample of research families indicates that the more depressed mothers in the study direct fewer nurturant behaviors to their children than the less depressed mothers in the study. There is also a suggestion that mother-child relationships, as viewed by the children, are less happy and intimate when mothers are depressed.

It is instructive to consider the nature of some of the highly stressful life events experienced by our small sample of women. These include: rape, beating by the husband, robbery, nervous breakdown, appearance in court, husband stabbed to death, children claimed by their father after many years, and desertion by the husband. Violence is not rare, and husbands or lovers are frequently the perpetrators of violence. Holmes and Rahe's (1967) widely used social readjustment rating scale, which measures recent life events such as business readjustment and taking a mortgage over $10,000 but excludes events such as evictions or rape, is hardly applicable to the experience of these women. Nor would scores on Holmes and Rahe's (1967) scale do justice to the life stress experienced by these women.

Examination of these life events also forces one to consider carefully the role of husbands or lovers in the lives of these women. Much of the data reviewed earlier in this chapter, particularly the discussion of husbands or boy-friends as emotional "buffers" against depression, might lead one to conclude that marriage is a safe haven for women, especially mothers. The incidence of threatening life events perpetrated by husbands certainly suggests that the issue is not so simple. We plan to analyze the ways in which our sample of women are supported by men: emotionally, financially, in help with child-care tasks, and the like, and the ways in which the women are stressed by the men with whom they share a home.

Any attempt to understand low-income mothers must take into account the diversity of the coping strategies that these women adopt. I will describe two very different women in the study. The first has explained her situation clearly to us. She feels that with all the problems in her own life (poor health, loneliness, joblessness) she is simply not able to deal adequately with her three preschool chil-dren. She believes she is not a satisfactory mother, but she sees no hope for improvement until she can get the other problems in her life under control.

This mother has, however, coped with her inability in a number of powerful ways. She has utilized her social net-work and her personal connections at social service agen-cies to provide other nurturant figures for her children. The respondent's adult brother is involved in caring for the children, and he visits frequently. Neighbors drop by often and spread around a bit of affection to both mother and children. The mother attends a women's group that discusses child-rearing problems and how to handle them. Without this group, the respondent feels she would have been "messed up a long time ago." A social worker has become very involved with this family and has even become godmother to one of the children.

This mother freely discusses her problems, recognizes the limits of her own ability to care for her children, and broadens the support networks of her children. At one point during the course of the study she sent her oldest child to spend several weeks with a close friend of hers in another part of the city. During this period the mother felt she was able to establish a workable routine with her younger children. This regime did not endure, however, after the return of the eldest child.

In contrast, another woman in our study who is also experiencing highly stressful conditions does not report herself to be depressed and does not express such dismay at her life situation or her ability to care for her children. This woman has chosen a very different strategy for coping with poverty and a large, young family without a husband. The mother's goal is to help her children move up and out of poverty, and her strategy involves a great deal of self-imposed isolation. Although she has lived in the same apartment for 9 years, she has very little contact with her neighbors. Her children are bused to school in distant suburbs and do not play with the neighbors' children. This mother generally sees her close friends less than once a month. She refuses to give up parenting tasks to others, and even forbids her older children to care for the younger children. Attempts to aid these very different mothers and their children will fail unless they take into account the different philosophies and strengths that these mothers possess.

In a research project such as ours, the relationship of researcher to respondent can be revealing. When we began working with families, we worried that we would be seen as child-care experts or social workers or clinicians. We worried about the signals we might give. We did not want to be seen as potential critics of child-rearing techniques or of housekeeping, and we wanted each woman to regard herself as the expert on the facts of her own life. Nor did we want to find ourselves conducting interventions instead of research. As work began, we were able to discard some of these worries. We received only rare queries about child care, and these seemed casual and easily deflected. We received apologies about the state of the apartment, but not the whirlwind cleanup that the social worker gets.

We apparently were not seen as experts or potential critics, but as people with access to information and power. In particular, we were enlisted to help with job searches, and employment possibilities were discussed with us. Over the period of one summer's work with eight families, two women took jobs, one woman began a serious search for training, and other women discussed employment options with us. The extent to which we were role models or catalysts in this process is unclear. What is clear is that jobs represented a bright hope to many of these women. Research such as that by Brown et al. (1975) and Radloff (1975) suggests that employment can actually protect women's mental health when other circumstances are difficult. To several of the women with whom we worked, the future looked dismal without a job to provide some way out of poverty, isolation, and low self-esteem.

We asked each woman, "What would you like to see your child doing when he or she is your age?" One of our respondents said she hoped her children would not be on welfare. "That deteriorates a person quick. Some people like being on welfare. I think it's a damn hang-up." For her daughter she said, "I hope she has kids. I hope she be established in a job or program to help her provide for herself. Then, if she find the right dude—if there is one— I hope she won't be in the depression I'm in."

I couldn't say it better.

References

Belle, D. Who uses mental health facilities? In M. Guttentag and S. Salasin (Eds.), *Families abandoned: The cycle of depression.* New York: Academic Press, 1978, in press.

Brown, G. W., Bhrolchain, M. N., & Harris, T. Social class and psychiatric disturbance among women in an urban population. *Sociology,* 1975, 9(2), 225–254.

Fox, E., Personal communication, 1976.

Guttentag, M., Salasin, S., & Belle, D. Executive summary: National patterns in the utilization of mental health services. Unpublished paper, Harvard University, 1977.

Holmes, T. H., & Rahe, R. H. The social readjustment rating scale. *Journal of Psychosomatic Research,* 1967, 11, 213–218.

Longfellow, C. Divorce in context: Its impact on children. In G. Levinger and O. Moles (Eds.), *Divorce and separation.* New York: Basic Books, 1978, in press.

National Council of Organizations for Children and Youth. *America's children 1976: A bicentennial assessment.* 1976.

Nye, R. I. *Role structure and analysis of the family.* Beverly Hills, Calif.: Sage Publications, 1976.

Pearlin, L. I., & Johnson, J. S. Marital status, life-strains and depression. Unpublished paper, 1975.

Pleck, J. Men's new roles in the family: Housework and child care. Unpublished paper, 1976.

Radloff, L. Sex differences in depression: The effects of occupational and marital status. *Sex Roles,* 1975, 1, 249–265.

U.S. Bureau of the Census. *Statistical abstract of the United States, 1976.* (97th ed.) Washington, D.C.: U.S. Government Printing Office, 1976.

3

The Experience of Abortion

Tamara E. Belovitch

The issue of abortion is one of the most highly controversial issues facing women today. It is also one of the most important and serious considerations a woman may have to make, because the consequences of her decision are irreversible: unlike a husband, a child cannot be divorced; unlike a job or career, a child cannot be changed; unlike a relationship, a child cannot be ended. On the other hand, it must also be remembered that once a pregnancy is terminated, the child that would have developed will never be; a woman may subsequently have other children, but not that one.

It is estimated that in 1976, 1.2 million abortions were performed by physicians—one abortion for every 2.8 live births. Of those women receiving abortions, 75% are unmarried, 67% are white, and 48% have no children. Age groups of these women seem to be evenly distributed; 32% are teenagers, 33% are in the 20 to 24-year-old bracket, and 35% are 25 or older (Center for Disease Control, 1976).

Abortions also appear to be safer than live births. For every 100,000 abortions performed, 3.2 resulted in the death of the mother, while for every 100,000 live births, death resulted for 12.8 of the mothers (Center for Disease Control, 1976).

At the crux of the proabortion-antiabortion debate is whether the fetus is a living person. This highly charged and intensely emotional issue will not be debated here; it has been unresolved for decades and may go unresolved for decades more. But it is important to examine the impact of the abortion issue on the lives of women, and the unwanted child.

IMPACT ON THE CHILD

The most damaging plight of a child is to be unwanted. Erikson (1958) has said, "The most deadly of all possible sins is the mutilation of a child's spirit" (p. 70), and the Group for Advancement of Psychiatry (1968–1971) reported:

> There can be nothing more destructive to a child's spirit than being unwanted, and there are few things more disruptive to a woman's spirit than being forced without love or need into motherhood. . . . The predicament of the future child should he be born cannot be ignored. . . . (O)ne significant study has been carried out in Sweden with 120 children born after an application for a therapeutic abortion had been refused. These children were born during the 1939–41 period and followed up until age 21 for assessment in terms of mental health, social adjustment, and educational level. They were compared to a control group composed of the very next same-sexed child born at the same hospital or in the same district to other mothers. The mothers of the control were not selected on the basis of their maturity, but simply by the criteria of proximity in time, in geography, and in the sex of offspring. The results of this study indicated that "The unwanted chil-

dren were worse off in every respect. . . . The differences were often significant (statistically) and when they were not they pointed in the same direction . . . to a worse lot for the unwanted child." This is certainly not unexpected since the adverse consequences of maternal rejection have long been recognized by psychiatrists as one of the major contributing elements of human psychopathology. In fact, some psychiatrists believe that one of the most important goals of preventive psychiatry is the prevention of unwanted offspring. (pp. 209, 219)

A woman who is not psychologically, physically, or financially capable of mothering, or one who simply does not want the task, should not and cannot be forced to mother. As Belle (1978) describes, there is a high proportion of depression and psychiatric disturbance among single parents living with children.

"Adoption not abortion" has been suggested as an alternative, but this can present equally serious problems for the woman who must carry her pregnancy to full term and then give up the child, and for the child if he or she does not get adopted. Orphanages and child welfare agencies are overloaded with "unadoptable" (older) children who are being shuffled from one foster home to another, still unwanted.

Impact on Women

Aside from all the politics is the human side—women who have actually had to come to grips with the question of an unwanted pregnancy and have had to make the decision to carry to full term or to terminate the pregnancy.

Emotions such as ambivalence, anxiety, guilt, anguish, fear, despair, and sorrow have all been attributed to the abortion experience (Denes, 1976; Francke, 1978). These are also the emotions that most frequently bring people (men and women) into psychotherapy. Therefore, for women, the psychological aftereffects of the abortion experience should be examined not only so that "informed social decisions about abortion can be made" (Shusterman, 1976, p. 80), but to give psychotherapists as much information as possible as to the psychological reactions of patients seeking help because of a contemplated or experienced abortion. During this time of crisis and upheaval women need knowledgeable support and empathy.

A paradoxical situation has arisen in this area because many people in the feminist movement have led women to believe that because control of our bodies is our right, abortion is free of conflict. "We are afraid to say that abortion is terrible—for the woman whose body undergoes the trauma, and (I think) for the other life involved. Afraid to give our enemies ammunition, we whisper these things to one another; we are afraid to say them out loud" (Harrison, 1978, p. 40).

In a review of the literature, Osofsky and Osofsky (1972) looked to studies done on the psychological reactions of patients to abortion. The studies were conducted in the United States, Scandinavia, England, the USSR, Eastern Europe, and Japan. Their investigations revealed scarce information and data, but what was available indicated that negative reactions to the abortion experience were scarce.

In her review of the psychosocial factors surrounding abortion and the psychological aftereffects, Shusterman (1976) found:

The literature on the psychological effects of induced abortion is quite contradictory: many studies conclude that there are severe psychological consequences; many conclude that there are mild or no consequences, and some conclude that the consequences vary with other factors. (p. 90)

She attributes the contradictions to "methodological differences, differences in the variables investigated, sample differences, and theoretical differences" (p. 90). She also faults the investigations on the basis that "Many conclusions have been drawn from shoddy or non-existent data" (p. 90). An important distinction is made by Fleck (1970), who reviewed the literature on abortion. He concluded that abortion itself can be a relatively simple medical procedure without negative psychological consequences. The psychological pain often reported was the result when women were forced to seek illegal medical treatment.

Given these different reports, it is important to treat each woman individually. Biological, psychological, and sociological dynamics differ for every woman; reactions to an experience such as abortion will also differ from woman to woman. The only certainty may be the uncertainty of a woman's reactions. And to this the health care delivery system must be attuned and sensitive.

The following section contains interviews conducted with women (whose identities are anonymous) who have had abortions. There is no claim that this is a random sample of women, or a controlled study. Rather, it is an attempt to present personal reactions from a few women. They have generously related their experiences and emotions before and after the fact. For some it was the first time the experience was shared with anyone, and for those and others it was not an easy task. The interviews reveal that even though women's new freedom allowed them to consider their own future and goals more than ever, equal if not more consideration was given to the future and well-being of the unborn child.

THE ADOPTION ALTERNATIVE

As mentioned earlier, adoption is often suggested as an alternative to abortion. However, it, too, carries with it its own trauma and pain. Many of the women interviewed were asked whether they had considered adoption over abortion, and they all felt, as one girl put it:

> I don't think I could carry a baby all that time and then give it up. I'd never be at peace not knowing what happened to it, if it was loved or happy or safe. No, that would be the worst thing and my last choice.

The following interview is with a woman who did choose adoption. Linda M. is a 50-year-old married housewife with two grown children. She said she wanted to share her story because "It may help someone out in the same boat."

> I was 17 when I became pregnant. At that time there was no pill, in fact, birth control wasn't even considered. I wasn't wild or anything, I just got caught. Neither my boyfriend nor I wanted to get married as we both wanted to go to college (I wanted to be a teacher). Abortions at that time were absolutely out of the question, not only because of the religious and moral taboos but because they were downright dangerous, not to mention expensive. I was too afraid so I "went abroad" for a year and had my baby and gave it up for adoption. I never saw it (I don't even know what sex it was). But I can tell you that the day hasn't gone by that I haven't thought about it and wondered if it was OK. After nine months that baby was a part of me and when I gave it up I gave up some of myself.

CONTRACEPTIVE IGNORANCE

Many young girls become pregnant because they have little or no knowledge about birth control or sometimes because the consequence of becoming pregnant simply does not occur to them.

Sandy A. is a 20-year-old black woman with an infant baby girl. She is unmarried and on welfare. The baby's

father is in the service, when he is discharged they plan
to be married.

> I got pregnant the first time because I just wasn't taking any-
> thing. Nobody had ever said anything about birth control, but
> then I never had sex with anybody except my boyfriend. When
> I got pregnant with my little girl I didn't even consider abor-
> tion. My boyfriend said it was OK to have the baby and he
> helps me out with his Army money. After I had the baby I
> started taking the pill but we had sex right away and I guess
> the pill didn't have time to work. So I got pregnant again but
> this time there was no way I could have another baby so he
> gave me the money to have an abortion. It was easier than
> having the baby, but even though I knew I couldn't have kept
> it I still felt kind of bad doing it. Maybe some day I'll be able
> to have more kids when we get married.

ABORTION WITHOUT CONFLICT

For some, abortion is taken in stride, as with Joan C., a
25-year-old single medical secretary. She leads an active
social life and says:

> I didn't have much luck taking the pill so I had an IUD put in.
> Well, somehow I got pregnant anyway. At the time I was going
> out with a Black guy and even though we had a great thing
> going we didn't want to get married and I certainly didn't want
> a kid. Even if I did, in that situation I don't think it would have
> been realistic to have the baby. Anyway, there was no question
> in my mind—I didn't have to give it a thought. I had a quickie
> abortion and that was that. No, I've never been sorry.

ABORTION AS A JOINT ISSUE

The majority of women seeking abortions are unmarried; however, there is that minority of married women

who have unwanted pregnancies. Not only does a decision have to be made but, if the woman consults her husband (which not all women who have unwanted pregnancies do), the decision must be a joint one.

Susan G. is a 21-year-old married woman. She works in an office full time to help put her husband through college.

Shortly after we were married I discovered I was pregnant. I was on the pill but I have to admit that some nights I'd just forget to take them. My husband and I wanted a family but not for a long time yet. We didn't know what to do. It was all we talked about. We weighed the pros and cons all the time. We felt as though we weren't ready emotionally, let alone financially for such a responsibility—then we'd see a young couple with a cute baby and we'd say well, they're doing it. We were so confused for awhile we didn't know what to do. We finally ended up talking to one of the counselor's at Jim's university and just having an objective third party to listen to us helped. We finally decided on the abortion. We don't feel guilty about it and we don't regret it because we feel as though we'll have more to offer our kids in the future—emotional support as well as financial support. But sometimes I get real sad thinking about it. I am very sorry that I had to do it.

ILLEGAL ABORTION

It is not so many years ago that abortions were illegal in all states in the United States. We have all seen in the movies, read, or heard about back-alley abortions, some of which result in death or sterility for the woman. The following interview is with a woman who had one of those abortions.

Dolores S. is a 34-year-old wife and mother. At the age of 19 she became pregnant and had to get an illegal abortion.

I was a very ignorant and naive 19. I got pregnant the first time I had sexual relations with anyone. I am a Roman Catholic and felt guilty enough about having pre-marital sex—then when I found myself pregnant! I was so shaken I didn't know which end was up. All my boyfriend could think of was to get rid of it. At that time abortion was not legal but he said he knew a good "doctor," who for the right price would perform abortions. My upbringing and religious beliefs told me it was wrong, yet going home to my family and telling them I was pregnant was out of the question—they'd have kicked me out or killed me. That was the ultimate sin—rob a bank, shoot someone, but don't get "in trouble." So I had my abortion thinking someday God would punish me. The man *was* a doctor and it was done in typical soap-opera fashion—late at night in his office. I was sick as a dog after—emotionally and physically. I had to tell my folks I had a stomach virus. And was I punished? Well, I have a good husband and a beautiful child, but I've never gotten over the guilt of what I did and I live with that every day. Today women are urged to seek help for their emotional problems, it's almost the thing to do. I only wish then I had someone to talk to, but even that was looked down upon a little—besides what reason could I give for getting help? I've been playing around with the idea of going to see a therapist now, but I think it's too late for me. I'll see.

Seeking Help

Because of the highly emotional and traumatic feelings that abortion or the thought of abortion evoke, many women find they need assistance not only for negative aftereffects but in helping them to decide in the first place.

Maureen A. is a 26-year-old divorced legal secretary. She became pregnant at the time she and her husband were about to be divorced.

I had been on the pill for a number of years but decided that since I was getting divorced and was not interested in going out with men for awhile, I'd give my body a break and go off the pill. This was during the period when my ex-husband and I were separated—we decided our marriage was not a good one and going nowhere. We were both agreeable to the terms and still friendly. One night he came over to discuss something and we ended up in bed. I had completely forgotten I was off the pill—I never had to think about contraception before. Well, needless to say, I got pregnant. I am not a particularly religious person but I really don't think abortion is right, yet when I was faced with the possibility of being alone with a child I didn't particularly want, that didn't seem quite right either. I didn't even know whether to tell my ex-husband or not. He probably would have wanted me to have the baby and not get divorced. I don't believe that children save a marriage so I didn't care for that prospect. But then sometimes I'd think I could have the baby, be divorced and still make it OK—but then the thoughts of going on welfare were repugnant. A girl-friend of mine worked for a psychologist and got me an appointment to talk to her. It was great. She let me weigh all my options and helped me to sort my feelings. I did have my abortion. I am also still seeing my psychologist. The support and insight I get from that relationship have been invaluable. I do not regret my decision to terminate the pregnancy. Maybe some day I'll be in a position to truly welcome a child into my life without so many ambivalent feelings—the way it should be.

The last two interviews are especially revealing, because the women relate their experiences right through to the procedures. One woman had a D&C abortion; the other had a saline abortion. The importance of staff and clinic support should be noted in both cases.

Alice P. is a 30-year-old woman who is married for the second time. Three years ago she underwent a D&C abortion. She relates her story and her day at the clinic.

I had been divorced for a couple of years when I started going out with my present husband. We had a good thing going when I discovered I was pregnant. I couldn't believe it—I was on the pill and hadn't missed a one. He was divorced also and we were determined not to make the same mistake twice. So while a part of me wanted the baby, another part knew it would be unwise to have it. I was only 2½ months pregnant so I knew I could get a quickie (D&C) abortion. I had to be at the clinic early in the morning with a urine sample. When I walked into the waiting room I couldn't believe my eyes—it was pretty full. There were girls there who didn't look old enough to have their period and women who looked like they were mothers many times over. After I was checked in I was told to have a seat and that I would be called. Sitting there was like sitting at a wake—deadly silence, no one looked up—if they did you saw the same expression—fear and/or sadness. Finally I was called in with a group of others to the clinic area. The whole section was nice and modern and everyone who worked there was terrific, it's the one thing that really stands out for me. They made you feel like you were doing the right thing instead of something criminal. Anyway, we were given a fairly complete physical—blood work and all—and a complete medical history was taken. We were put into groups of about seven and led to a room where a woman talked to us about birth control. When they asked if any of us were using contraceptives at the time we became pregnant and I told them I was on the pill they looked a little skeptical until I told them what I was on. They said they had had a lot of trouble with that pill and shortly after my abortion it was taken off the market. The woman explained every form of birth control from coitus interruptus to the pill. She used diagrams, plastic models and everything. We were to choose which form we wanted, with the pill being stressed. After that we each saw a social worker privately to discuss our feelings about the abortion—were we sure, etc. That was the last stretch before the "procedure." We were offered a mild nerve relaxer while we waited. My group was waiting in one area and by now we were pretty nervous—this was it—and we finally started talking and swapping stories. None of us wanted to be there but we all felt it was the best thing to do. One feeling we all felt was that we were very glad to have had the opportunity to have a safe abortion in a clinic such as this one. My turn came up and I was shown into an examining room. I put on my johnnie and waited for the doctor and nurse. They were both soft-spoken and pleasant. As I lay back the doctor explained to me just what was going to happen and what I could do to make it easier and before I knew it, it was over. I got dressed and had to rest for awhile before they would let me leave. Cookies and soda were waiting (it was now late in the day and we weren't allowed to eat all day). I went to the pharmacy, got my pills and went home. As I look back on it now, I know I did the right thing. When I think back to the other girls I met that day at the clinic I know that for whatever reason, none of us were happy with what we felt we had to do and I often wonder how they're doing now. We did not want to "kill our babies"— whether we felt that way because society had brainwashed us into thinking that way, or whether our religious beliefs tell us it is wrong, it was something that was not done lightly.

The final interview is with a 33-year-old single woman who shares what she considers to be "the worst thing that ever happened" to her—a saline abortion performed several years ago.

I had a good job as an administrative assistant in an advertising firm, a nice apartment of my own—my only problem was that I was involved with a married man (no divorce in sight). I was on birth control pills but this was at the time when doctors thought it was a good idea to take a break from the pill for a month or two a year. When my boyfriend had to go away on business for a while I decided to take my break. It was also felt at that time that when a woman went off the pill after being on them for a long time she would have trouble getting pregnant right away until her body adjusted. My boyfriend came back a little earlier than expected and I guess my body adjusted quicker than expected because I soon found myself pregnant. My boyfriend said "abortion" immediately. Abortion was not legal in my state but was in a neighboring state. My first reaction was anger—I felt betrayed by the medical profession and even by my own body—and I was angry at my boyfriend and men in general who could be so detached and cool when my life had turned upside down. I am not a formally religious person and I have always believed that a woman should be able to choose whether or not she wants children even if this ultimately results in abortion. The question of whether the fetus was a "child" is something I never gave much thought to. Yet when I found myself pregnant I was suddenly overcome with all kinds of maternal feelings. I didn't know what to do. Sometimes I felt I really wanted the baby even though it would mean an entirely different life than I had planned for myself, and yet at other times I just couldn't see my way clear to go ahead with it. I agonized over it constantly. I didn't sleep for three months straight—I'd lie awake either crying or trying to visualize what my life would be like with a baby and without a baby. I also found myself agonizing over the fear that something might go wrong (punishment?) and I'd never be able to have children. For this first time in my life I thought I was cracking up. I procrastinated for so long that when I finally did decide to have an abortion I was four months pregnant and discovered I would have to have a saline abortion. I had heard so many horror stories about that, that I almost changed my mind again, but I didn't. So I took what seemed like the longest train ride of my life to an out-of-state hospital. It was old and pretty run down and the admitting staff was cold as I got shuffled around (again I almost changed my mind). It was late afternoon and I was finally put into a room with two other women—we were all relieved to see each other. A nurse came in to tell us we would be receiving the procedure shortly and to get ready. We were taken to a minor surgery room in what looked like the basement and again I wanted to bolt. There were three beds and we each went to one. Three doctors came in. I had a very soft-spoken Oriental woman who very carefully explained everything she was doing to me and what was going to happen. A saline solution was being injected into my abdomen (almost painless) and without realizing it the first thought that came into my mind was "my poor baby, I'm so sorry." We were told that at some point soon, possibly the next day, we would start to feel labor pains and our water would break. When the pains got very bad and close together we would be taken to the delivery room—the fetus would be delivered as if it was a baby. The whole process would take about three days. So for the next 24–48 hours we just had to sit around and wait—wait for the pain. The other two girls and I got along fine—misery loves company—and the nurses on our floor were very nice and accommodating. Two days later the pains started to get bad so one of the girls called a nurse. I am not one to carry on if I'm in pain and though I wasn't carrying on the pains were sharp and took my breath away. The nurse on seeing me thought I could wait a little longer before going to delivery. The next thing I knew something was oozing out of me and one of the girls ran for the nurse again. I had aborted in bed. The room filled with doctors and nurses—it was a mess—but one of the nurses held my hand the whole time. When it was over she said, "You're free now." I was on intravenous for a while and the next day I was sent home. A couple of weeks later I hemorrhaged and had to go back to the hospital—they hadn't gotten all of the afterbirth out. For a long time I couldn't think about it without crying. I couldn't stand to read or hear about abortions or babies being born. I'm sorry I didn't get some counseling either before or right after—I think it would have helped—but at the time I felt it was something I had to work out on my own. Today I do not regret my decision—very sorry it happened—but no regrets.

These few interviews would support Fleck's (1970) conclusion that the women who were forced to have illegal abortions suffered the most psychological damage. As mentioned above, the universal feeling of women who had obtained legal abortions was gratefulness to have had safe, therapeutic abortions made available. Yet in 1977, new Health, Education & Welfare guidelines limited the use of federal medicaid funds for abortion to only three circumstances: (1) when a woman's life is endangered; (2) when, in two physicians' opinions, the pregnancy would be highly detrimental and long-lasting to her *physical* health; and (3) when pregnancy was the result of rape or incest reported within 60 days ("Abortion Under Attack," 1978). This restriction points out the terrible possibility that abortion may become illegal once again. As long as we live in a society that still believes that a woman's primary (if not only) role is that of wife and mother; as long as we live in a society where one of the most powerful and affluent religious institutions uses its tax-exempt status and pours thousands upon thousands of dollars into a campaign that tries to impose its religious doctrines on all people; as long as we live in a society where the Equal Rights Amendment still cannot get passed in some of the states—as long as these and other injustices exist, the psychological impact of abortion on women must be addressed with support and sensitivity by mental health professionals and the health care delivery system at large.

REFERENCES

Abortion under attack. *Newsweek,* June 5, 1978, pp. 36–47.

Belle, D. Who uses mental health facilities? In M. Guttentag and S. Salasin (Eds.), *Families abandoned: The cycle of depression.* New York: Academic Press, 1978 (in press).

Center for Disease Control. Abortion data. Washington, D.C.: U.S. Government Printing Office, 1976.

David, H. P. Abortion in psychological perspective. *American Journal of Orthopsychiatry,* 1972, 42(1), 61–68.

Denes, M. *In necessity and sorrow.* New York: Basic Books, 1976.

Erikson, E. *The young man Luther.* New York: W. W. Norton, 1958.

Fleck, S. Some psychiatric aspects of abortion. *Journal of Nervous Mental Diseases* 1970, 151, 42–50.

Francke, L. B. *The ambivalence of abortion.* New York: Random House, 1978.

Group for the Advancement of Psychiatry. Report #75, Vol. VII, 1968–1971, pp. 203–227.

Harrison, B. G. On reclaiming the moral perspective. *Ms.,* June 1978, pp. 40, 97–98.

Osofsky, J. D., & Osofsky, H. J. The psychological reaction of patients to legalized abortions. *American Journal of Orthopsychiatry,* 1972, 42(1), 48–60.

Shusterman, L. R. The psychosocial factors of the abortion experience: A critical review. *Psychology of Women Quarterly,* 1976, 1(1), 79–105.

White, R. Comments on abortion and psychiatry. In R. E. Hall (Ed.), *Abortion in a changing world.* Vol. 2. New York: Columbia University Press, 1970.

4

Women and Employment
Some Emotional Hazards

Jeanne Parr Lemkau

" To love and to work"—this was Sigmund Freud's reported reply when asked what a normal person ought to be able to do well (Erikson, 1950, p. 265). Ironically, in his considerations of women, Freud himself overlooked the relationship of work and emotional health. Since his day, the emotional well-being of women has continued to be discussed largely in terms of the "love" component of his dictum and the nurturant and expressive aspects of wife and mother roles. When the employed woman has been studied, the focus has been on how her working status affects her "important" roles as wife and mother, and the "myth of the career-woman freak" (Laws, 1976) has been manifested in repeated attempts to explain why a woman would become so "deviant" as to take employment seriously (Almquist & Angrist, 1970)! In contrast, discussions of men and employment have assumed the basic healthi-

I would like to thank Bernice Lott, Jane B. Parr, and Robert G. Parr for their helpful comments on an earlier draft of this chapter.

ness of male participation in the labor force and have focused on the impact of their particular occupational roles on job satisfaction and emotional well-being. Little attention has been given to men as husbands and fathers, roles assumed to require little more than their passive cooperation.

This situation in the literature of social science bears an uncanny resemblance to the cultural stereotypes that hold competency-related characteristics to be more typical and ideal for men (Broverman, Vogel, Broverman, Clarkson, & Rosenkrantz, 1972). While in the early part of the century paid employment was an experience shared by the majority of men but a minority of women (U.S. Department of Labor, 1975), thus providing the "kernel of truth" behind the differential emphasis in the literature, traditional assumptions about women are becoming increasingly discrepant with the realities of their lives. Today, at every stage in the life cycle, the American woman is more likely to work than ever before (Hoffman, 1977).

I wish to contribute to a more balanced view of women by discussing some of the stressful consequences of female participation in the work place. My focus is on the emotional liabilities of women's employment rather than on the joyful and life-enhancing aspects and on the stressful situations commonly experienced by highly educated, employed women. In the context of portraying some of the more extreme and stressful situations that the educated working woman may encounter, issues are raised of general relevance to the emotional well-being of employed women.

A brief overview of current trends in female labor force participation provides a context for discussing the emotional ramifications of employment. In 1976, over 38 million women were in the U.S. labor force (Women Entering the Job Force, 1976), more than half of the women in the prime working years from 20 to 64 years old (Stencel, 1977). The labor force participation of women has expanded dramatically over the past several decades, due almost entirely to the increased employment of married women and mothers.

Prior to World War II, most women entering the work force were either single, middle-class, white-collar workers who worked only until marriage, or poor women employed in factories or domestic service. Since World War II married middle-class women have increasingly entered the labor market and remained there, taking less and less time out for childbearing. Whereas in 1940 less than 15% of married women with husbands present were employed, this figure had climbed to over 30% in 1960 and 43% in 1974 (U.S. Department of Labor, 1975).

Married women and also mothers of young children are more likely to work than ever before. Between 1940 and 1974, the labor force participation of working mothers quintupled, "probably the most significant labor force change the country experienced during this period" (U.S. Department of Labor, 1975, p. 26). In fact, in the early 1970s, the percentage of women with school-age children and husbands present who worked passed the 50% mark and, for the first time, a woman was more likely to be employed if she had children less than 18 years of age than if she did not. Maternal employment rates are even higher among mothers without husbands present, and such female-headed households are ever increasing (Hoffman & Nye, 1974). In 1974, one out of every eight families was headed by a woman (U.S. Department of Labor, 1975).

The trends of greater participation in the work force of women of all ages, particularly married women and those with school-age children, are of a long-term nature. Various explanations have been offered. Hoffman (1977) sees the employment of wives as an inevitable outcome of improved fertility control and more limited family size, increased health and longevity, and technological advances that have streamlined housekeeping. Others have pointed to the role of interrelated factors such as economic necessity (Seifer, 1973), the permission-giving aspect of the women's liberation movement, and the greater education of women (Harbeson, 1971).

These figures alone justify considering the implications of work on the mental health of educated women. The factor of education, however, further enhances the likelihood that a woman will be employed. In 1974, over 60% of women with college degrees were in the labor force. The higher a woman's educational attainment, the more likely she is to be employed, a fact that may reflect a stronger work orientation among women who are seeking education and the greater access to interesting and better paying employment for those with higher education.

When more women are working than ever before, to dismiss employment as peripheral to women's mental health or as ipso facto evidence of "penis envy" and disturbed sex role identification is as absurd as suggesting that every working woman is a paragon of mental health. As Helson (1972) has written of the career woman, "simplistic evaluation of them as good or bad, well-adjusted or neurotic, feminine or not should become obsolete" (p. 48). The reason a particular woman works, the nature of her employment, skills, and aspirations, the relationship of employment to marital and family demands, and the particular cultural, situational, and intrapsychic stresses that she faces as a function of her job status all influence the degree to which her employment fosters satisfaction, self-esteem, and growth and/or depression, alienation, and distress.

STATUS, STRESS, AND EMOTIONAL WELL-BEING

Frustrations, conflicts, and pressures that block the satisfaction of psychological or physical needs place stress, or "adjustive demand," on the individual (Coleman, 1976). In elaborating sources of stress, Coleman (1976) points to many factors common in employment situations; stress may result from prejudice and discrimination, from the lack of skills necessary to attain one's goals, or from internal psychological barriers that prevent a person from meeting needs. Conflicts generated by the necessity of choosing among different options are stressful, as are environmental or intrapsychic pressures to achieve certain goals or to behave in certain ways. Extreme stress has been demonstrated to precipitate psychological decompensation in basically "healthy" individuals, while preexisting emotional difficulties are presumed to make one more vulnerable to the deleterious effects of additional stress (Dohrenwend & Dohrenwend, 1974).

When groups of people face different sets of stresses in their work and family involvements, one would expect the result to be different patterns of emotional disturbances. Thus, given the different situations of men and women, it is no surprise to find distinctive "men's" and "women's" emotional difficulties (Chesler, 1972). According to a number of reviewers, women suffer from many categories of "mental illness" at higher rates than men in the United States. Gove and Tudor (1973) concluded from their survey that women, more frequently than men, are diagnosed as suffering from neuroses, functional psychoses, transient situational disturbances, and psychophysiological disorders. Weissman and Klerman (1977) review available studies on depression and conclude that the greater incidence among women is "real and not an artifact of reporting of health care behavior" (p. 109). Further evidence of greater distress among women is the fact that in 1973, 29% of American women as compared to 13% of American men took psychotropic drugs (Stellman, 1977).

Several writers have pointed to the influence of women's disadvantaged status on the different patterns of emotional difficulties between the sexes and the greater numbers of women in most major categories of emotional distress. The "social status hypothesis" (Weissman & Klerman, 1977) proposes that women's situations are generally depressing and that the psychological distress that results is exacerbated by the discrimination that women encounter if they attempt to cope through direct action and self-assertion. In their elaboration of the social status hypothesis, Gove and Tudor (1973) note that few roles are culturally sanctioned sources of satisfaction for women, and that the one "legitimate" role, that of housewife, is low in status, income, and visibility and is likely to be frustrating, because of the boring and repetitive nature of housework and the minimal use of intellectual capabilities and educated skills. They cite the higher rates of emotional disturbance among married women as evidence of the deleterious effects of their status position.

Although Gove and Tudor (1973) deal only tangentially with employed women, their analyses aptly apply. "Legitimate" work is limited to a few narrow roles. Income, status, and visibility for these positions are usually low, and the work itself is often frustrating. Women are more likely than men to be employed in positions that make only minimal use of their training and intellect.

In some feminist circles, employment has been lauded as a solution to the housewife ennui, which Friedan (1963) has called "the problem that has no name" (p. 15). It has not lived up to its promise. The structure of the present labor market combined with the impact of sex role stereotypes limits options and rewards for the employed woman, creating stresses that women might not tolerate if their options outside of the labor force were any better (Kreps, 1971; Stellman, 1977).

Some of the potential hazards to emotional well-being engendered by various aspects of women's employment status are elaborated in the pages that follow. Specifically, a number of similar and distinctive difficulties faced by women employed in either traditional or pioneer fields for women are considered. Consistent with the social status hypothesis, I assume that the pressures, conflicts, and frustrations experienced by women as a result of their status in the work force are vitally related to their emotional health, and that different adjustments are demanded of different employment situations. In addition to the stressful impact of the job itself, be it a traditional or nontraditional one, the combination of work and family demands places additional burdens on many women. The role conflicts that result are discussed along with several coping styles women use in attempting to cope with role proliferation and discontinuity.

WOMEN'S WORK ROLES: FROM THE FRYING PAN TO THE FIRE

Occupational Segregation

One source of stress in women's work stems from women's position within the labor market. American women tend to be restricted to a narrower range of occupational roles than men. Whereas the 57 most frequent occupations for women represent 75% of the working female population, the top 57 occupations for men describe barely half of the working male population (U.S. Department of Labor, 1975). Furthermore, the participants in roles most frequently occupied by women are overwhelmingly female—the most frequent work roles for women are as secretaries, waitresses, nurses, elementary school teachers, stitchers and sewers, salesladies, cashiers, typists, bookkeepers, or private household workers!

The picture of occupational segregation (i.e., the separate labor market for men and women) does not change when just educated women are considered. In 1973, one-sixth of college-educated women still held clerical positions. While education increases access to the professions, the greater proportion of women professionals in recent years is largely accounted for in terms of more women in the traditionally female occupations such as teaching, social work, nursing, and other health-related fields (U.S. Department of Labor, 1975). When a woman occasionally enters a male-dominated field, she is still part of a very small minority in spite of slight inroads by women over the past decade in management (Garfinkle, 1975) and in professional disciplines such as medicine, law, and engineering (Parrish, 1975; Stencel, 1977).

Occupational segregation has implications for the emotional well-being of the woman worker. At a general level, the narrower range of "legitimate" options decreases the likelihood of a woman finding employment well-fitted to her skills, interests, and aspirations. Second, the separation of the sexes is accompanied by the devaluation of "women's work"; markedly lower income, status, and power are generally available to women employed in female-dominated fields. Innovation in "male" occupational domains, on the other hand, is met with emotional hazards of a different variety. An examination of the emotional liabilities associated with traditional and nontraditional employment illuminates problems common to most working women in varying degrees while simultaneously suggesting areas of conflict likely to be most salient for women in particular segments of the labor force.

Women in Traditional Employment

The emotional well-being of educated women in traditionally female fields such as clerical work, nursing, home economics, and library science is likely to be compromised by factors such as (1) low income and status, (2) the underutilization of one's abilities, and (3) the lack of autonomy and meaningful decision-making responsibility.

Income. The lower status of "women's work" is reflected in lower average incomes for female-dominated fields (U.S. Department of Labor, 1975). This discrepancy holds even at professional levels, where education is held constant. In a recent study comparing 135 women with master's degrees employed in either "male" or "female" professions, a substantial pay differential in favor of women in "male" occupations was found, in spite of the fact that the more traditionally employed women had significantly more job experience (Lemkau, 1977).

A double discrimination is incurred by women in traditional employment; in every occupational category, a woman earns only two-thirds of the wages of her male counterpart. Thus, even in clerical work, the most frequent employment area of women, a secretary earns 65% of the salary of the average male secretary! Lest one think this is not the case for educated women, Stellman (1977) points out that "women with college degrees make less than men with high school degrees in every occupational category, and about half of the wages of equally educated college males" (pp. 77, 78).

Financial hardship is itself a source of stress and, in spite of myths to the contrary, most women work because of economic need. "Two-thirds of all women workers are either single, divorced, widowed, or separated or have husbands who earn less than $7,000 per year" (Griffiths, 1976, p. 9). A college-educated woman with a family to support may not earn enough to maintain them above the poverty line working as a secretary. The lack of financial security without a husband's greater income may be a major factor in keeping a woman from leaving a stressful marriage.

On a more emotional level, to the extent that a woman has accepted the work ethic belief that one earns one's just reward, her low income may foster an underevaluation of her capabilities and worth. Furthermore, low financial reinforcement and low income ceiling may foster the realization that one's work efforts make no difference, and "learned helplessness," anxiety, and depression will result (Seligman, 1975).

Underutilization. To work in a position where one's natural abilities or trained expertise are underutilized can be frustrating and unsatisfying. The inherent dissatisfactions of such work are compounded by disappointment among women who anticipated more meaningful roles when they were in school. Andrisani and Shapiro (1978) followed 5000 employed women in their thirties and forties over a 5-year period; they found that job dissatisfaction was much higher among women whose skills were being underutilized than among those whose jobs required greater use of their training.

Underutilization is not limited either to women or to those in "feminine" occupations, but it is more prevalent in this group. The college-educated secretary who spends her day filing and typing or the nurse or social worker overwhelmed with paperwork and other "maintenance" functions of her role at the bottom of the bureaucratic totem pole are cases in point. Frequently, the woman in a traditionally female profession finds herself performing functions not unlike those of the traditional housewife (i.e., taking care of others' needs, managing daily routines, and making life more comfortable for higher-status men), leaving her neither the energy nor the opportunity to exercise different skills and specialized training.

Power. Top administrative posts in social work, library science, and nursing are disproportionally held by men, and many "female" occupations are auxiliary to "male" occupations. The nurse is expected to "follow doctor's orders." For the secretary, "he's the boss!" The teacher reports to the (usually male) principal. Few women are in positions with legitimized power to make decisions about working conditions or policies related to the execution of their jobs.

This situation represents another aspect of the underutilization of female talent. In addition, where one's responsibilities involve the welfare of others, as when the nurse, secretary, or teacher mediates between "higher-ups" and the public, the stressful effects of having little say may be accentuated (Stellman, 1977). Frustrations may be particularly acute for women who consciously desire greater decision-making power and are confronted with discrimination in their attempts to gain greater control.

Where legitimized power is out of reach, more covert tactics may be used that capitalize on the expected weaknesses of women (Wilson, 1971). It is common knowledge among nurses, for example, that direct recommendations regarding patient care are often perceived as presumptuous by physicians. One may frequently observe a nurse cleverly manipulating a communication so that the physician "spontaneously" offers her idea, which she then flatters and supports. While such a coping style may be effective in an immediate sense, the nonassertive, self-minimizing, and feigned helplessness that are perpetuated are likely to have long-term consequences deleterious to self-esteem.

Women in Nontraditional Employment

Stresses stemming from low income and low status are attenuated somewhat among educated women in male-dominated professions. Income discrimination is not of the "double" variety although within a particular field, women still come out on the bottom. A recent review of the status of women in college administration, for example, revealed that even female affirmative-action officers earn less than their male counterparts (On campus with women, 1978). Women in nontraditional fields may be more sensitive to whatever income discrimination they do experience due to greater daily contact with the more privileged sex than is common for traditionally employed women.

The stresses which are discussed in regard to women in nontraditional employment are those generated by discrepancies between traditional "femininity" and the requirements of "masculine" work roles. Broverman and her colleagues have shown that the typical and ideal woman is perceived as less competent and more nurturant than the typical and ideal man (Broverman, Vogel, Broverman, Clarkson, & Rosenkrantz, 1972). Thus women are expected to be less rational, assertive, self-confident, logical, etc. than men as well as more expressive, gentle, and sensitive to the needs of others. Other research has confirmed the prevalence of such shared assumptions about the "nature" of the two sexes and the persistence of such stereotypes over time (McKee & Sherriffs, 1957; MacBrayer, 1960; Bem, 1974).

Traditional assumptions about women have persisted in spite of rapid changes in the actual roles in which women have been involved, creating both intrapsychic and interpersonal conflicts. The working woman of the 1970s, even in a nontraditional field, is likely to have internalized some aspects of traditional sex role stereotypes that are dissonant with the requirements of her job, and she must certainly deal with friends, colleagues, and the like who have difficulty seeing a "real woman" doing "man's work."

The discrepancies between stereotypic femininity and the demands of nontraditional employment are great: assertiveness, rationality, independence, and self-confidence are essential for adequate job performance in fields such as medicine, law, and architecture and also for survival as a "pioneer." Even though similar issues affect women in traditional occupations, especially those who excel and/or hold leadership roles, the fact that these women hold "legitimized" female roles, which capitalize on the "warmth-expressive" dimensions of traditional femininity, suggests less deviance from normative expectations and less potential stress.

In elaborating some of the more specific areas of conflict

and stress that occupationally nontraditional women are likely to experience, I draw heavily on the analysis of Bunker and Seashore (1977), who propose that the contradictions between sex role stereotypes and the demands of employment generate conflicts in four areas—"power, collusion, intimacy-sexuality, and support" (p. 356).

Power. The detrimental emotional effects of *not* having the opportunity to participate in policy and decision making have already been mentioned. Different emotional liabilities are faced by the woman who has such opportunities by virtue of her job role (e.g., the woman executive in a "male" corporation, or the woman physician who holds a crucial decision-making position on a health care delivery team).

Although women have often wielded power informally and indirectly ("the power behind the throne"), legitimate power defined by a woman's occupational role is usually a new experience for which she may be ill-prepared. New roles and new behaviors are stressful in themselves. To the degree that she has accepted the prevalent ideals of "appropriate" female behavior or has lacked training and experience in the exercise of power, she may feel awkward and guilty as she explores being decisive and assertive rather than reactive.

Even when her style becomes practiced and appropriately refined for her authority position, she may be called "pushy" where a man would be called "assertive," "hard" where a man would be called "cool and decisive," and so forth. Such feedback is likely to exacerbate internal conflicts as a woman finds herself in the precarious position of being punished for exhibiting the behaviors required to execute her responsibilities.

If a woman, through her competence and leadership, wins the approval of her co-workers, it is often at the expense of her femininity in their eyes. Norma Mann, the president of a large steel company, reports, for example:

People will ask my men how they feel about working for a woman. They'll say, "I don't work for a woman. I work for Norma." I haven't figured out yet whether that's an insult or a compliment. (Medsger, 1975, p. 11)

Further conflict in regard to power is engendered by the competitive context in which power is exercised in "male" work settings (Bunker & Seashore, 1977), since women have been brought up to "play dumb" (Komarovsky, 1946) and to leave competition to men, lest they lower their desirability in the sexual marketplace. The "fear of success" literature, originating with Horner's (1972) work, has documented the hesitancy of women to compete in male-identified endeavors when success is perceived as threatening a woman's esteem in the eyes of men.

A final source of stress in regard to the exercise of power is the necessity for a woman to be "boss" for either men or women. In spite of the fact that comparisons of male and female leaders do not support the myth of the mean woman boss (Tavris & Offir, 1977), both men and women continue to hold negative attitudes about women in supervisory roles. For a male to have a female boss is so contrary to the accepted relations between the sexes that, at least initially, anxiety and resentment are likely to be generated in both parties—in the man, who feels "less like a man" for "taking orders from a woman," and in the woman, who senses that her subordinate does not respect her authority. The woman boss of other women finds herself in an equally stressful role, given the accepted equation of "authority" and "male" and the devaluation of women shared by both sexes.

Collusion. When a women behaves according to her expectations of others with little regard to her own needs or desires, the result is often stressful. One's behaviors may conform to the sex role expectations of others on the job or to internalized standards of what a woman "should" do; in either case the result may be collusive (i.e., constituting a denial of one's own needs). The woman architect who agrees to make coffee while the male architects discuss an important project, the female engineer who hesitates to request a prestigious and challenging assignment, and the woman lawyer who laughs at sexist jokes about female clients are all involved in collusion to the extent that their responses are dictated by sex role pressures in conflict with the felt needs of the women themselves. Over time such collusion may breed resentment and lowered self-esteem. Refusing to collude, on the other hand, may elicit the surprise, disappointment, and resentment of others who may accuse the woman of being a "poor sport" or a "women's libber," a term rarely used in a complimentary manner. Thus, however a woman handles issues of collusion, conflict and frustration may result, requiring the expenditure of emotional energy on issues peripheral to job performance.

Intimacy-sexuality. Differences in socialization combined with the natural attraction between the sexes contribute to potentially stressful situations for women in close contact with men on the job. Women are brought up to self-disclose and share feelings in both friendship and sexual relationships, while men are socialized to *do* things with friends and to restrict emotional sharing to sexual relationships. Few men are accustomed to having women friends. These different orientations cause difficulty when a woman's eagerness for camaraderie and emotional support evokes sexual overtures from male colleagues. The tendency of men to see women in sexual terms and to associate friendliness with sexuality may also generate anxiety among men who work closely with women, especially when wives at home disapprove of their daily contacts and/or business trips with women. Such troublesome responses may occur with only a small proportion of males, in situations where there are few women and large numbers of men, but the resulting stress may be considerable.

Issues of intimacy, power, and collusion converge when sexual liaisons occur between women and the men with whom they work. Unfortunately, "when there are only a few women in an organization and they are in lower status positions, it is not uncommon to find that sex is the wampum being exchanged for advancement" (Bunker & Seashore, 1977, p. 365). In such situations sex is power. When a woman participates in collusive sex (i.e., concedes sex in exchange for a special consideration), the psychological cost may be substantial. A woman may well attribute subsequent job success to her sexual concessions and not to her job-relevant abilities, an attribution hardly likely to foster self-esteem. And whereas the male's image may be enhanced by his sexual exploits, the woman is likely to be devalued. The "bargain" often backfires as each collusion perpetuates the myth that female success can only be the result of sex; I was recently told of a male psychiatrist who, after briefly meeting the attractive mother of one of his clients, turned to his female colleague and remarked, "Well, you know how *she* got to be a surgeon, don't you?" In a system where sexual submission is rewarded, the woman who refuses to "play the game" may nonetheless suffer emotional consequences, to the extent that she perceives her job-related skills as making no difference in advancement.

Support. Emotional support and encouragement from others may be crucial in enabling a woman to stay in a position long enough to work through some of the issues already mentioned. Yet support may be a scarce commodity on the job. Women in male-dominated occupations are generally excluded from the "old boy" friendship and apprenticeship network. And relations with men are further hampered by the intimacy-sexuality dilemma already discussed. Support from other women is problematic, since there are few women with whom to relate in "male professions." Because the scarcity of women increases as one moves up the occupational hierarchy, career advancement may mean decreased opportunities for female support when the stress of change makes it all the more critical.

Considering that a supportive reference group is often lacking, it is hardly surprising that women in nontraditional occupations have frequently been found to be more self-reliant and socially aloof than other women (Lemkau, 1979, in press). However, since even highly independent people need support, one might expect husbands to be important, and there is some evidence that this is the case. In my study, women employed in male-dominated fields more frequently mentioned the enthusiastic support of their husbands when citing reasons for their current occupational involvements than did women in female-dominated fields (Lemkau, 1977). Adrisani and Shapiro (1978) found that an unfavorable attitude of a woman's husband toward her working was more strongly related to job dissatisfaction than her own attitude or whether she had young children at home. These data suggest that a husband's support, or lack thereof, may relate to the type of work a woman feels comfortable pursuing and to her overall job satisfaction.

Because of the inherent conflicts between traditional femininity and the demands of nontraditional professional employment, it is not surprising that few women anticipate entering such careers and even fewer succeed. One might expect that those who do are highly resilient, exceptionally qualified, and less socialized to accept the constraints of sex role stereotypes. Indeed, occupationally nontraditional women tend to come from enriched family backgrounds where they were encouraged and supported in developing their talents and interests without regard to "appropriate" roles (Lemkau, 1979, in press). As a whole they tend to be more independent, socially aloof, adventurous, and assertive than other women, and to show even more of the traits that "appear to be adaptive to their professional life styles and role expectations" (Bachtold, 1976, p. 78) than their male counterparts.

In reviewing the relevant literature, I found no general trend for nontraditional women to be less emotionally healthy on trait measures than other women (Lemkau, 1979, in press). However, some evidence of role strain was suggested in several studies using situationally sensitive measures of stress and/or looking at exceptionally creative women in nontraditional fields (Helson, 1971) or those in fields where isolation from other women was most severe (Standley & Soule, 1974). The pressures, frustrations, and conflicts engendered by a nontraditional career choice seem to block many women from actualizing such aspirations, and those who persist and do not drop out appear to be those who are most resistant to these stresses.

ROLE PROLIFERATION AND DISCONTINUITY

Relative to women, expectations for men are clear-cut and follow a natural evolution over the adult life span. Typically, a young man is encouraged to excel in school and to enter the most prestigious and well-paying employment possible. The more advanced his academic or occupational status, the more desirable he will be as a prospective husband. He is encouraged to marry a woman who promises to be an asset to his career, that is, an eager caretaker of his home and children, a gracious hostess, and an emotional support for his arduous climb up the occupational ladder of success. When he becomes a father, this does not alter his job status except perhaps to heighten his motivation to "succeed" in order to meet growing financial responsibilities. He will probably work continuously until retirement. Although the stereotype male role is not without its emotional liabilities (Jourard,

1974), they are minimally related to issues of role proliferation and discontinuity.

In comparison to the prototypic male, the young woman's developmental road is a rocky one. As a child she is encouraged to do well in school, but by adolescence, she is expected to anticipate marriage and children eagerly and to value these goals above all others. She is urged to prepare herself for work only as an "insurance policy" in case Mr. Right makes a late appearance or dies at an early age, and she is warned not to excel academically so as not to be considered an "egghead." Early career socialization is rarely geared to the unique capabilities of a young woman, but is more frequently shaped by the nature of the sexually segregated labor market and considerations of maximizing eligibility on the marriage market. The more prestigious a woman's employment, the narrower the range of men who will consider her as a potential marriage partner (Safilios-Rothschild, 1976).

According to a National Longitudinal Survey (U.S. Department of Labor, 1975), our typical young woman works for 3 or 4 years after finishing school before she marries. Following marriage and the birth of her first child, she may leave the work force for 5 to 10 years. During this time she is expected to find major gratification in child rearing and homemaking. The last of her children will enter school when she is about 35 years old, at which time she will return to work on at least a part-time basis. She will remain in the labor force another 20 to 30 years.

In brief, over her adult life a woman usually experiences considerable segmentation of roles as she moves through various permutations of worker, wife, and mother. For a man, being a good worker, spouse, and parent are synchronous; for a woman, these are mutually incompatible roles insofar as one aspires to meet culturally prescribed standards for the enactment of each. As Stein and Bailey (1973) conclude, "there is no path that a woman can choose that is as highly rewarded and relatively con-

flict-free as high occupational achievement is for a man"
(p. 351).

Role Discontinuity

Three sources of stresses related to role discontinuity
are (1) change in general, (2) the nature of particular
changes, and (3) the lack of institutionalized social supports to assist in transition. Change is itself stressful
(Toffler, 1970). With shifting demands, a woman must
learn new skills (child care, housekeeping, job hunting),
form new relationships (with co-workers, husband's colleagues, children's teachers), exchange old responsibilities for new ones (shifting from financial independence to
child rearing and financial dependence on her husband),
and sustain marked alterations in daily routine (juggling
child care with the demands of a profession).

Aside from the fact of change, the nature of the specific
change can make a difference. In a study of 40 women's
attitudes about housework, Oakley (1974) found that dissatisfaction with housework was much higher among
women who had previously been employed, suggesting
that the housewife role may be experienced as more
stressful for those who have known paid work alternatives.

The transition from homemaker to employed woman
may be a difficult one, especially for the woman who has
not been employed for several years. She may be unable to
locate work consistent with her earlier interests, or she
may no longer be motivated to work in the area of her
prior training or experience, a likely possibility when earlier choices were made to maximize chances of "finding a
man." If she seeks retraining at this juncture, she will find
few educational or training programs flexibly geared to
her needs.

Major shifts in the nature of a woman's employment may create conflicts in other areas of a woman's life. One of my therapy clients, in the midst of a tumultuous marriage, explained,

> When I was a secretary, it didn't bother me if my husband treated me like a child. But once I got used to being my own boss as an insurance agent, I began to like being on my own. I don't want him to treat me like a little girl anymore!

The lack of institutional supports to smooth the transitions between roles and to broaden a woman's options is another source of stress. Relative to other industrialized countries, organized child-care facilities are poorly developed in the United States (Safilios-Rothschild, 1974). Thus, not only does the responsibility of making child-care arrangements invariably fall on women but, in the vast majority of cases, private arrangements must be made for the care of young children. Many women work in situations with poor or nonexistent maternity benefits and/or no maternity leave. Others, particularly in the male-dominated professions, have limited opportunities for part-time employment. Such factors force women to make either-or decisions about working when they might otherwise choose to integrate work and parenthood according to their equal financial and emotional needs.

Role Proliferation

Some combination of wife-mother-worker roles is the dominant pattern among American women today. According to the standards perpetuated by television, popular magazines, and advertising, fulfilling any one of these would involve one completely. As a wife and mother, a woman is expected to maintain a restful haven to which family members can return for physical and emotional replenishment. The "good" wife not only cooks, cleans, and does the wash, but graciously maintains the social life of the family, handling correspondence, entertaining, and making sure that birthdays and holidays are properly celebrated. She is supposed to know that her husband really *does* notice when his t-shirts are soft, when he gets stuffing instead of potatoes, and when he can see his reflection in the china!

A wife is expected to be totally devoted to her husband's success and to gain satisfaction vicariously through his achievement. If a move is required for his career, the "good wife" gladly follows. She may be "allowed" to work as long as it does not interfere with wifely duties, but she would not think of competing with her spouse in terms of income, prestige, or the seriousness of her work commitment.

As the caretaker of the children, she is an expert, as aware of the dangers of "maternal deprivation" as the perils of being "overpermissive." During a child's illness, she is at her child's side, shielding her husband from such inconvenience. She volunteers time to the Girl Scouts, assists in the PTA, and is always at home when her children return from school.

The professional role is tailor-made for a person with a "wife" at home to fill the supportive functions just mentioned. A professional is expected to be devoted to a career, taking work home to "keep up" in her field, attending professional meetings and, in many professions, such as medicine and law, being available on evenings and weekends. Many professions are accurately characterized as "two-person careers" (Papanek, 1973), requiring one paid employee and an "auxiliary" to entertain, maintain the necessities of daily life, and provide sufficient emotional support to enable the first person to "succeed."

From this brief characterization of major role expectations confronting the professional employed woman with a family, the inevitability of conflict should be clear. A woman may respond to the multitude of demands by attempting to be a "superwoman," striving to excel simultaneously as a wife, mother, and worker. Or a woman may decide that her career is as important as her husband's, eschewing the unattainable standards of other roles and seeking accommodation with family members in regard to home responsibilities. Other coping styles are possible, but I wish to focus on the emotional liabilities associated with these two strategies.

"Superwoman." Although employment may be a threat to a woman's sense of "femininity," being a model wife and mother besides may have the reassuring effect of minimizing her feelings of deviance and the negative responses her career evokes in others. The "superwoman" coping style may be an exhausting one for the individual woman, but at least it lessens the necessity for other family members to stray from traditional roles. In fact, this adaptation is often a response to the man who says "Sure you can work, as long as you can still keep up the house and take care of me and the kids." The excessive demands on a woman's time and the inevitability of conflicting priorities are the emotional hazards that go along with this coping style.

To appreciate the demands on a superwoman's time, one must only survey the data on housework. Oakley (1974) notes that the working hours of a housewife are "among the longest in contemporary society" (p. 72). Among 40 subjects, the least amount of time spent on housework each week was 48 hours by a woman holding a full-time job! In Vanek's (1974) sample, the average working woman spent 26 hours weekly doing household chores, with increases between 5 and 10% for each child. Vanek (1974) found working wives to be no more likely to have paid help or a helpful husband than housewives, suggesting that the superwoman status is common.

The superwoman inevitably finds that "a woman's work is never done!" The sheer demand on her time leaves little opportunity for leisure and emotional replenishment. Even the woman who accepts this situation as proper may feel resentful of her spouse who has only one job, or she may feel guilty and anxious whenever she does not enjoy "womanly" responsibilities or when thoughts of relinquishing her duties cross her mind.

Inevitably occasions arise when even the most efficient and energetic of women must choose among conflicting demands. Her husband asks her to entertain his colleagues when she has an important deadline to meet, or he may have an opportunity for a career advancement in another city just when she has settled into a fulfilling position. If she puts priority on her own professional performance, she may feel guilty and unsure of her position as a wife and mother. If she opts to fulfill wifely and motherly duties, she may feel frustrated and resentful that her own career possibilities are hampered.

Dual-career compromise. The superwoman does not expect her spouse to make accommodations to her career, but other women do believe that their own careers have equal importance to those of their husbands; they require their spouses to make major compromises and adjustments so that parenting and household responsibilities may be more equitably shared. A woman may either select a mate whom she believes is open to such accommodation, or she may place new demands on an already existing marriage as her career commitment evolves.

In all likelihood, the educated woman in a profession will be married to someone with an equally demanding career, and stresses generated by the dual-career compromise are inevitable. Three interrelated sources of difficulty may follow: (1) psychic vestiges of traditional sex role socialization, (2) unanticipated changes and issues in the marital relationship, and (3) the impact of the "deviant" on others outside of the marriage.

Even the most "liberated" individuals have been reared in a culture where a sexual division of labor is salient, and the process of moving away from traditional marital roles regarding child care, decision making, competition, and dependency is likely to generate anxiety, doubt, and feelings of guilt in even the most ardent supporters of equality between the sexes. One woman reported to me that it was easy to let her husband *help* her do the dishes, but it took several years before she could relax and not feel guilty when he did the dishes alone, even though he was comfortable doing so. Other women report feeling guilty when their own careers are going better than their husbands' careers. As these two examples indicate, the gap between intellectual acceptance of new roles and emotional comfort is often a difficult one to close.

Unanticipated repercussions to the marital relationship are a second source of conflict. When there are two careers to consider and decisions are not automatically based on the assumed greater importance of one, decisions about where to live, who takes care of the children, and the like, are not simple. An element of "overchoice" is introduced as the number of "negotiable" issues increases. This in itself may be stressful (Toffler, 1970).

While a man may genuinely accept his wife's right to a life of her own, he may resent the decreased autonomy this represents, and his response may evoke unresolved guilt and anxiety in his wife. As Hunt and Hunt (1977) have noted, "(I)nasmuch as dual-careerism increases the domestic responsibilities of men, it reduces their insulation from the acute role-conflict women experience when pursuing careers and may simply make such conflicts a problem for both spouses" (p. 412). The inevitability of conflict logically follows from Papaneck's (1973) analysis of two-person careers, because in the two-career couple there are actually two, two-person careers, or *four* roles to consider. Career success is maximized when each formally employed person has an auxiliary person to support them. The superwoman may be exhausted by attempting to fill three out of the four roles (performing the auxiliary housekeeping, entertaining, etc., for both formal work roles); in the dual-career relationship, these four roles are juggled between two people. This may offset the exhaustion of the superwoman, but it is hardly a solution because it at least potentially undercuts the career possibilities of both spouses (Hunt & Hunt, 1977).

A final source of difficulty concerns the relationship of the couple to persons outside the marriage. Assuming that husband and wife have developed a harmonious working relationship to accommodate their two careers, they must still live in a social network, and they still need friends. Hunt and Hunt (1977) note that

> the dual-career family's "deviance" constitutes a barrier to its ready assimilation and acceptance within traditional social circles, which may work to make this family even more isolated than its more conventional counterpart. (p. 412)

The circle of potential social supports for the "deviant," unconventional couple is narrowed. The potential social isolation is exacerbated by the scarcity of time for socializing. In balancing the tasks of employment, child care, and home management, what is frequently squeezed out is the pursuit of joy, leisure, and social pleasure. The "task orientation" of the dual-career marriage, along with the couple's deviant status, may contribute to social isolation, stress, and a loss of the *joie de vivre* that makes it all worthwhile.

Mental Health: Blaming the Victim?

All employed women must cope with stresses inherent in their occupational roles, whether they are traditional, nontraditional, or somewhere in between. And all working women must respond to the conflicting expectations of "femininity" and "competence," employment and motherhood, if only to select one of several roles. Most women cope with such stresses privately or informally. For some, conflicts may become so debilitating or painfully confounded by other emotional, medical, or sociological problems that they turn to mental health professionals for assistance.

A new client in a counseling relationship is often naive with respect to the value-laden nature of the psychotherapy enterprise and the impact of sociocultural factors on her emotional well-being. Typically, by virtue of her socialization, a woman is quick to blame herself for her distress, and she has probably already tried to overcome her symptoms by being an "even better" wife-mother-lover, and so on. One of my clients, for example, attempting to cope all at once with a full-time job, a traditional husband, and adolescent children, dated the onset of severe depression to when she decided to become a "total woman" (Morgan, 1975); it was only after the dismal failure of this self-help attempt that she sought professional help.

The mental health professional to whom the distressed working woman turns may be similarly unaware of the role of his or her own values in the psychotherapeutic enterprise and may well share the sex role stereotypes that perpetuate the oppression of women (Broverman, Broverman, Clarkson, Rosenkrantz, & Vogel, 1970). If the therapist is a graduate of a traditional psychiatric residency or clinical psychology training program, attention to intrapsychic difficulties within a mental illness framework may be cultivated to the point of producing tunnel vision, which impedes effectiveness with a woman whose difficulties are generated or exacerbated by her employment situation. Take, for example, the client who reported to me that, as a secretary, "I felt like I wasn't a person." Is this a sign of depersonalization symptomatic of a mental disease or a healthy perception in an alienating employment environment? The professional who focuses on curing the "sick" may be blind to the healthy and adaptive aspects of a woman's symptoms and to the necessity of social instead of or in addition to individual change. Such a therapist may actually add to a woman's difficulties by reinforcing her sense of responsibility and by indiscriminately supporting her efforts to be a "better woman," when an examination of the environmental sources of stress and the stereotypic expectations she holds for herself would be more appropriate.

To be of assistance to an emotionally distressed woman, the mental health worker must be as attuned to the social forces that create stress as to the impact of intrapsychic and family dynamics. Some of the emotional hazards of employment for women have been surveyed in order to sensitize prospective therapists and clients to the critical importance of work to the emotional well-being of women. Several issues common to a variety of employed women have been discussed, including the stressful dilemmas of simultaneously or sequentially combining work and family commitments or of being competent on the job without jeopardizing one's "femininity." In addition, some of the issues that are particularly salient for different types of employment have been elaborated, such as the loneliness of being a pioneer on male professional turf or the demoralizing aspects of being employed in a low-status, traditionally female field. It should be clear from this review that only the professional who is familiar with the different cultural influences that impact on the sexes, who has dealt with his or her own sex role issues, and who can see both person and environment as figure and ground is qualified to assist women whose distress is the result of trying to "work things out" in the world of work.

REFERENCES

Almquist, E. M., & Angrist, S. Career salience and atypicality of occupational choice among college women. *Journal of Marriage and the Family,* 1970, **32**, 242–249.

Andrisani, P. J., & Shapiro, M. B. Women's attitudes toward their jobs: Some longitudinal data on a national sample. *Personnel Psychology*, 1978, 31, 15–34.

Bachtold, L. M. Personality characteristics of women of distinction. *Psychology of Women Quarterly*, 1976, 1, 70–78.

Bem, S. L. The measurement of psychological androgyny. *Journal of Consulting and Clinical Psychology*, 1974, 42, 155–162.

Bunker, B. B., & Seashore, E. W. Power, collusion, intimacy-sexuality, support: Breaking the sex-role stereotypes in social and organizational settings. In A. G. Sargent (Ed.), *Beyond sex roles*. St. Paul: West Publishing, 1977.

Broverman, I. K., Broverman, D. M., Clarkson, F. E., Rosenkrantz, P. S., & Vogel, S. R. Sex-role stereotypes and clinical judgments of mental health, *Journal of Consulting and Clinical Psychology*, 1970, 39, 1–7.

Broverman, I. K., Vogel, S. R., Broverman, P. M., Clarkson, F., & Rosenkrantz, P. Sex-role stereotypes: A current appraisal. *Journal of Social Issues*, 1972, 28, 59–78.

Chesler, P. *Women and madness*. New York: Doubleday, 1972.

Coleman, J. C. *Abnormal psychology and modern life*. Glenview, Ill.: Scott, Foresman, 1976.

Dohrenwend, B. S., & Dohrenwend, B. P. *Stressful life events: Their nature and effects*. New York: John Wiley, 1974.

Erikson, E. *Childhood and society*. New York: W. W. Norton, 1950.

Freidan, B. *The feminine mystique*. New York: Dell, 1963.

Garfinkle, S. H. Occupations of women and black workers, 1962–74. *Monthly Labor Review*, 1975, 98, 25–35.

Gove, W. R., & Tudor, J. F. Adult sex roles and mental illness. In J. Huber (Ed.), *Changing women in a changing society*. Chicago: The University of Chicago Press, 1973.

Griffiths, M. W. Can we still afford occupational segregation? Some remarks. In M. Blaxall and B. Reagan (Eds.), *Women and the work-place: The implications of occupational segregation*. Chicago: The University of Chicago Press, 1976.

Harbeson, G. E. *Choice and challenge for the American woman*. Cambridge, Mass.: Shenkman, 1971.

Helson, R. Women mathematicians and the creative personality. *Journal of Consulting and Clinical Psychology*, 1971, 36, 210–220.

Helson, R. The changing image of the career woman. *Journal of Social Issues*, 1972, 28, 33–46.

Hoffman, L. W. Changes in family roles, socialization, and sex differences. *American Psychologist,* 1977, **32,** 644–657.

Hoffman, L. W., & Nye, F. I. *Working mothers.* San Francisco: Jossey-Bass, 1974.

Horner, M. S. Toward an understanding of achievement-related conflicts in women. *Journal of Social Issues,* 1972, **28,** 157–176.

Hunt, J. G., & Hunt, L. L. Dilemmas and contradictions of status: The case of the dual-career family. *Social Problems,* 1977, **24,** 407–416.

Jourard, S. Some lethal aspects of the male role. In J. H. Pleck and J. Sawyer (Eds.), *Men and masculinity.* Englewood Cliffs, N.J.: Prentice-Hall, 1974.

Komarovsky, M. Cultural contradictions and sex roles. *American Journal of Sociology,* 1946, **52,** 184–189.

Kreps, J. *Sex in the marketplace: American women at work.* Baltimore: Johns Hopkins University Press, 1971.

Laws, J. L. Work aspirations of women: False leads and new starts. In M. Blaxall and B. Reagan (Eds.), *Women and the workplace: The implications of occupational segregation.* Chicago: The University of Chicago Press, 1976.

Lemkau, J. P. Personality and background characteristics of women in asextypical occupations. Unpublished doctoral dissertation, University of Rhode Island, 1977.

Lemkau, J. P. Personality and background characteristics of women in male-dominated occupations: A review. *Psychology of Women Quarterly,* 1979, in press.

MacBrayer, C. T. Differences in perception of the opposite sex by males and females. *Journal of Social Psychology,* 1960, **52,** 309–314.

McKee, J. P., & Sherriffs, A. C. The differential evaluation of males and females. *Journal of Personality,* 1957, **25,** 356–371.

Medsger, B. *Women at work: A photographic documentary.* New York: Sheed and Ward, 1975.

Morgan, M. *Total woman.* Old Tappan, N.J.: Revell, 1975.

Oakley, A. *The sociology of housework.* New York: Random House, 1974.

On campus with women. *Project on the status and education of women.* Washington, D.C.: Association of American Colleges. No. 19, March 1978.

Papanek, H. Men, women, and work: Reflections on the two-person career. In J. Huber (Ed.), *Changing women in a changing society.* Chicago: The University of Chicago Press, 1973.

Parrish, J. B. Women in professional training: An update. *Monthly Labor Review,* 1975, **98,** 49–51.

Safilios-Rothschild, C. *Women and social policy.* Englewood Cliffs, N.J.: Prentice-Hall, 1974.

Safilios-Rothschild, C. Dual linkages between the occupational and family systems: A macrosociological analysis. In M. Blaxall and B. Reagan (Eds.), *Women and the workplace: The implications of occupational segregation.* Chicago: The University of Chicago Press, 1976.

Seifer, N. *Absent from the majority: Working class women in America.* New York: National Project on Ethnic America, 1973.

Seligman, M. E. *Helplessness: On depression, development and death.* San Francisco: W. H. Freeman, 1975.

Standley, R., & Soule, B. Women in male-dominated professions: Contrasts in their personal and vocational histories. *Journal of Vocational Behavior,* 1974, **4,** 245–258.

Stein, A. H., & Bailey, M. The socialization of achievement orientation in females. *Psychological Bulletin,* 1973, **80,** 345–366.

Stellman, J. M. *Women's work, women's health: Myths and realities.* New York: Random House, 1977.

Stencel, S. The changing American family. In *Editorial research reports on the women's movement: Achievements and effects.* Washington, D.C.: Congressional Quarterly, 1977.

Tavris, C., and Offir, C. *The longest war: Sex differences in perspective.* New York: Harcourt Brace Jovanovich, 1977.

Toffler, A. *Future shock.* New York: Bantam, 1970.

U.S. Department of Labor Women's Bureau. *1975 Handbook on women workers.* Women's Bureau Bulletin No. 297. Washington, D.C.: U.S. Department of Labor, 1975.

Vanek, J. Time spent in housework. *Scientific American,* 1974, **231,** 116–120.

Weissman, M. M., & Klerman, G. L. Sex differences and the epidemiology of depression. *Archives of General Psychiatry,* 1977, **34,** 98–111.

Wilson, V. An analysis of femininity in nursing. In F. Fidello and J. Delamater (Eds.), *Women in the professions: What's all the fuss about?* Beverly Hills, Calif.: Sage, 1971.

Women entering job force at "extraordinary" pace. *New York Times,* September 12, 1976, p. 1.

5

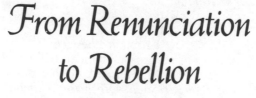

From Renunciation to Rebellion
The Female
in Literature

William A. Shuey III

Franklin Pierce's wife never came downstairs.
She never came upstairs either.

—Ishmael Reed
"Mystery 1st Lady"

Those who restrain desire, do so
because theirs is weak enough to be
restrained; and the restrainer or
reason usurps its place & governs
the unwilling.

—William Blake
The Marriage of Heaven and Hell

$\mathcal{M}$uch of human life is characterized by conflict, and it is a central concern in literature as well. Different people—in real life and in books—respond to conflict in different ways: some talk, others prefer to fight physically, some avoid it, and others seem to seek it out. Indeed, there are probably as many different responses to conflict as there are individuals to respond to it. However, certain stereotypical human responses to conflict also exist, and one of them is renunciation. By this we usually mean either the abandonment of the conflict altogether, or the internalization of the tension generated by the conflict. Renunciation is just about the opposite of standing one's ground and fighting; to renounce is to avoid conflict.

Mental health professionals agree that conflict is best dealt with when it is brought out into the open—unless this process would involve physically destructive violence, of course. For example, if a married couple is involved in serious strife it would be best to work out the conflict as openly as possible (Lederer & Jackson, 1968). If this were not done, and one or both partners were to *renounce* the struggle—either by abandoning it or by internalizing it— most mental health professionals would not consider the conflict satisfactorily resolved. They would expect difficulties to follow such irresolution sooner or later.

It is often the experience of mental health workers that women are more likely than men to be renunciatory in conflict situations. Even if this premise were disputed, few would disagree that historically and culturally women have been and are still expected to be more renunciatory than men. This chapter will illuminate the issue of womanly renunciation by considering its importance in several English and American novels. It will argue that our perspective on female renunciation has changed radically since the nineteenth century, and that the way certain novelists have created their heroines is evidence of this broader cultural change.

Two definitions of "renunciation" given by the *Oxford English Dictionary* are particularly relevant to the more specialized matter of female renunciation. The first definition is "to give up" or "to resign" in the sense of abandoning or repudiating something. The great literary example of this is Nora's renunciation of her home and her family in Ibsen's (1879) *A Doll House.** But in a second definition of the term—and here we are closer to the way most of us use the word in our everyday speech—to renounce is to give up the very struggle that Nora so passionately undertakes. Rich (1976) has described this sort of maternal renunciation in *Of Woman Born,* her study of motherhood: "We learn, often through painful self-discipline and self-cauterization, those qualities which are supposed to be 'innate' in us: patience, self-sacrifice, the willingness to repeat endlessly the small, routine chores of socializing a human being" (p. 19). The word "renunciation," then, can be seen in widely divergent ways when applied to women. In the pages that follow, an evaluation is offered of how certain novels have mirrored or transcended the notion of womanly renunciation that their era adhered to.

CHARLES DICKENS AND THE VICTORIAN NORM

To deprive oneself of pleasure by renouncing the things that are desired by all the world is to invite ridicule, and this is true even in societies less pleasure-oriented than our own. Nonetheless, renunciatory females are numerous in literature, particularly in the novels of the so-called Victorian era, a great age in the English novel, as the names Dickens, Thackeray, Eliot, and Bronte attest. Obviously the perspective of authors and readers on the appro-

---

A Doll House rather than *A Doll's House,* as it is usually translated. As Richard Gilman writes on page 32 of *The New York Times Book Review* (April 16, 1978), reviewing a new translation of Ibsen: "Mr. Fjelde ... make(s) a small, important correction, translating Ibsen's best known title as *A Doll House* ... for the original Norwegian ... conveys the play's sense of a place where all the inhabitants, not just the protagonist, live like children."

priateness of female renunciation has changed since the 1800s, but renunciatory women characters seem to have remained. There seems to be something in the female condition in our culture that has made womanly renunciation a preoccupation of many writers.

An interesting if extreme example of renunciation appears in *Little Dorrit,* one of Dickens' greatest novels (1855–1857). The case of Mrs. Clennam is a caricature of what is in theory a virtue. Nunlike, she has renounced the "hollow vanities" (p. 31) of the world to an incredible extent: although of sound body, she has not left her bedroom for more than 12 years! She has still been able to run the family business from this self-imposed prison. For Mrs. Clennam renunciation is *the* virtue. As she says to her 30-year-old son (the novel's main male character) when he suggests that she examine her conscience and think about reparation for any wrongdoing she may have committed:

> "Reparation," said she. "Yes truly! It is easy for him to talk of reparation, fresh from journeying and junketing in foreign lands, and living a life of vanity and pleasure. But let him look at me, in prison, and in bonds here. I endure without murmuring, because it is appointed that I shall so make reparation for my sins. Reparation!" (pp. 45–46)

Dickens' treatment of renunciation and the renunciatory female in this case is worth at least a glance. He portrays a puritanical and powerful woman of will and shows how she is able to get what she wants at the same time she is renouncing the world. As her son perceives, she is actually renouncing very little; her self-sacrifice is a facade behind which writhes a tortured conscience. We see in *Little Dorrit,* in the character of Mrs. Clennam, one of the more grotesque examples of female renunciation.

Lessing (1952), a contemporary novelist and master of twentieth-century family pathology, does something related in *Martha Quest*. Martha, the novel's 17-year-old

heroine, and her father are discussing another renunciatory female *par excellance,* Martha's mother.

They were both remembering the first occasion, when he had
demanded angrily, "Well, don't you love your mother, then?"
And Martha had burst into peals of angry laughter, saying,
"Love? What's love got to do with it? She does exactly as she
wants, and says, look how I sacrificed myself. She never stops
trying to get her own way, and then you talk about love." (p.
68)

Again, as in *Little Dorrit,* we see renunciation used by a
woman for her own ends—the perversion of a concept sup-
posedly meaning self-denial or resignation. Such
pseudorenunciation beats society at its own game, since it
ultimately is used to control people. Females like Mrs.
Clennam or Mrs. Quest may be called passive-oppressive
personalities, parodies of the renunciatory female.

Although the two characters are parodies, we may remind ourselves that a parody is only possible where something to parody exists. Indeed, there is ample evidence in
nineteenth-century English and American novels that
female renunciation and resignation were highly es-
teemed values, values held by the entire culture. Certainly
Amy Dorrit, known in the novel as "Little Dorrit" (because
she is so short), is the very picture of "active resignation,
goodness, and noble service" (p. 766), the ideal Victorian
heroine. Born in the Marshalsea debtor's prison to a family whose nominal head was ruined financially before she
was born, she learns about poverty by living it, although
she is not embittered as a result. Instead, she functions as
the unacknowledged head of the pathetic household, supporting her incompetent and totally impractical brother,
sister, and father (her mother died when Little Dorrit was
8 years old) by going out of the prison during the day to
work as a seamstress. During the course of the story, she
falls in love with Arthur Clennam, son of the aforemen-

tioned Mrs. Clennam, who leaves her unrequited for 800 pages until he notices her and returns her devotion by marrying her.

Unlike Mrs. Clennam, Little Dorrit is never consciously renunciatory. She seems to be selfless to the core, apparently quite content to support her family and get little thanks for it. There is no stuffiness or oppressively self-conscious morality behind her renunciation, but kindness and resignation to her lot as a virtual servant to her family. Dickens describes her youthful recognition of this.

> What her pitiful look saw, at that early time, in her father, in her sister, in her brother, in the jail; how much, or how little of the wretched truth it pleased God to make visible to her, lies hidden with many mysteries. It is enough that she was inspired to be something which was not what the rest were and to be that something, different and laborious, for the sake of the rest ... impelled by love and self-devotion to the lowliest work in the lowliest way of life. (p. 65)

We see here one of the great examples of the renunciatory Victorian heroine in all her glory. Many writers used the stereotype, but Dickens' great gift as a caricaturist makes his creations impossible to surpass.

One of the principal definitions of renunciation is to withdraw from worldly interests to lead a spiritual life. It is worth considering that little Dorrit, as opposed to the rest of her family, is not a renouncer of certain concrete realities that they would rather not think about—particularly money and work. Indeed, Dorrit supports her family emotionally and economically and is therefore more part of the world than they ever are. Her timidity, virtue, and unobtrusiveness do not make her otherworldly in this crucial sense. And yet she *is* renunciatory in two typically Victorian ways: (1) the pleasures of the flesh do not interest her, and (2) she gives up her own life for her family's.

This brings us to the final aspect of Little Dorrit's renunciatory personality: sexual renunciation. She is certainly no rounded figure of a woman in this respect. All one need do is consider the sexually vibrant (exaggeratedly so, perhaps) females of twentieth-century writers such as Faulkner, Joyce, or Lawrence to feel that Little Dorrit is positively asexual. But we must not forget the tradition out of which Dickens was working, the one that held that all "good" women were sexually renunciatory by definition. If real women in the nineteenth century knew the pleasures of sexual or even sensual activity, the literary convention and cultural situation forbade overt mention of the fact.

HENRY JAMES' AND THOMAS HARDY'S NINETEENTH CENTURY RENUNCIATORY HEROINES

The literary tradition of the renunciatory female probably peaks in the work of James (1881). Isabel Archer, the heroine of *The Portrait of a Lady*, is one of the great non-comic renunciatory female figures in American literature. She embodies the argument for self-denying renunciation as a virtue, as Mrs. Clennam does for that sort of renunciation as a vice.

Isabel has been criticized as being frigid in the clinical sense (Millett, 1966). Those who think her character to be so constituted would perhaps also agree with Blake, the visionary Romantic poet of the late eighteenth-century, when he said that only those whose desires are weak are capable of restraining them. But Blake's interesting remark makes little sense in connection with Isabel because she is, in fact, strong-willed and passionate. Her passion, however, is all resistance. In one of the last scenes in the novel Isabel is pursued and cornered by one of her unrequited lovers, Caspar Goodwood.

He glared at her a moment through the dusk, and the next instant she felt his arms about her and his lips on her own lips.

His kiss was like white lightning, a flash that spread, and spread again, and stayed; and it was extraordinarily as if, while she took it, she felt each thing in his hard manhood that least pleased her, each aggressive fact of his face, his figure, his presence, justified of its intense identity, and made one with this act of possession. (p. 436)

At this point Isabel flees, heading back to Italy and to her depressing marriage to Gilbert Osmond. We can only discern two motives for this return: her affection for Pansy, her stepdaughter, whom she feels she must protect as best she can from Osmond; and her love of resistance, either for its own sake or because she feels that it alone constitutes real freedom.

It should be understood that Isabel's consciousness is no simple thing, and that the sort of renunciation she represents is not precisely of the religious ilk, such as the kind taken to cultivate the spirit or mortify the flesh. When she visits her stepdaughter, who has been virtually imprisoned in a convent as punishment for falling in love with a man not rich or important enough to suit her father, Isabel is not pleased with the renunciatory atmosphere of the convent. Instead, she is depressed by the "benevolence and acceptance" (p. 382) of the Mother Superior, whose voice "fell with a leaden weight on Isabel's ears; it seemed to represent the surrender of a personality, the authority of the Church" (p. 382).

Thus Isabel is not renunciatory in any overtly Christian sense. Neither is she ready to renounce her marriage *à la Nora,* however richly deserving it may be of such a fate. Instead, she chooses to renounce her lovers and most of her friends. We thus find Isabel in the position of the intelligent and fully aware victim who chooses to be victimized. In one important scene, where she has just finished arguing with her husband about a trip she feels she must make to England to see her dying cousin Ralph, we see her consciousness in action.

Isabel went to her room where she walked up and down for an hour. It may appear to some readers that gave herself much trouble, and it is certain that for a woman of high spirit she had allowed herself easily to be arrested. It seemed to her that only now she fully measured the great undertaking of matrimony. Marriage meant that in such a case as this, when one had to choose, one chose as a matter of course for one's husband. (pp. 360–361)

Isabel very clearly is not happy with the state of affairs here; she would prefer to resist her husband and go to England rather than submit for the sake of her marriage. Self-sacrifice is her duty, but not her impulse at this point. In fact, Isabel *does* defiantly go to England to see her cousin. The reader hopes, along with her friends, that her dreadful marriage is over. But no such luck; as the novel ends she is going back to Italy and her supposed duties as stepmother and wife.

What are we to make of this high renunciation, this submission? It is not as though Isabel were a passive, weak woman, friendless and alone. On the contrary, she has many sympathetic and supportive admirers; she is "adored" (p. 417), as Ralph Touchett tells her on his deathbed, and she is independently wealthy. She is renouncing the world and choosing suffering from a position of strength; this makes her brand of renunciation different from the submission a more vulnerable woman would almost have to make. It is a little as if Nora—if she had enjoyed financial independence—had decided to stay married to Torvald. But Isabel's position is even more purely and perversely renunciatory, since Osmond is a good deal nastier than Torvald and has no love for her. Returning to Osmond is very close to being an act of martyrdom. As some submit to the Church or to death, Isabel submits to a formal concept: the indissoluability of marriage.

When it comes to renunciation verging on martyrdom, however, we may turn to a second nineteenth-century renunciatory female character: Sue Bridehead, heroine of Hardy's (1895) *Jude the Obscure.* The fact that this novel was published at the end of the century is significant, because its concerns are those of the twentieth century. The character of Sue is one of modern elements; she is an intellectual, a student of religion who has heretical tendencies. Nor is marriage her aim in life, as it was for many other nineteenth-century women in literature. The other modern element in *Jude the Obscure* is Hardy's willingness to deal fairly openly with sexuality. Compared to the treatment of sexuality by James and Dickens, the novel is at least frank, if not by our current standards explicit.

A brief plot summary is perhaps in order here. Jude Fawley, a stonemason with intellectual interests, falls in love with Sue, who is very advanced in matters of theology and also rather ethereal in her attitude toward men and sexuality. But the sexual reality of her marriage to an older schoolteacher is so horrible that she annuls the marriage and lives "in sin" with Jude, with whom she has two children. Their social situation and their high-mindedness—she objects to marriage on principle—make them outcasts, but they live a nomadic and happy existence for several years. The novel comes to a horrible turning point when a strange older child living with them (Jude's son by a previous marriage) hangs himself and the other two children. Sue views this as punishment for the way she and Jude have lived for love, so she goes back to her husband, the now elderly schoolteacher.

Sue, then, is a renunciatory female in two very different senses of the word "renunciatory." On the one hand she renounces marriage as a degrading institution that binds people together who should not be so bound. On the other hand she ultimately renounces passion as sinful and, in a perverse parody of the idea of mortification of the flesh, martyrs herself to marriage with a man she loathes sexually, thus atoning for her fleshly sins with the man she did love.

This reductive treatment of Sue's character is oversimplified; it does Sue and the novel as a whole less than justice, but it does get at something that is at the heart of many twentieth-century novels: female sexuality. Nearly all nineteenth-century novels leave this out. In its place we find the renunciation of all such desires by women; we may find strong women, but they are usually decorously restrained when it comes to sex. Of course, there are a few women who are frankly sexual beings, but the inability of Becky Sharp *(Vanity Fair)* or Maggie Tulliver *(The Mill on the Floss)* to make the appropriate womanly renunciation of sexual expression costs them more dearly than it would most twentieth-century heroines.

Sue Bridehead's self-sacrifice is a species of quasireligious martyrdom. It is based on the notion that Blake, among others, had so vociferously attacked: the artificial and impossible flesh-spirit dichotomy. The idea is widely held even today that one must deal with the spirit and the flesh as opposites, that when one is healthy the other is at least dormant. St. Paul, whose platonism pervades *Jude the Obscure,* objected to marriage because it pulled men away from the things of the spirit and only reluctantly supported it as a necessary evil. ("It is better to marry than to burn" p. 417.) The misogyny of Paul and the monastic portion of church fatherhood is well known.

There is very probably a link between the flesh-spirit dichotomy and misogyny. Indeed, the latter seems to follow from the former. Women and sexual pleasure are easily perceived as evil because they interfere with spiritual truth. Women must be renounced, unchaste, carnal creatures that they are. This line of "reasoning" has been attacked by people like Blake but, for Sue Bridehead, it becomes the truth. As a woman who believes in the evil of pleasure she is in a self-contradictory position; she must renounce herself because she is capable of the degrading pleasures of the flesh. To become the spiritual being she feels herself to be, she must give up the flesh. As she says to Jude:

I have thought that we have been selfish, careless, even impious in our courses, you and I. Our life has been a vain attempt at self-delight. But self abnegation is the higher road. We should mortify the flesh—the terrible flesh—the curse of Adam! . . . Self-renunciation—that's everything! I cannot humiliate myself too much. (pp. 410–411)

This extreme renunciatory stance is the product of the flesh-spirit dichotomy, particularly in a sensibility such as Sue's, and this same dichotomy goes a great distance to explain the number of renunciatory females one finds in nineteenth-century English and American novels. The cases of Little Dorrit or Isabel Archer are not as extreme as Sue's, but neither are those two renunciatory women as obsessed with and as conscious of their sexuality as she is.

THE TWENTIETH CENTURY: D. H. LAWRENCE AND DORIS LESSING

For the great and liberating step into the subject of female sexuality and the consequent destruction of traditional ideals of renunciatory womanhood, we turn to the work of Lawrence. Lawrence fiercely attacked the idea that the self-denying species of renunciation was a virtue, or even a possibility for women. Influential feminists have been severely critical of Lawrence (de Beauvoir, 1949; Millet, 1970) but, if we look at *Sons and Lovers* (1913) and *The Rainbow* (1915), we find that his perceptions, if to some extent "sexist," are nonetheless worth considering. Lawrence felt that attempts somehow to renounce the flesh for the spirit were insane, so he rebelled against any official support of the conventional dichotomy. Female renunciation, either in the sense of self-sacrifice by women in the interests of family or in the sense of female emancipation from traditional family ties, interested him a great deal, particularly in the two novels just mentioned.

In spite of the fact that Lawrence had no commitment

to the self-sacrificing renunciatory female as an ideal, he still portrays such figures in his novels. Perhaps the most moving of these is Mrs. Morel, in *Sons and Lovers.* We see in her a woman who is not renunciatory by choice, but by necessity. As a working-class woman and mother, she simply has no choice but renunciation, but she does not resign herself willingly. This fact separates her clearly from the other renunciatory females that we have discussed. It is true enough that they are all expected to renounce certain things, but their attitudes about it are different from Mrs. Morel's: Sue Bridehead is ecstatic, Little Dorrit is cheerful and unobtrusive, and Isabel Archer is stoical.

Of what does Mrs. Morel's renunciation consist? Primarily of putting up with being married to a man she learns to hate and having to give up her individual life to those she does love, her children, and particularly the younger, artistic son, Paul. It is not fair to say that she surrenders. Instead, Mrs. Morel pushes her children toward some sort of life outside the drudgery of the coal mining village that provides the setting of the novel. For Paul, this means that she exposes him to farm people, urges him to pursue painting and drawing, and encourages him to work outside the village as a clerk in a factory in a nearby city—a step up socially and economically from life in the coal pits. This sort of renunciation, a mother fighting for her children, trying to force them to achieve what she never can because she is exclusively a mother, is akin to the maternal self-sacrifice that Rich (1976) speaks of in *Of Woman Born.*

Lawrence makes it clear that the ambitious, embittered Mrs. Morel, trapped by marriage and children, is not really going to renounce anything voluntarily, however. She is neither of the upper classes—and thus not about to renounce marriage *per se* as, for example, do Ibsen's Nora, and Tolstoy's Anna Karenina—nor of the race of apparently passive or quasireligiously motivated females like Sue Bridehead, Little Dorrit, or Isabel Archer. Instead, her renunciation is a forced thing, so that we can speak of her as being renunciatory only in the way a prisoner is renunciatory: he cannot escape, so he submits out of necessity. Mrs. Morel's passionate dreams are passed on to at least one of her children; aside from that, her own life is too bitter to bear. Her attitude toward her death is not unlike her attitude toward life.

> Sometimes as she lay he (Paul) knew she was thinking of the past. Her mouth gradually shut hard in a line. She was holding herself rigid, so that she might die without ever uttering the great cry that was tearing from her. He never forgot that hard, utterly lonely and stubborn clenching of her mouth, which persisted for weeks. Sometimes when it was lighter, she talked about her husband. Now she hated him. She could not bear him to be in the room. . . . She thought of the pain, of the morphia, of the next day; hardly ever of the death. That was coming, she knew. She had to submit to it. But she would never entreat it or make friends with it. (pp. 385–86)

Mrs. Morel is a different kind of renunciatory woman than we have been looking at so far; she is an unwilling victim, and external circumstances alone force her to submit. But in this unwillingness to submit she is rather more characteristic of women as they are beginning to be portrayed in twentieth-century literature. The myth of the willingly submissive female is finally starting to take a long-deserved beating.

The myth further deteriorates in Lawrence's *The Rainbow*. For the women of that novel sexual awareness and sexual power are central, and the notion of seeing them apart from these elements—merely as minds—is impossible. Lydia Lensky, Anna Brangwen, or even the relatively emancipated Ursula are women who are deeply involved with their biological nature as procreators and profoundly sexual beings. One thinks of Anna's passionate dance among the corn sheaths and her sensual bliss as a young mother, for example. The power of this novel as it explores the ebb and flow of sexual life is considerable. Nothing could be further from renunciation in the sense of Victorian sexual restraint than the sexuality and maternity of Anna Brangwen and her mother.

The character of Ursula—a schoolteacher and college student as well as a potential mother—sheds further light on the question of female renunciation as it has been considered here. Easily as aware of her sexuality as her mother, she is also a good deal more willing to experiment with it, as her lesbian affair with Winifred and her premarital liaison with Anton demonstrate. As the novel ends, she breaks off the affair with Anton because she can not bear to marry him only "out of fear of herself" (p. 475), that is, for fear she will become promiscuous. This certainly is a kind of renunciation, perhaps comparable to Sue Bridehead's antipathy toward the social form of marriage that reduces one's passions to habits. Bourgeois restraint is not for Ursula.

> She was the naked, clear kernel thrusting forth the clear, powerful shoot, and the world was a bygone winter, discarded, her mother, her father and Anton, and college and all her friends, all cast off like a year that has gone by, whilst the kernel was free and naked and striving to take new root, to create a new knowledge of Eternity in the flux of Time. And the kernel was the only reality; the rest was cast off into oblivion. (p. 492)

This is renunciation of a variety approaching the feminist position. It is not renunciation in the sense of self-sacrificial motherhood, nor is it the renunciation of sexual restraint. It is an open-ended form of abandonment, the abandonment of dead forms in favor of living ones. It is in this way affirmative renunciation, the only variety that many highly passionate women nowadays would find tolerable. Perhaps Nora and Ursula are closer than we originally suspected. Their notion of female renunciation has one thing in common: it eliminates the legitimacy of sexual puritanism or female submission to male definitions of the proper place for females.

Before bringing this chapter to a close, we may profitably look at one more twentieth-century novel in relation to this issue of female renunciation. *Martha Quest* by Lessing (1952) may be selected for three reasons: (1) the novel is utterly matter-of-fact about sexuality, as opposed to Lawrence's tendency to exaggerate and glorify the subject (particularly in *The Rainbow*); (2) Lessing's heroine is more intellectual than any of Lawrence's women and is also a good deal more capable of sophisticated and radical political and social judgments and, finally, (3) contradictory as it may seem, Martha is caught up in the pleasures of the very society she condemns. In short, Lessing's novel takes us one step further into the twentieth century: the character of Martha Quest is *very* convincing because it is very authentic.

The novel is set in South Africa, and Martha is the daughter of English-speaking farmers, not well-to-do enough to suit her snobby mother, but prosperous compared to the blacks who work the land and more socially important than the Afrikaaners who are their neighbors. Martha, although she does not like to acknowledge it, is a member of the ruling class, but she is intelligent and rebellious, and questions many of the racist and socially discriminatory values held by her parents. She also questions (and this is significant in relation to the idea of renunciation) their sexual biases, which are essentially puritanical.

In an earlier quotation from this novel we saw Martha's pseudorenunciatory mother held up for ridicule: maternal self-sacrifice, when it is rhetorical only and masks determined manipulation, is obviously a bad joke. What is less amusing is the way Martha has been unable to rid herself of the sexual renunciation her mother has so carefully taught her, even though she is very consciously the defiant daughter. Lessing, in describing Martha's two love affairs, makes us understand just how deeply influenced the young woman is by the peculiar combination of puritanical and romantic attitudes that is her heritage. Observe the following.

> She arranged the facts of what was occurring to fit an imaginative demand already framed in her mind. Nor was she disappointed. For if the act fell short of her demand, that ideal, the-thing-in-itself, that mirage, remained untouched, quivering exquisitely in front of her. Martha, finally heir to the long romantic tradition of love, demanded nothing less than that the quintessence of all experience, all love, all beauty, should explode suddenly in a drenching, saturating moment of illumination. And since this was what she demanded, the man himself seemed positively irrelevant—this was at the bottom of her attitude, though she did not know it. For this reason, then, it was easy for her to say she was not disappointed, that everything still awaited her; and afterwards she lay coiled meekly beside him like a woman in love, for her mind had swallowed the moment of disappointment whole, like a python, so that he, the man, and the mirage were able once again to fuse together, in the future. (p. 192)

This description of Martha's loss of her virginity to the Jewish musician, Adolph, foreshadows the inevitable failure of her more socially appropriate marriage to Douglas Knowel. Perhaps it is oversimplifying to declare that the heavy freight of the renunciatory tradition sinks the ship of their marriage, but it does contribute significantly to all that is wrong between this couple. She is "shocked" (p. 232), for example, when the 30-year-old Douglas confesses to her that he was chaste until they made love. Here it is the male who is heir to renunciatory sexual tradition, and Martha is disgusted by the fact that men, too, are subjected to the repressive middle-class norm of sexual renunciation.

But mostly it is Martha, by virtue of being female, who

is subjected to the renunciatory tradition. For example, she is unable to stop the slide toward marriage, because the tradition that women ought to go along with male impulses is so hard to fight. Martha is at several points quite ready to call the great event off, but she passively submits, unable to express her severe internal reservations. Throughout the pages leading up to the wedding, Lessing's prose moves with a kind of horrible intensity as she depicts the truly insurmountable social and personal forces pushing Martha toward submission. She is "lost and afraid" (p. 245), "deflated" (p. 242) when about to argue, "unhappy and restless" (p. 251), and so forth. Among all her friends and family there is no one willing to talk to her about how she really feels on the eve of her marriage; indeed, they have a veritable genius for avoiding the subject. In place of honesty, there is a mindless, socially condoned movement toward marriage that is characteristic of the painful movement of the novel as a whole.

Martha is unhappy in her position of renunciation; she is forced into it. In this way she is victimized by the traditional female renunciatory position—by marriage and by sexual repression. However, her defiant nature and her intellectual curiosity make her renunciatory in the opposite sense of the word as well. That is, she is also renunciatory in Nora's sense, in the sense of being ready to abandon traditional forms in order to pursue her identity as a human being rather than as a member of a submissive subspecies. This at least is what we feel her to be potentially, considering her deeply felt internalization of all her doubts about marriage and the radically unjust society in which she is placed.

It seems clear that *Martha Quest* is very far from the traditional nineteenth-century position on female renunciation, that respectable virtue practiced by all decent women. *Martha Quest* and the two Lawrence novels eliminate that sort of renunciation from the list of virtues once and for all. In its place we find a healthier, more open form of renunciation—something closer to rebellion—held up as the goal for women. Martha is, of course, suffering a set-back as the novel ends; we may even say that she is acting out the role of the traditionally renunciatory female. But nearly every line in the novel emphasizes how wrong this course is for her, and any reader must feel this to be the case. Certainly we also suffer when Little Dorrit, Sue Bridehead, or Isabel Archer engage in renunciatory acts in the interests of destructive social norms. But perhaps we suffer more keenly when this occurs in a contemporary setting, as in *Martha Quest*. As the women portrayed in literature become more well-rounded, as they are portrayed in more fully human and complex ways, as we begin to believe in their sexual, intellectual and, traditional in literature, emotional legitimacy, we find ourselves less able to bear their renunciation of the things that we know we ourselves would be unwilling to renounce.

In a word, the heyday of passive renunciation as a way of dealing with conflict is gone for good. In our everyday lives we cannot but feel this is a good thing, that it is long overdue. The implications for literature are also profound; it has meant and will continue to mean the disappearance of a certain sort of renunciatory heroine. We can no more mourn her passing than we can the passing of the patriarchal society that forced her into existence in the first place. In her place we will doubtless continue to see renunciatory females being created by novelists. However, these new renunciatory females will renounce the values of the patriarchy and espouse new values designed by themselves. Ibsen's Nora was the beginning of a new tradition of renunciatory womanhood, a tradition that is still working itself out in our time and place.

REFERENCES

deBeauvoir, S. *The second sex*. New York: Random House, Vintage Books Edition, 1974. (Originally published, 1949.)

Dickens, C. *Little Dorrit.* New York: Odyssey, 1969. (Originally published, 1855–57.)

Erdman, D. V. (Ed.). *The poetry and prose of William Blake.* New York: Doubleday, 1965.

Hardy, T. *Jude the obscure.* New York: Random House Modern Library Edition, 1943. (Originally published, 1895.)

Ibsen, H. *"A Doll House,"* in *Six Plays by Henrik Ibsen,* translated by E. La Galliene. New York: Random House Modern Library Edition, 1951. (Originally published, 1879.)

James, H. *The portrait of a lady.* New York: Random House Modern Library Edition, 1951. (Originally published, 1881.)

Lawrence, D. H. *Sons and lovers.* New York: Viking, Viking Critical Library, 1968. (Originally published, 1913.)

Lawrence, D. H. *The rainbow.* New York: Viking, Compass Books Edition, 1961. (Originally published, 1915.)

Lederer, W. J. and Jackson, D. D. *The mirages of marriage.* New York: Norton, 1968.

Lessing, D. *Martha Quest.* New York: Simon & Schuster, 1964.

Millet, F. B. *Introduction to the Modern Library College Edition of the portrait of a lady.* New York: Random House, 1966.

Millet, K. *Sexual politics.* New York: Doubleday, 1970.

Rich, A. *Of woman born.* New York: Norton, Bantam Edition, 1977.

6

Toward Choice and Differentiation in the Midlife Crises of Women

Sophie Freud Loewenstein

Social scientists have recently become interested in developing typical stages of adult development that are comparable to the well-publicized childhood stages. We must be somewhat wary of this attempt; social science descriptions become cultural prescriptions, and we do not want to accept lightly new norms of which we may fall short. The norms of the terrible twos and the delightful threes also did not always match our children and caused us much anguish. In addition, we have learned that women and men usually have different timetables and that stages constructed with men in mind may not fit many women.

Women's lives tend to be organized around events in the family life cycle and choices that a particular woman has made in this area. A woman who remains single and or childless or one who postpones childbearing until her late thirties in order to consolidate a career will have a different middle life than a woman 40 years old who has followed traditional role prescriptions and is just beginning to discover a larger world at that age (Barnett & Baruch, 1976).

There is increasing evidence from studies of the life cycle patterns of men, that men experience a midlife crisis (Gould, 1972; Levinson, 1978; Vaillant, 1977). It has been suggested that crisis intervention is the proper helping technique for such situations (Strickler, 1975). Women's midlife crises had traditionally been associated with the climacterium and menopause, long regarded as "a narcissistic mortification that is difficult to overcome" (Deutsch, 1945, p. 457). However, since this biological event has been discarded as an essential organizing life experience (Neugarten, 1968a) we have come to feel some uncertainty regarding the existence, the distinguishing characteristics, and the meaning of a midlife crisis for women.

With due regard to the previous warnings about age norms, there is nevertheless the universal experience of aging and being faced with one's mortality (Jaques, 1965). It has been suggested that midlife starts when one is tempted to count one's age from the end, "time left to live," rather than "time since birth" (Neugarten, 1968b, p. 97), and both women and men come to such a realization. The midlife crisis or, more accurately, midlife crises, are thus cross-gender experiences, but their meanings and manifestations may be very different for women and men. Sheehy (1974), as did Jaques (1965), places the midlife crisis at the age of 35 years, but this strikes me as premature. No doubt the particular age of the social scientist contemplating the life cycle is an important variable, since many of us feel ourselves to be in crisis much of the time! I suggest here that we think of midlife as the age period from 40 to 60 years and that we consider the internal and external upheavals that women experience during this time period as midlife crises.

THE MEANING OF IDENTITY CRISIS

Identity and identity crisis have remained powerful but illusive concepts in people's minds. Erikson (1959) posited a major identity crisis in adolescence, defining identity as a sense of knowing who one is, a sense of continuity of self, and a sense of purpose. The identity crisis, he thought, consists of the challenge and struggle of finding and establishing such an identity. With changing times this is now seldom done in adolescence but, instead, in young adulthood; this is Levinson's (1978) "novice phase," which he defines as lasting from 17 to 33 years of age, at least for young men.

Parkes (1971), an English social scientist who had focused on the crisis of bereavement, renamed the identity crisis psychosocial transition, which he defined as "those major changes in life space which are lasting in their effects, which take place over a relatively short period of time and which affect large areas of the assumptive world" (p. 103). Levinson (1978) has called these psychosocial transitions marker events and suggests that they can be divided into three categories.

1. Biological events, such as adolescence, menopause, illnesses.
2. Family cycle events, such as births, deaths, divorce, children leaving home.
3. Work- and career-related events, such as promotions, unemployment, success, retirement.

These do not acquire importance by themselves, but through the specific interpretation given to them by a particular woman. Thus a certain biological event such as menopause, or a social event such as children leaving home or even a mastectomy may have very different impacts, depending on the symbolic meaning that a woman attaches to her menses, the significance of the mothering role, or the intactness of her feminine body (Bailyn, 1976; Parkes, 1971).

Levinson (1978) introduces the concept of commitment and hypothesizes four major tasks for the novice phase of men. By broadening Levinson's ideas and changing them to fit women's lives, I suggest to you the following four types of commitments that are usually made by women in this novice phase.

1. There is a commitment to basic social values that are to guide one's life. Religion belongs here, as well as other ideals and ideologies and one's allegiance to certain reference groups. These basic beliefs will influence all other areas of commitment such as decisions on marriage, having children, modes of child rearing, work patterns, and consumption patterns.

2. There is usually a commitment to one or several human relationships, such as a life partner, friends, and perhaps children. I think commitments to causes, organizations, and institutions could sometimes belong here, when these acquire strong personal meanings.

3. There is a commitment to certain areas of interest, work, and productivity. This commitment may be expressed through taking a job, acquiring a certain education, developing or neglecting certain talents, and through the amount of energy devoted to work. Commitment to domesticity and child rearing can be one choice.

4. There is a commitment to a personal style. We must decide on our appearance, our manner, and our general way of presenting ourselves to the world. This would encompass physical and emotional realms, including how we take care of our bodies, how we dress, and our assumed attitudes, such as being assertive, submissive, abrupt, smiling, expressive, or controlled.

I believe it is the kinds of commitments we make in these areas, through deliberate decisions or through simple compliance to assumed expectations, that eventually crystallize and define our identity. Wheelis (1969, p. 58) suggests that such an identity will feel stable and harmonious if these various modes or areas of commitment are congruent, well-integrated, and not in conflict.

We experience an identity crisis whenever one of these areas of commitment is questioned or changed either by our own initiative or by circumstances that we cannot control. Identity crises can thus be expected all through the life cycle as a normal aspect of development, not just in adolescence. Wheelis (1969) expresses this changing view well: "Adolescence, traditionally, is the time of greatest freedom, the major choices thereafter being progressively made, settled, and buried, one after another, never to be reopened. These days, however, an exhumation of such issues in later life has become quite common, with a corresponding increase in freedom which makes life again as hazardous as in youth" (p. 61). In this view, identity crisis is a reopening of commitments that were once considered settled, and a new awareness of choice. We no longer need to feel ashamed, or "adolescent," which implies immaturity, when we have these identity crises at unexpected times, such as experiencing an unexpected passion at 40 years of age. I am emphasizing this point to prepare my argument against the concept of "menopausal acting out," which has been for a long time an insidious part of the psychology of the midlife woman.

In his pioneering book on crisis theory Caplan (1964, p. 86) stresses that crisis intervention must be guided by specific knowledge of a particular crisis. As a woman in midlife, I will draw on my own experience, on my extensive clinical consultations with women of my age, on my research projects, and on existing social science and fiction literature (Bawden, 1967; Lessing, 1973; Mann, 1956; Martin, 1977; Moore, 1964) to guide younger mental health professionals to understand some of the issues and conflicts that women experience at this stage of their lives. I will discuss the universal changes in commitment that all women face in midlife and as the particular crises of commitment faced by women with various kinds of prior lifestyles.

THE CHANGING COMMITMENT TO ONE'S BODY IMAGE

The Crisis of Physical Aging

It is only through medical advances in the last 50 years that we have acquired the luxury of planning for a longer life. The current average life expectancy for women is now 75 years (Huyck, 1974, p. 2); it was only 49 years at the turn of the century (Weideger, 1976, p. 198). If we have a midlife crisis at 45 years of age, we must contemplate perhaps 30 years more life, indeed a large chunk of our whole life.

Mortality becomes symbolized by our physical aging. All of us, women and men, have a narcissistic investment in our bodies, in remaining healthy, mobile, intelligent, and attractive. We dread, I dread, to lose these aspects of our identity. It is a comfort to learn that intelligence barely deteriorates if one keeps using one's mind. Another source of comfort is the realization that one's good spirits, optimism, and sense of purpose are closely related to physical health, although the cause and effect relationship remains in question (Blau, 1973).

Contrary to common belief, aging is not equivalent to being sick (Blau, 1973). Sick old people in our society are outnumbered by healthy old people. The number of completely incapacitated old people is quite small, less than 10% (Blau, 1973, pp. 134–142). It is true that some sicknesses incubate earlier and emerge with age, and other minor physical difficulties that could be contained by the young seem more difficult, less manageable, and more threatening to one's bodily integrity when one is older. I cannot expand on the physical aspects of aging here, but the literature stresses the importance of treating one's body with respect and wisdom throughout life. This includes proper food and exercise and moderation or abstinence in the use of drugs, alcohol, and cigarettes. Taking care of one's body is a major feminist value that increases in urgency as one ages (Weg, 1977). Mental health professionals should pay more attention to this aspect of people's lives. The emphasis on choice and responsibility in the care of one's body is expressed well by Dubos (1978).

> In the final analysis we can make choices concerning our behavior and surroundings, choices that will prevent or minimize undesirable changes in our milieu interieur. Thought processes ... can profoundly alter hormonal secretions and consequently physiological mechanisms.... Human health transcends purely biological health because it depends primarily on those conscious and deliberate choices by which we select our mode of life and adapt, creatively, to its experiences. Many have affirmed the human ability to create our own selves and shape our own lives. As George Orwell and Albert Camus independently observed, by the age of fifty we have the faces we deserve (pp. 80–81).

We might be especially alert to this last sentence; for women, the prospect of loss of beauty or at least attractiveness as defined by our society is particularly threatening. Our sense of self-esteem is tied up with our looks (Israel, 1977; Nowak, 1977). Beautiful women who have received much admiration for their appearance are particularly vulnerable in this respect; Marilyn Monroe is a tragic example. I grew up with a beautiful mother who, in spite of being a professional woman, sat for hours in front of the mirror plucking out white hair as it grew in. Watching her demoralizing fight against aging, I allowed my hair to

grow white, but the threat of "shriveling up" is nevertheless a reality of my life. When a wiser friend challenged
my fear, I realized that trying to look attractive (meaning
youthful) is part of my assumptive world, an adolescent
commitment that is difficult to relinquish. Peck (1968), in
discussing the tasks of middle age, comments that "the
optimum course for people who reach this first stage of
physical decline is to switch from physique-based values
to wisdom-based or mental-based values, in their self-defi-
nition and their behavior" (p. 89). He refers to men need-
ing to give up physical strength as a high value, but the
thought is equally valid when applied to women giving up
the ideal of physical beauty. The thought that our faces
will reflect above all our feelings about ourselves, about
others, and about life will be reassuring to many women.

Menopause

The themes of the body, health, and beauty direct our
thinking to menopause, again a universal biological event
faced by all women. Deutsch (1945), for many years the
best-known psychoanalytic speaker on the psychology of
women, considered the climacterium "a narcissistic mortification that is difficult to overcome" (p. 457). "Woman
has ended her existence as bearer of future life and has
reached her natural end—her partial death as servant of
the species. She is now engaged in an active struggle
against her decline" (p. 459). This seems an outrageous
statement to all of us, but it stood practically unchallenged
until the recent feminist writings. Even today the con-
temptuous destructive attitude against middle-life women
is still widespread. As recently as during a 1971 conference
on menopause sponsored by the U.S. Department of
Health, Education, and Welfare, a gynecologist characterized menopausal women as being "a caricature of their
younger selves at their emotional worst" (Bart & Gross-

man, 1976, p. 3). It is not clear why the menopausal woman is such a threat to men. Perhaps men who sometimes begin to experience a decline in energy at 50 years old are jealous of women who may be performing at peak capacity in every way at that age, probably because they had a later start. Women in our society tend to be late bloomers.

The physiological changes of menopause used to be associated with depression in middle-aged women, a condition formerly called involutional melancholia. Currently, however, this psychiatric syndrome is being dropped from the official psychiatric nomenclature (Spitzer, 1976). The emphasis on understanding menopausal distress, when it occurs, has shifted from a biological event to seeing it as a social event, associated with role loss and self-esteem loss. The research on menopausal symptoms is still in its beginning stages.

Weideger (1976) reports that "eighty percent of women passing through menopause have one or more symptoms but only ten percent have such severe symptoms that they interfere with daily routine" (p. 58). In a survey of 100 pre- and post-menopausal women, aged 43 to 51 years, menopausal status was not found to be a contributing factor in the self-evaluation of middle-aged women (Neugarten, 1967, pp. 46–49). The women's reactions to menopause were related to previous health problems and to difficulties with menses, sexuality, pregnancy, and childbirth; the possibility existed that these links were either attitudinal or physiological.

There is speculation that women's attitude toward aging and menopause may be as important as hormonal changes. Women with low self-esteem and low life satisfactions were found to be the most vulnerable to menopausal depression and physical symptoms (Neugarten, Wood, Kraines & Loomis, 1963). In a 1974 mail survey of 638 women of all socioeconomic levels in England, they found that the only *consistent* menopausal physiological symptom was that of hot flashes, experienced by 75% of the women and sometimes continuing for as long as 5 years. The other six symptoms that are most frequently associated with menopause and that were specifically inquired about, headaches, dizzy spells, palpitations, sleeplessness, depression, and weight increase, showed no direct relationship to menopause but did tend to occur together; each symptom was reported by approximately 30 to 50% of the respondents (Bart & Grossman, 1976, p. 5). Similarly, in a survey conducted by the Boston Women's Health Collective (1976), two-thirds of the 484 respondents mentioned hot flashes. No other symptoms were consistently reported. However, vaginal dryness seems to be another objective change that women feel is underreported because it is not always associated with menopause.

Menopause, like other aspects of female sexuality, is thus experienced in very diverse ways by different women. We must be cautious about the suggestions, in some literature, that menopausal symptoms are primarily psychosomatic. A healthy, vital, 63-year-old woman reported to me her shame and upset when she experienced severe headaches during menopause after having been told by her (male) doctor that physical symptoms were not to be expected. She had felt personally inadequate for not living up to the standards and expectations that had been set up for her.

Although we do not want to convert menopause into yet another "sickness" or emphasize the physical disabilities of menopause, we also do not want to discount the frequent physical symptoms that occur at that time as psychosomatic, which has a stigmatizing connotation. Menopause is accompanied by physiological changes that affect different women in different ways.

CHANGING COMMITMENTS TO RELATIONSHIPS

Mourning for Children

There are different contradictory research findings regarding the effect of children's departure, the so-called "empty-nest syndrome," on women. The majority of women tend to feel a sense of relief from the burden of motherhood, especially after the tumultuous adolescent years (Glenn, 1975; Radloff, 1975). They become less, not more, depressed, and we know that marital satisfaction over the life cycle rises after the departure of children from home in those marriages that have survived that long (Rollins & Feldman, 1970).

However, the empty nest is depression-inducing to women who invested all their energies into the maternal role and find it difficult to find other substitute roles. Contrary to what Deutsch (1945) had thought, women who had been most invested in motherhood were found to be most distressed by menopause (Bart & Grossman, 1976, p. 6). Sometimes such depressions seemed to focus not so much on mourning for children as on the lack of alternate meaningful activities (Barnett & Baruch, 1976).[1]

The process of differentiation of self is a lifelong process; it is the very essence of personal growth (Bowen, 1973). Some women remain closely fused to their children in a passionate, ambivalent love relationship that gives meaning to their lives but is ultimately imprisoning to both mother and child (Loewenstein, 1977; Stierlin, 1972). Such children are narcissistic extensions of their mothers. They are a woman's major emotional investment, and their departure may face them with great emotional emp-

[1]The recent phenomenon of young adult children "coming home to roost" either because of economic hardship or personality difficulties or a combination of the two, appears to be much more unsettling and upsetting to mothers than the children's original departure, which most mothers had, after all, fostered and anticipated for many years.

tiness, even though geographic distance does not equal emotional separation. It can be a most liberating aspect of middle life and an act of dramatic maturational impact on mothers, sons, or daughters if a woman can grow to differentiate herself in middle life. Even excessive guilt about mistakes made in one's child rearing can become a binding force. Women in middle life who have held on to their children must now let them go, and mental health professionals must help them in this process. Mothers must release their anxious control and let their children make their own decisions and mistakes and bear their own pain (Szasz, 1959).

The approach of menopause may be more of a real threat to never-married, childless women. Such women are usually reported to have high life satisfactions (Birnbaum, 1975). My current research on single women bears this out, but some (by no means all) of them suffer from the poignant regret of not having borne children. This may be a serious midlife issue for these women. In our research, more single women mentioned having remained childless as a source of regret instead of having remained unmarried. Such women may become favorite aunts to their relatives' or friends' children, or they may become "big sisters" to children in need of extra parenting. Two women I recently interviewed, both in their early forties, considered the possibility of single-parent adoption of an older child. We know, of course, from the infamous Ann Landers (1976) survey that some parents who *did* have children have regretted *that* decision.

Sex and Love in Middle Life

The findings on menopause and the empty nest are ambiguous, but there is no uncertainty about the findings that menopause does not correspond to the end of potential sexual satisfaction, although this association was firmly embedded in women's minds for a long time (Mann, 1956). On the contrary, it seems that women in the middle years from 35 to 60 years old are sexually more interested, more responsive, and more orgasmic than younger women (Huyck, 1977a; Loewenstein, 1978). Our repressive culture has arranged it so that many women need 15 years of sexual practice before losing their inhibitions sufficiently to enjoy their sexual capacity (Bardwick, 1971, p. 58). We learned from the Kinsey research that women who are widows or divorcées become more orgasmic in their post-marital sexual encounters than they had been during their marriages (Gebhard, 1966). Marital intercourse in later years appears to be unsatisfactory for many women (Huyck, 1977). It is possible that the devitalization of some midlife marriages may find its most tangible expression in the sexual arena. There is need to renegotiate frequently sexual patterns that have become habitual—along with other midlife marital patterns. We might need to consider that sexual monogamy at this later stage of marriage might actually be more oppressive to women than to men. Even more to the point is the fact that many women find themselves alone in middle life, having lost a marital partner through death or divorce.

Aging women are not sought-after sexual partners; finding a suitable sexual partner may become a problem to them, even if they are emotionally and physically ready for such encounters. Some women do not enjoy independent sexuality, and some women are now learning to turn to other women for sexual satisfaction (Huyck, 1977, p. 55).

Menopausal women have a reputation for frantically seeking last-minute sexual adventures before the clock strikes. My own research on passionate love experiences for women includes 129 women over 40 years old; they range in age from 40 to 84 years. Fifty-two of these women reported passion experiences past the age of 40 years, 39 of the women (one-third of this sample) had sexually consummated passions; 25 of the 39 were married.

Of special interest are situations in which a woman encounters passionate love for the first time in midlife, after the age of 40 years. Mann (1956), in *The Black Swan,* described the drama of such an experience with great poignancy, and my research confirms the intensity and importance of these midlife events. In my sample there were five women, three who were still married at that time, one who was divorced, and one who had never married, who had a first passionate love at this later age; this love included sexual consummation for three of them. Two of these women were freed by this first love experience to terminate long-time unhappy marriages. Here is what one of these women writes at the age of 44 years about her sexual love, the first and only love of her life, for a married man when she was 40 years old.

(I had been) depressed by feelings of mental and soul stagnation. The experience gave me a will to live. I will be eternally grateful to have known what it is/was to feel—really feel. The person who loved me brought me back to being a whole person —allowed me to be me—gave me back a feeling of worth. I am grateful for my life.

The majority of women in middle life, however, are starting to give up the idea of passion. In the age group of 46 to 72 years, only 35% of the women answered the question whether they hoped for another passion in the future in the affirmative, compared to twice as many younger women. Here is what some of them wrote.

It is too distracting, too painful. (45-year-old)
I am too old! (72-year-old)
No, too energy consuming. (44-year-old)
I would be surprised at my age—would rather like to meet someone with whom I could share my interests and be a true friend. (55-year-old)
I think to be in the state of emotional arousal in the mid-fifties would be confusing. (56-year-old)

Why should I want such an upheaval at this time of my
life? (64-year-old)
I plan to avoid it. I disliked the loss of self-control, use of
emotion instead of reason. I became too dependent, too
vulnerable. (43-year-old)

Many women do not want to jeopardize their marriages
for the sake of another passion, but they feel conflicted
about this.

Sometimes I think I would like to be courted by another
man, but I avoid it, as I am happy in my marriage and
wouldn't want to jeopardize it. The romance is intrigu-
ing but the reality is not. (53-year-old)
I don't hope for passion outside my marriage except sometimes in my most secret self and I don't expect it in my
marriage. (43-year-old)

Yet, there are the 35% who still hope for another passion.

More passions please—they enhance enjoyment of life,
oneself and other people, even though mine tend to be
painful. (45-year-old in a satisfactory marriage)

Marriage in Middle Life

I have so far alluded to two possibilities for marriages
that have gone through and survived the child-rearing
years. There may be a new honeymoon and a new mutual
appreciation now that the children no longer interfere in
the relationship and no longer create the typical stresses
of the child-rearing years. Another possibility to be faced
is the increasing growing apart that may have been going
on through the years but was masked by focusing on the
children and their constant problems. Two strangers may
face each other in middle life, each alone across the break-
fast table.

The development of men and women in opposite directions may contribute to this process of estrangement. Neugarten (1968a) found in her research that both men and
women, in the process of gaining autonomy, reclaim earlier disowned parts of themselves, specifically the attributes of the opposite gender. Men allow themselves to
become more tender, nurturant, expressive, and more focused on house and domesticity. Women, however,
become more self-seeking and assertive and look for satisfactions outside the home, especially if they had a late
emergence. Once again, as in an earlier stage of marriage
when the situation may have been reversed, the needs of
the marital pair may not really mesh and may create conflicting wishes and expectations.

A third possibility is that excessive closeness may exist
in the marriage, creating a kind of fusion of personalities
that was described earlier in relation to a mother and her
child. Such a fusion might have had a protective function
earlier in life, meeting dependency and security needs, but
it can come to feel oppressive and restrictive in middle
life. Some family theorists have suggested that the explosive conflicts that arise in marriages are frequently a defense against such fusion (Fogarty, 1976). In fused
marriages the spouses perform emotional tasks for each
other, and the process interferes with the full development of each partner. Fusion also makes each spouse, especially the woman, extremely vulnerable to loss; we all
know couples where one partner could not survive the
death of the other (Pincus, 1974).

For many women new economic independence makes
the single life-style a possibility, either as a lifelong choice
or as a new choice in middle life. The new climate of
greater trust and communication among women has
broken through the isolation in which each woman used
to live. Women are starting to share their marital and
sexual unhappiness and are gaining new perspectives on
their own lives. No longer is it taken for granted that the

preservation of marriage into old age for better or for worse is the ideal solution for everyone. Livson (1977) thinks that marriages may come to hold a transitional function—a bridge stage between childhood and dependency and later life autonomy. However, this is an alien thought for most of us.

One of the difficulties that corrupts women's relationships to their husbands and children is the possessive mode that we have adopted in our industrial, consumer-oriented society. We do not only own cars, houses, and television, but also, and especially, human beings (Fromm, 1976). Mental health professionals might help people to understand that one way of growing into maturity and preserving precious human relationships is through a release of this sense of ownership. It is a mark of wisdom in middle life when enjoyment in relating to others and acceptance of their separateness replaces control and exclusive possessiveness.

Some women and men find it possible to renegotiate their marital relationships, vitalize them, and rebuild them on a new basis. Others find it impossible to become separate within the old relationships, and they see breaking the relationships as their particular solution. Wives or husbands feel a bitter sense of betrayal when their partner of many years suddenly wants to leave the relationship without an obvious reason. Traditionally, only men have acted on such feelings but, with women's new economic and emotional independence, it can now happen to either partner. Mood (1975) quotes the poet Rilke who reconciles the dilemmas between excessive distance and excessive closeness:

> the highest task of a bond between two people: that each should stand guard over the solitude of the other ... even between the closest human beings infinite distances continue to exist ... if each can succeed in loving the distance between them ... [it] makes it possible for each to see the whole and against a wide sky. (pp. 27–28)

Betrayal in Middle Life

A sense of betrayal in middle life may be the special fate of the traditional woman, whether she faces middle life alone or with a marital partner. I have so far talked about issues faced by all women, housewives and career women alike, but there are also differences. Many of today's middle-life women grew up with one set of assumptions about their role in society; now that they have come into middle life, they are faced with another set of values that undercut the earlier ones—the rules of how to live a good life have changed. Middle-life women handle this dilemma in different ways—denying the conflict, feeling angry and sorry, blaming women's liberation for making trouble, or becoming "total women" in Morgan's (1975) sense. Many of these women (but not all, by any means) experience a sense of deep betrayal. They feel that early faithful social role conformity has not offered the originally promised and expected rewards in middle life, just as 100% devotion to motherhood did not produce the perfect children we had been promised. Bitterness about betrayal is especially acute for women who become single in midlife not through autonomous choice, but because they have been abandoned through death or discarded by divorce; they are unprepared by their past life to assume independent, adult lives on the economic, social, or emotional level. Unlike men in similar positions, they may not be able to find a new marital partner, because the men in their age group prefer younger partners. Sheehy (1974, p. 306) hints that it might be because midlife women would be sexually too demanding for midlife men.

Some never-married or divorced single women use up enormous physical and emotional energy hunting for the elusive "right man," which is often a humiliating and demoralizing pursuit. Midlife could be a time when the possibility of remaining alone may be confronted and accepted.

Most women are tough and resilient, and many so-called traditional women, still married or not, are catching up for lost years. They are affirming their identity in small ways, such as using their own first name instead of their husband's. Or they are taking big steps, such as going back to school for pleasure and recreation or for professional or occupational training. An interesting job in middle life can provide the meaning and drama that love, marriage, and raising children had perhaps provided in earlier years (Atchley & Corbett, 1977; Hendricks, 1977). With some luck, a job, paid or volunteer, can turn out to be an emotional, social, intellectual and, indeed, economic resource if it is adequately paid. It can also lead to major conflicts regarding commitments to aging husbands, aging parents, parents-in-law, and grandchildren.

A colleague psychiatrist has urged me to tell my women students to have children in *early* adulthood so that the children can enjoy long-lasting warm grandparental relationships; he felt really happy that he could call on both his own mother and his wife's mother to help out in family emergencies, such as his wife's recent sickness. I told him that if I were a grandmother, which I theoretically could be, I could give grandmother emergency help on Sundays from 2:00 to 4:00 P.M., and that only with advance planning. We all have to make choices in life.

Building Friendships Against Loneliness

Loneliness can be a major hurdle in midlife and can cause much suffering. There is the loneliness of the single woman who has lost her husband through death or divorce (Caine, 1974; Lopata, 1969). There is the acute loneliness of the married woman in an estranged marriage (Gordon, 1976). There is also the loneliness of the never-married woman, although she may have learned by midlife to deal with loneliness (Campbell, 1975). The fear of becoming old under conditions of social or emotional isolation is present in all of us (Townsend, 1973). Friends are not a guarantee against loneliness, but they are certainly a great resource all through life. Some women find it hard to reproduce in adult life the intensity and intimacy of the best-girlfriend relationship of childhood and adolescence (Lopata, 1977). However, women do have a lifelong precious talent for friendship that is superior to men's capacity for friendship, regardless of all the talk about male bonding (Seiden & Bart, 1975). Research indicates that the major confidant of a man is his wife, and the major confidant of a woman is another woman (Blau, 1973, p. 72). In my research on passion I also asked a question about friendship. The great majority of the 700 women of all ages had either two or three intimate friends, while only 10% of the younger women and 16% of the older women indicated that they had no "close friend with whom they shared important feelings." Almost half of my sample had both men and women friends, but as the women grew older they were more likely to have exclusively women friends. When the women were asked whether they considered their husbands as friends, about three-fourths of the married women said yes and one-fourth said no. This correlated closely but not totally with the satisfaction the women described in their marriages.

Friends can definitely be a "lifeline" for each other (Caine, 1978). Some literature has emphasized the importance of friends in widowhood and divorce (Lopata, 1973, 1977), but they are just as important for married women as a safeguard against overloading the marital relationship. Caine (1978), in her useful prescriptions against loneliness, warns us not to overload friendships, either. She recommends several friends in adult life, each perhaps meeting different kinds of needs, instead of the one best friend of girlhood. Blau (1973) points out that having even one intimate peer relationship in old age is a better protection against loss of morale than the presence of one's adult children, with whom a relationship of true mutuality and equality is seldom easy to establish, considering the history of the relationships. Sharing pain, for example, can become difficult in a relationship in which both participants are apt to feel the pain of the other too keenly, as happens between parents and children. Building friendships take time and patience and nurturance. Superficial friendships are not nourishing to the soul. Women are fortunate to have acquired in childhood this talent for friendship as a partial protection against isolation. The world is full of potential friends. Midlife is an important time for the building and strengthening of friendships for the years ahead.

We must also give recognition to the increasing importance of support groups in our society. Support groups may hide in all kinds of disguises apart from those that come under that name. There are women's consciousness-raising groups, of course, and there are church groups, ethnic identity groups, cooking classes, tennis clubs, and political action groups. All of these, with the right ingredients, can function as support groups. I conduct an adult education class that secretly functions as a support group for both the students and myself. Support groups have become an integral part of our daily lives. No woman should have to function without belonging to at least one of these groups.

THE CHANGING COMMITMENT TO WORK

Midlife Conflicts for Career Women

Many women who maintain a career throughout their child-rearing years experience intense conflict between their loyalty, love, and commitment to their families and their interest in their jobs, in achievement, and in career advancement. The conflict is apt to abate as the children grow older; these women might experience great satisfaction and fulfillment in their fifties, reaping the rewards of earlier efforts. It is these women, however, whose life vicissitudes conform most closely to the typical male pattern. With the emphasis on exploring the housewife's midlife shift from household to career pursuits, the professional woman's conflicts have been given little attention, and fear of success is of limited value as an explanatory model (Horner, 1972). There is, of course, the obvious fear that excessive devotion to work has impoverished or deprived us of valued human relationships (Durbin, 1976; *The New York Times,* 1978). Jong (1977) and Caine (1978) have described, in different ways, the emotional hazards and potential emptiness of sudden fame and acclamation. The conflict is usually expressed in narrow terms of marriage and children versus career; it should be extended to encompass a whole range of love relationships and friendships for which there may be no time or energy, leaving professional women vulnerable to eventual emotional isolation. Not all women are socialized toward traditional roles. Many women get programmed by a parent in childhood toward high achievement and, by midlife, they start to feel as imprisoned as anyone else who is a faithful parental delegate (Stierlin, 1972).

Then we find women who entered traditional female occupations and start to regret in midlife that they had not set their sights toward other less predictable directions. In connection with our research on single women, I talked to a nurse whose Irish Catholic immigrant parents had given her a choice between working for the telephone company or becoming a nurse. She now longs to go back to college for a liberal arts education. I talked to a 45-year-old high school teacher who experienced boredom and stagnation. She wondered why she had not developed her considerable early musical talent. "Where has the promise of my youth gone?" she asked. It is too late for her to go back to a musical career, but she wonders whether she will have the courage to leave a secure, tenured job in order to join some friends who are starting a business selling antique musical instruments. A social work professor in the Boston area recently quit her job, just after receiving a major promotion, to pursue an old dream of running her own inn on Cape Cod.

Professional women are also not immune to questioning the meaning and social usefulness of their particular field of endeavor. I know a woman physicist who has lost faith in the usefulness of science and a woman psychiatrist who has lost faith in the efficacy of psychotherapy. It is frightening to arrive at midlife and feel that one has wasted one's talents on a futile social enterprise. Many successful women also wonder if they have sold their souls to the patriarchal establishment. The consciousness raising of the women's movement has no doubt contributed to women's needs to create a better world instead of perpetuating the existing one.

Professional women, just like professional men, also fear that life will lose its meaning in retirement. To age with a sense of becoming useless is a threatening thought; perhaps some thoughtful advance planning can help us carve out some meaningful roles for ourselves. I have decided that I will enjoy becoming a student again after so many years of being a teacher, but in a different field!

IN DEFENSE OF THE MIDLIFE WOMAN

The vitality of the midlife woman whose children have grown up and who can finally focus on self-development and emotional and intellectual growth has been maligned by being called a defensive, desperate measure against the inevitable decline. Here are Deutsch's (1945) alarmed words, quoted at length because I would like mental health professionals to be wary of this kind of thinking, even in disguised form.

This second puberty, just like the first is marked by all kinds of oddities of conduct; . . . One type of climacteric woman displays a quasihypomanic activity. She herself has the feeling of heightened psychic vitality. . . . She is suddenly seized by an urge to make her life richer, more active. She feels like a young girl, and, as she says, wants to begin her life all over again. . . . She becomes enthusiastic about abstract ideas, changes her attitude toward her family, leaves her home from the same motives as in her adolescence. . . . Narcissistic self-delusion makes her painted face appear youthful to her in the mirror . . . after thirty years of happy marriage she may raise the problem of whether her husband is worthy of her, suggesting that her marriage was a degrading mistake. Sometimes, amidst the difficulties of existence, she begins sentimentally to go back to the first days of her marriage, trying to repeat her experiences or to make up for what she has missed. (pp. 461–462)

Contrast this statement with Mead's (1977) recent comment that "the most creative force in the world is a postmenopausal woman with zest." There is thus unanimity in recognizing the vitality of the menopausal woman and some of the difficulties of midlife marriages. It is just the interpretation that varies.

You might feel that I am using unnecessary vigor to fight a battle that has now been won. However, in a brand-new, much acclaimed book, another prominent woman psychoanalyst renews these accusations against the selfish preoccupations of the midlife woman. Following are Fraiberg's (1977) sarcastic comments on this subject. She talks about an imaginary delegation of mothers from all over the world. The customs of the United States, Tribe D, are explained to mothers in other countries.

. . . It is a beautiful tradition in Tribe D that the wisdom of one generation should not obstruct the path of the next generation. When a woman becomes a grandmother, she can now fulfill her deepest longings. She can take courses in creative writing and pottery. She can learn to play tennis. She can go to the land of the sun every Winter. (p. 15)

Selfish concerns by women must not be tolerated not in midlife or at any other time. They seem to be especially objectionable to other women who have devoted their lives to highly fulfilling intellectual pursuits.

CONCLUSION: THE POSSIBILITY OF CHANGE IN MIDLIFE

Most people, men and women, spend their lives carefully following the scripts that society has laid out for them and conforming to everyone's expectations. Then, suddenly, the idea of mortality becomes a reality; we stop to take stock and start to wonder whether life has been worthwhile. Middle age, like adolescence, can indeed be a period of change and role transition. However, adolescents have to make decisions without really knowing what life is all about. By midlife we know the difference between what only glitters and what really counts. I suggested at the beginning of this chapter that there are four key areas of commitment in young adulthood: commitment to certain values and beliefs; commitment to relationships; commitment to work; and commitment to personal appearance and style.

Some of the commitments made earlier seem to be irrevocable. We cannot undo our lives. We have to live with mistakes that we made in earlier years. But there may also be room for change. Wheelis (1969) points out that different people have different capacities for change. "Throughout our lives the proportion of necessity to freedom depends upon our tolerance for conflict: the greater our tolerance the more freedom we retain" (p. 61). Both living in the realm of freedom and choice or the realm of necessity and tranquility have its particular hazards.

Leaving too many choices open keeps us in a state of imbalance and tension. But "as we expand necessity and so relieve ourselves of conflict and responsibility, we are relieved also, in the same measure, of authority and significance. . . . The more we are strong and daring the more we will diminish necessity in favor of an expanding freedom. 'We are responsible' we say, 'for what we are. We create ourselves. We have done so, and by so doing become what we are'" (Wheelis, 1969, pp. 61–62). Huyck (1977b) expresses very similar ideas in relation to changes of commitment in midlife.

> The challenge is to weather the midlife transition having reaffirmed, more maturely, the prior choices, or having developed the strength and ability to alter one's life to meet the needs of the next half of adulthood. If this challenge is met well, the middle years are often experienced as most rewarding. . . . If the midlife transition is dealt with superficially, there may be lingering unhappiness and bitterness over lost opportunities. (p. 6)

I have recently read *The Goat, the Wolf and the Crab* (Martin, 1977), a book on the midlife crisis that captured my imagination. A 42-year-old woman learns that she has cancer of the cervix. An operation could save her life. She has to decide whether life is worth living and under what conditions it might be worth living. For me the book carried the message that the decisions one makes in midlife may be a matter of life and death, since there are many ways of dying, actually or symbolically.

It is the very essence of crisis theory that life crises, if mastered adequately and creatively, are an opportunity for personal growth and change to a richer life (Rapoport, 1962). Mental health professionals must be alert to the elements of choice in clients' midlife crises. There is a frequent wish and fantasy, in all of us, for excitement, adventure, and expansion of our life space. But, simultaneously, we have a need for sameness, safety, continuity, and restriction of and withdrawal into our accustomed private world. I hope all of us, professionals and clients, can meet the challenges of the midlife crises with courage and wisdom.

REFERENCES

Atchley, R. C. and Corbett, S. L. Older women and jobs. In L. E. Troll, J. Israel & K. Israel (Eds.), *Looking Ahead,* Englewood Cliffs, N.J.: Prentice-Hall, 1971.

Bailyn, L. Some thoughts on adult development. Discussant's Comments on the Symposium: Will the real middle-aged woman please stand up? Towards an understanding of adult development in women. Eastern Psychological Association, New York, April 22, 1976.

Bardwick, J. *Psychology of women.* New York: Harper & Row, 1971.

Barnett, R. & Baruch, G. Women in the middle years: Conceptions and misconceptions. Symposium: Will the real middle-aged woman please stand up? Eastern Psychological Association, New York, April 22, 1976.

Bart, P., & Grossman, M. Menopause. *Women and Health,* 1(3), 3–11, 1976.

Bawden, N. *A woman of my age.* New York: Harper & Row, 1967.

Birnbaum, J. Life patterns and self-esteem in gifted family oriented and career committed women. In M. Mednick, S. Tangri, and L. Hoffman (Eds.), *Women and achievement: Social and motivational analyses.* New York: Halstead, 1975.

Blau, Z. *Old age in a changing society.* Chicago: New Viewpoints (Franklin Watts), 1973.

Boston Women's Health Collective. *Our bodies, ourselves.* New York: Simon & Schuster, 1976.

Bowen, M. (Published under Anonymous). Toward the differentiation of self in one's own family. In J. L. Framo (Ed.), *Conference on systematic research on family interaction.* New York: Springer, 1973.

Caine, L. *Widow.* New York: William Morrow, 1974.

Caine, L. *Lifelines.* Garden City, N.Y.: Doubleday, 1978.

Campbell, A. The American way of mating. *Psychology Today,* 1975, **8,** 37–43.

Caplan, G. *Principles of preventive psychiatry.* New York: Basic Books, 1964.

Deutsch, H. *Psychology of women.* Vol. II. New York: Grune & Stratton, 1945.

Dubos, R. Health and creative adaptation. *Human Nature,* 1978, **1,** 80–81.

Durbin, K. Love and work. *Working Woman.* November 1976.

Erikson, E. The problem of ego identity. *Psychological Issues,* 1, Monograph 1, 5–100.

Fogarty, T. Marital crisis. In P. Guerin (Ed.), *Family Therapy.* New York: Gardner Press, 1976.

Fraiberg, S. *Every child's birthright: In defense of mothering.* New York: Basic Books, 1977.

Fromm, E. *To have or to be.* New York: Harper & Row, 1976.

Gebhard, P. Factors in marital orgasm. *The Journal of Social Issues,* 1966, **22**(2), 88–95.

Glenn, N. Psychological well-being in the postparental stage: Some evidence from national surveys. *Journal of Marriage and the Family,* 1975, **37,** 105–109.

Gordon, S. *Lonely in America.* New York: Simon & Schuster, 1976.

Gould, R. The phases of adult life: A study in developmental psychology. *American Journal of Psychiatry,* 1972, **129,** 521–531.

Hendricks, J. Women and leisure. In L. Troll, J. Israel, and K. Israel (Eds.), *Looking Ahead.* Englewood Cliffs, N.J.: Prentice-Hall, 1977.

Horner, M. The motive to avoid success and changing aspirations of college women. In J. Bardwick (Ed.), *Readings on the Psychology of Women.* New York: Harper & Row, 1972.

Huyck, M. Aging: The ultimate experience. *Vassar Quarterly,* 1977, **73,** 3–7. (a)

Huyck, M. *Growing older.* Englewood Cliffs, N.J.: Prentice-Hall, 1974.

Huyck, M. Sex and the older woman. In L. Troll, J. Israel, and K. Israel (Eds.), *Looking Ahead.* Englewood Cliffs, N.J.: Prentice-Hall, 1977. (b)

Israel, J. Confessions of a 45-year-old feminist. In L. Troll, J. Israel, and K. Israel (Eds.), *Looking Ahead.* Englewood Cliffs, N.J.: Prentice-Hall, 1977.

Jaques, E. Death and the midlife crisis. *International Journal of Psychoanalysis,* 1965, **46**(4), 502–513.

Jong, E. *How to save your own life.* New York: Holt, Rinehart and Winston, 1977.

Landers, A. *The Boston Globe,* January 23, 1976.

Lessing, D. *The summer before the dark.* New York: Knopf, 1973.

Levinson, D. Growing up with the dream. *Psychology Today,* 1978, **11**, 20–31.

Levinson, D. *The seasons of a man's life.* New York: Knopf, 1978.

Livson, F. B. Coming out of the closet: Marriage and other crises of middle age. In L. E. Troll, J. Israel & K. Israel (Eds.), *Looking Ahead,* Englewood Cliffs, N.J.: Prentice-Hall, 1977.

Loewenstein, S. An overview of the concept of narcissism. *Social Casework,* 1977, **58**(3), 136–142.

Loewenstein, S. An overview of some aspects of female sexuality. *Social Casework,* 1978, **59**(2), 106–115.

Lopata, H. Z. Loneliness: Forms and components. *Social Problems,* 1969, **17**(2), 248–261.

Lopata, H. Z. The meaning of friendship in widowhood. In L. Troll, J. Israel, and K. Israel (Eds.), *Looking Ahead.* Englewood Cliffs, N.J.: Prentice-Hall, 1977.

Mann, T. *The black swan.* New York: Knopf, 1956.

Martin, G. *The goat, the wolf and the crab.* New York: Scribner, 1977.

Mead, M. Comment made during a talk at the Harvard School of Public Health, April 7, 1977.

Mood, J. L. (Ed.), *Rilke on love and other difficulties.* New York: W. W. Norton, 1975.

Moore, B. *The lonely passion of Judith Hearne.* New York: Delta, 1964.

Morgan, M. *Total Woman.* Old Tappan, N.J.: Revell, 1975.

Neugarten, B., Wood, V., Kraines, R. J. and Loomis, B. Women's attitudes towards the menopause. *Vita Humana,* 1963, **6**, 140.

Neugarten, B. A new look at menopause. *Psychology Today,* 1967, **1**, 43–48.

Neugarten, B. Adult personality: Towards a psychology of the life cycle. In B. Neugarten (Ed.), *Middle age and aging.* Chicago: University of Chicago Press, 1968. (a)

Neugarten, B. The awareness of middle age. In B. Neugarten, (Ed.), *Middle age and aging.* Chicago: University of Chicago Press, 1968. (b)

The New York Times. Women and success: Why some find it so painful. January 28, 1978.

Nowak, C. A. Does youthfulness equal attractiveness? In L. Troll, J. Israel and K. Israel (Eds.), *Looking Ahead,* Englewood Cliffs, N.J.: Prentice-Hall, 1977.

Parkes, C. M. Psychosocial transitions: A field for study. *Social Science and Medicine,* 1973, 5, 101–115.

Peck, R. C. Psychological developments in the second half of life. In B. L. Neugarten (Ed.), *Middle Age and Aging.* Chicago: The University of Chicago Press, 1968.

Pincus, L. *Death in the family.* New York: Pantheon, 1974.

Radloff, L. Sex differences in depression: The effects of occupation and marital status. *Sex Roles,* 1975, 1, 249–265.

Rapoport, L. The state of crisis: Some theoretical considerations. *The Social Science Review,* 1962, **36**(2), 211–217.

Rollins, B., & Feldman, H. Marital satisfaction over the life cycle. *Journal of Marriage and the Family,* 1970, **32**, 20–27.

Seiden, A., & Bart, P. Woman to woman: Is sisterhood powerful? In N. D. Glazer-Melbin (Ed.), *Old Family/New Family.* New York: Von Nostrand, 1975.

Sheehy, G. *Passages.* New York: E. P. Dutton, 1974.

Spitzer, R. L. More on pseudoscience in science and the case for psychiatric diagnosis. *Archives of General Psychiatry,* 1976, **33**.

Stierlin, H. *Separating parents and adolescents.* New York: Quadrangle, 1972.

Strickler, M. Crisis intervention and the climacteric man. *Social Casework,* 1975, **56**, 85–89.

Szasz, T. The communication of distress between child and parent. *The British Journal of Medical Psychology,* 1959, **32**, 161–170.

Townsend, P. Isolation and loneliness in the aged. In R. S. Weiss

(Ed.), *Loneliness. The Experience of Emotional and Social Isolation.* Cambridge, Mass.: MIT Press, 1973.

Vaillant, G. *Adaptation to life.* Boston: Little, Brown, 1977.

Weg, R. More than wrinkles. In L. Troll, J. Israel, and K. Israel (Eds.), *Looking Ahead.* Englewood Cliffs, N.J.: Prentice-Hall, 1977.

Weideger, P. *Menstruation and Menopause.* New York: Knopf, 1976.

Wheelis, A. How people change. *Commentary,* 1969, **56,** 56–66.

III

From Traditional Psychoanalysis to Alternatives to Psychotherapy

In Part I, the introduction, I traced the relationship and the battle between women's rights and psychoanalysis. Many feminists have criticized not only psychoanalysis as a specific type of psychotherapy, but also psychotherapy as a process. It is important, therefore, to make
distinctions between the process of psychotherapy and the
different schools of psychotherapy. In this section, chapters have been chosen to reflect a wide range of views—
from psychoanalytically oriented authors to behaviorists,
as well as educators and social scientists. Psychotherapy
and consciousness raising, which has been presented as
an alternative to psychotherapy, are discussed. In this section it is not possible to discuss intensively the differences
between the psychoanalytic, behavioral, humanistic, and
systems views of women. However, the five chapters can
be seen as highlighting some of the different ways of dealing with women's mental health problems.

TURNING AWAY FROM TRADITIONAL PSYCHOANALYSIS

Salzman's chapter on the psychoanalytic view of
women represents an ego-analytic perspective. Some of
the material was originally published as a paper in 1967.
Thus, it was one of the earlier writings within psychoanalytic circles to challenge directly many of the psychoanalytic concepts discussed in Chapter 1.
Salzman's chapter reflects the ego-analytic or neoana-
lytic perspective in several ways. He begins by discussing
the social changes in women's roles. This position immediately pays more attention to the environment, something that Freud neglected to do. Salzman's views are
interactional—a woman exists in a society, and thus cultural and interpersonal factors affect her development. He
traces the negative effect that psychoanalysis, religious

dogma, and pseudoscientific observations have had on women's lives. He points out that Freud, too, was affected by his culture, and therefore exhibited social biases toward women. Freud attributed much of women's behavior to biological differences, whereas Salzman sees behavior as being frequently socially determined.

Salzman then discusses the biological and sexual issues in women's lives. He disputes the belief that psychological differences between the sexes are based on the anatomical differences of the sexes; this is the primary point of his chapter. He challenges the notion of penis envy as an ubiquitous controlling factor in the female psychology. Salzman suggests that Freud was using the penis as a metaphor for social privileges and did not believe that women actually desired a penis. [This position, however, is difficult to accept after reading some of Freud's earlier papers on this subject (Freud, 1925, 1931).] Nonetheless, Salzman adds that penis envy is an unfortunate concept that still exists within some psychoanalytic circles. Similarly, the emphasis on masochism in women's sexuality is viewed as a reflection of the ignorance regarding the sexual responses of women. These comments are now well known due to the work of Masters and Johnson (1966, 1970) and other sex researchers (Brecher & Brecher, 1966; Kline-Graber & Graber, 1975; Sherfey, 1972).

Finally, Salzman emphasizes the childbearing capacity of women. He writes that women have the choice of whether to bear children or not and that women must confront this issue. By focusing on choice and the decision-making process, Salzman again reveals his ego-analytic perspective. No longer is biology or unconscious motivation emphasized alone. Cognitive factors such as thinking and choice are seen as important determinants of personality. The issue of childbearing is then a crucial one according to Salzman, but the role of mother is not seen as the only psychologically healthy role for women.

Salzman begins to untie anatomy from destiny. Although he still pays a lot of attention to biological issues, many of his comments are similar to those made by feminist critics of Freud. It should be recognized that there is much debate over the role of women within psychoanalytic circles and that not all psychoanalysts are in favor of the maintenance of traditional sex roles.

THE BEHAVIORAL PERSPECTIVE

In Gambrill and Richey's chapter on assertion training for women, a completely different perspective from the psychoanalytic one is presented. The behavioral viewpoint discusses problems that can be observed and measured. Therefore, unconscious motivation and underlying problems that cannot be observed are not seen as the focus of psychotherapy. Gambrill and Richey's chapter can be seen as representative of the behavioral perspective in several ways. First, they identify a specific measurable behavior—the problem of being unassertive. A woman who does not express her thoughts, feelings, and needs is unassertive. Assertion training is a treatment that identifies assertive and unassertive behaviors and involves the client in learning to express herself more effectively. Behavior therapists assume that new behaviors can be learned and that therapy is a process of learning new, more adaptive ways of dealing with individual and interpersonal problems.

The emphasis on individual assessment is also an important part of the behavioral approach. Each person is seen to be an individual who may be affected by some biological variables but, more significantly, by a history of learning. Therefore, individual assessment becomes crucial because it leads to a treatment plan. For example, one woman might be unassertive because although she knows how to express herself, she becomes anxious in specific situations, such as dealing with her employer. Another woman might not possess the actual verbal and nonverbal skills to express herself well to anyone. Two different treatment plans would be needed in these cases. In the behavioral approach, assessment leads to individualized treatment that can be measured. Specific tasks and goals are determined, and both client and therapist can judge whether the client is making progress.

The components of assertion training also mirror several important trends in behavior therapy. Anxiety reduction procedures involve learning techniques that are incompatible with high-anxiety behaviors such as muscle relaxation or by practicing new positive self-statements. This pairing of anxiety-provoking situations with new techniques that are incompatible with anxiety leads to anxiety reduction. These procedures are based on classical conditioning and are often used to control anxiety-based problems. A second approach involves social support and reinforcement of assertive behaviors, since many women have been punished for being assertive. This reflects the principles of operant learning. Finally, skills development and feedback encourage a client to learn and practice new ways of dealing with others. Through new, small steps and feedback by either video replay or coaching and modeling from the therapist, new behaviors for self-expression can be developed.

Assertion training involves women individually and in groups—targeting a problem, working on it with the therapist and others, and changing their environment by changing their own behavior. Thus, behavior therapy involves continued practice and activity on the part of the client and the therapist. This is a much more direct approach to treatment and is consistent with much of the demand for new types of therapy for women. One advantage of behavior therapy for women is that both client and therapist can actually observe and discuss specific desired behavior change. In addition, problems are clearly seen in the context of the individual within the environment. Finally, there is nothing within learning theory that is sexist as there was within psychoanalytic theory.

It should be noted, however, that prior to the focus on assertion training there was little research in the behavioral school of psychotherapy that addressed women's issues. This reflects the individual nature of behavioral assessment but, in the desire to treat each person individually, the special needs of certain groups have been neglected. Assertion training, however, as described by Gambrill and Richey, offers the advantages of the behavioral approach for problems of specific concern to women.

The popularity of assertion training programs is reflected by the many self-help books in this area (Alberti & Emmons, 1974; Cotler & Guerra, 1976; Galassi & Galassi, 1974; Phelps & Austin, 1975; Smith, 1975). Several of the books specifically address women's problems. The consumer should be cautioned, however, to determine whether a particular self-help book has been validated. Research on a book's therapeutic value should be included in the book before it can be assumed to be effective (Brownell, Heckerman, & Westlake, 1978; Rosen, 1976). Recently, researchers such as Alberti (1977), as well as Gambrill and Richey, have discussed the ethical principles involved in assertion training.

HUMANISTIC PSYCHOTHERAPY

Humanistic psychotherapy, or the third force within psychotherapy, refers to the works of theorists such as Rogers (1961), Maslow (1968), and May (1961). According to humanistic theory, an individual will develop and grow toward self-fulfillment or self-actualization. Emotional problems develop when a person's family or other forces in the environment prevents this natural growth. Maslow (1968) suggests that after the basic needs such as food and shelter are met, higher needs such as love, creativity and, finally, self-actualization will emerge. According to the humanist school, psychotherapy through the therapeutic relationship removes the barriers to growth. This involves a focus on the present relationship between client and therapist. Humanistic therapists emphasize the need for the client to take responsibility for her behavior. Anxiety must be faced directly and, with it, life's different possibilities and choices. Humanistic therapists believe that too often individuals do not truly confront the meaning of their lives and do not choose or act according to their beliefs and values. More often they live lies based on expediency or on other people's expectations (May, 1961).

The democratic values and goals of the humanists, such as freedom, the ability to choose, and individual growth, are similar to those described by human liberation movements and are therefore consistent with the goals and values of the women's movement. Burlin and Guzzetta (1977) suggest that there are three specific values of existential psychotherapy that make it appropriate for women: the emphasis on acting as a subject, not an object; the belief that people are free and responsible; and the search for meaning. Women are frequently socialized to view themselves by their relationship to others; thus, they are objects —a man's wife, a child's mother—before becoming a person. The passive dating and mating behavior that was once the norm also objectified women—a woman would want to be telephoned, would hope that a man would ask her to marry him, and would rather be attractive than active.

Burlin and Guzzetta (1977) add that the emphasis on freedom and responsibility suggests that although women must realize that social forces have affected their behavior, ultimately they must and can choose their values and actions. Humanistic psychotherapy resembles feminist psychotherapy as described by Williams (1976). Both emphasize removing the barriers toward growth and an equal and honest basis between client and therapist. Feminist therapy, however, emphasizes the need for a therapist who is aware of specific problems of women. In addition, it is a therapy in which the specific barriers to growth are seen as coming from institutions such as school systems, the traditional marriage, and religious groups. Feminist therapy specifically includes raising the client's awareness or consciousness of the social and political injustices as the first step toward growth.

Although humanistic psychotherapy emphasizes the values of growth and change, it should be pointed out that growth is seen as a goal of psychoanalytic and behavior psychotherapies as well. Sugarman (1977) describes the way current psychoanalytic theorists emphasize humanistic values. Mahoney and Thoreson (1974) similarly point out the ways in which behavioral techniques can be used to expand an individual's choices.

Although a chapter discussing humanistic psychotherapy is not included in this section, chapters 1 and 6 by Loewenstein reflect a humanistic orientation. Loewenstein's chapters also demonstrate the overlap between humanistic and feminist approaches to psychotherapy.

ALTERNATIVES TO PSYCHOTHERAPY

What about psychotherapy as an institution or process? The process of individual psychotherapy involves one client and one therapist with the goals of helping the client feel better or behave differently. The client usually pays some fee for the services of the therapist.

One criticism of this process is that by the very definitions of the roles, the woman is defined as "troubled" or in some cases, "sick"; in actuality, the discrimination and limitations that women endure force them into unhealthy patterns or positions of powerlessness and, therefore, alienation, depression, and other mental health problems. By going to an individual or even to traditional group psychotherapy, this argument goes, the notion of the woman being sick instead of the society being sick is reinforced. Alternatives to going to a mental health professional might be politically and logically more consistent with this position. These alternatives might include support groups in a health cooperative, organized political activity, or consciousness-raising groups.

The next two chapters deal with the phenomenon of consciousness raising. Both chapters empirically examine the effectiveness of consciousness raising as an alternative to psychotherapy. Bond and Lieberman, two social scientists, discuss consciousness raising and whether it is self-help, psychotherapy, or political activation in their chapter. Consciousness-raising groups were, according to Bond and Lieberman, originally seen as social action groups where women would come together to discuss the experiences they have had as women and to understand the environment and its impact on their lives, specifically with relationship to discrimination. They discuss consciousness raising in general and try to discover why women enter these groups and what they get out of them. They also discuss the results of one survey of almost 1700 women who have participated in consciousness-raising groups. Questionnaires and detailed scales were collected on all subjects. Factor analysis was done in order to see what the reasons for joining the groups were. They found that in addition to a general interest in women's issues, one of the important factors was help-seeking, or the desire to solve certain problems. Although the women were not experiencing more life stress than a normative sample, they did express more general feelings of difficulties with self-esteem and role dissatisfaction, and had somewhat higher scores on a symptom distress scale than the normative sample. This help-seeking is reflected in the fact that over half of the women in the study had been in psychotherapy at one time and that one-third of the women were in psychotherapy at the time the groups took place.

When studying the changes that occurred, the primary changes were seen to be increased self-esteem and self-reliance. Women came away from the groups feeling greater self-respect and independence and knowing more about themselves, but Bond and Lieberman did not find that the group members became specifically less anxious or depressed. The changes were of a more general nature. Similarly, few changes took place in the women's value systems or marital relationships. Thus, the authors did not find that consciousness raising was an alternative to psychotherapy.

First, women involved in consciousness raising were not as distressed or as interested in seeking help as women entering psychotherapy or a growth center. The main reason given by women in consciousness-raising groups is not help-seeking, but an interest in women's issues. The results of consciousness raising were a more generally improved self-image and greater feelings of autonomy, not symptom relief. Bond and Lieberman conclude that consciousness raising does not fit any of the three models—self-help, political activation, or psychotherapy—but is a unique phenomenon. They add that for those women in psychotherapy, dual involvement with psychotherapy and consciousness raising seemed to be particularly beneficial.

On the other hand, the women did find an increased identification with the women's movement. As Bond and Lieberman point out, it seems that self-disclosure was an important component of the consciousness-raising group experience. Thus, whereas self-help groups begin with an awareness of the common interests of the group, this awareness is the goal, or the result of consciousness-raising groups. Although the authors write that they find this somewhat puzzling, this process of increased sharing and awareness of the female experience is virtually synonymous with the expression consciousness raising.

CONSCIOUSNESS RAISING AND DEPRESSION

In the chapter by Weissman, similar results were found. She discusses the specific problem of depression. Depression has been documented as a problem that is more prevalent for women than for men. Weissman cites the prevalence of depression as 3%. The ratio of depression in women to men is approximately 2 or 3 to 1 (Weissman & Klerman, 1977). A review by Weissman and Klerman (1977) found that this did not seem to be an artifact of a health care reporting system, but was in fact a true sex difference. In her chapter, Weissman reviews the nature of depression and the depressive syndrome. She clarifies the difference between feeling a general sense of malaise, or feeling sad, with the depressive syndrome, which includes depressed mood, changes in appetite, disturbed sleep, loss of pleasure, loss of interest in work, and decreased ability to concentrate. These symptoms can be quite severe and can lead to serious interference with functioning.

Weissman reviews various treatments for the syndrome depression and compares data for the efficacy of consciousness raising with respect to depression. She points out that the consciousness-raising model would be consistent with the learned helplessness model of depression, which emphasizes that social discrimination and the stereotypical views of women as passive and dependent lead to an inability to gain reinforcement from the environment. This lack of gratification leads to depression. Consciousness raising, by focusing on these learned and social factors, would give women a new sense of selfesteem and might lead to less depression. Weissman cites research which indicates that although depressive symptoms were common in women in consciousness-raising groups, the symptoms were not a primary reason for attendance, and it did not seem that consciousness raising was an alternative for traditional psychotherapy. Instead, the same patterns as those of Bond and Lieberman's study were found.

Weissman then reviews the research indications with respect to psychotherapy alone, psychotherapy and drug treatment, and drug treatment alone. It should be noted that she compares many different kinds of psychotherapy, including supportive psychotherapy and rational emotive therapy. She concludes that preliminary evidence reveals that although both psychotherapy and pharmacotherapy are valuable in the treatment of the syndrome of depression, the combination of drugs and psychotherapies seems to be more effective than either treatment alone. Note also that she is discussing women with the syndrome of depression, not women who are feeling mildly depressed and whose functioning is not severely impaired. Weissman also points out that psychotherapy and pharmacotherapy are not mutually exclusive. One criticism has been that too many women are receiving medication instead of engaging in psychotherapy. Weissman suggests that there may be an additive effect of the two types of treatment. Women who have the syndrome of depression may be more able to become involved in psychotherapy when some of the acute symptoms are treated pharmacologically.

We can conclude that consciousness raising is not an alternative to psychotherapy. Nor is it strictly a political experience. Perhaps it can be better described as a supportive and growth-promoting experience. Women gain feelings of self-esteem and autonomy as well as a greater understanding of women's issues from consciousness raising. Consciousness raising can also be seen as a preventative measure. Women in consciousness-raising groups are not like women in therapy, yet they report somewhat more distress than a control group. Thus, the increase in self-esteem and greater feelings of autonomy derived from consciousness raising may prevent more serious distress.

The final chapter in Part III, by Donady, Kogelman, and Tobias, addresses a similar type of prevention. In addition to depression and other mental health problems, women have problems in the areas of competence and education. One specific problem is math anxiety or math avoidance. Math anxiety is learned. Often, it is a conditioned fear; educational experiences in math may have been associated with a teacher who did not expect girls to do well. These low expectations could lead to a fear and avoidance of math and of associated subjects such as science. Similarly, there are few role models for women in the areas of math and science. If the anxiety is severe, however, it can be associated with more general feelings of incompetence. As Erikson (1950), White (1959), and others have pointed out, the feelings of competence and mastery are particularly important for healthy development in children during the later grades of grammar school. If a child feels inferior and incompetent in school, the scars can be serious. But as Donady, Kogelman, and Tobias discuss, it is at this same stage that many girls begin to doubt their capabilities in math, even though they perform well in other subjects, and sometimes these doubts generalize to other areas of competence.

In their presentation concerning treatment, the authors emphasize the need for individual assessment. Some women can be successfully treated by teaching them to relax and making them aware that this is a socially conditioned fear. An emphasis is made on separating the person's emotional and intellectual feelings from her actual ability to do the work. By bringing the women closer to math itself, they can demystify the experience of math, thus allowing the women to see that it is not such a frightening situation after all.

In more serious cases, the feelings of anxiety can be quite intense and can severely limit a woman's educational and occupational options, make her feel inferior, and lower her self-esteem. This might require longer-term counseling.

In their discussion of policy implications, Donady, Kogelman, and Tobias discuss the need for better math teachers in elementary school and for the elimination of sexist beliefs that certain school subjects are "more appropriate" for boys than for girls. Considering the massive impact that the educational system has on the personality development of children, these changes can lead to increased areas of strength for girls and boys. By removing what the authors refer to as institutionalized intimidation, the education of schoolchildren will be improved and mental health problems resulting from feelings of inferiority can be prevented.

The implications of these chapters can be reviewed briefly if we examine them in reverse order, from the perspective of preventive community mental health. What policy changes or efforts can be made to prevent and treat women with psychological problems? The chapters can be organized into a system that resembles a funnel (see Figure 1).

As one goes through the funnel, each level represents a smaller segment of the population. For example, primary prevention might involve all school-age children (an entire population), whereas tertiary prevention involves a specific, relatively small group of people who have already manifested specific psychological problems (Caplan, 1964).

Donady, Kogelman, and Tobias suggest primary prevention. They would like to see changes in the educational system. These changes can encourage learning and bolster the feelings of mastery in school-age children. These changes can prevent problems such as math anxiety and might prevent mental health problems, which often are

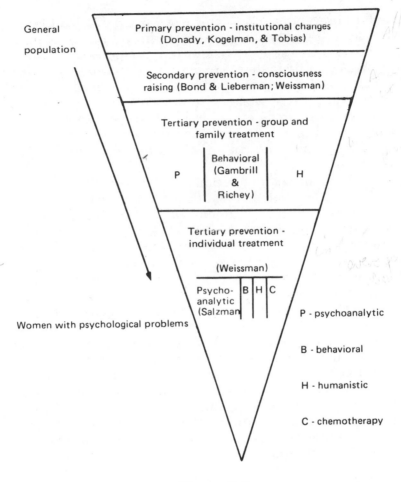

Figure 3–1

A Preventive Model of Mental Health Services for Women

school-related. Such changes would represent a primary prevention effort.

For adult women who are beginning to feel some low self-esteem or general malaise, consciousness raising as described by Bond and Lieberman might be seen as secondary prevention. Consciousness raising can lead to increased self-esteem and greater feelings of independence. It can serve as a support system and can increase women's awareness of their shared experiences. In addition to this function and to the political functions, consciousness raising might prevent women from developing more severe psychological problems. Finally, as Weissman suggests, the groups can help women identify their problems at an early stage, and thus can serve as a secondary preventive technique.

For women who are seriously impaired by symptoms such as depression, anxiety, or assertion problems, however, more specific treatment, or tertiary prevention, is indicated.[1] The treatment may take place in a group or family system, or on an individual basis. Within each of these levels of treatment are the different schools of psychotherapy that can take place in either a group or on an individual basis. For example, Gambrill and Richey describe cases where groups of women learned the behavioral skills of assertion training. They also describe specific family systems where communications can be improved through assertion training. Finally, on an individual basis, ego-analytic psychotherapy, humanistic psychotherapy, or chemotherapy might be able to help women who are experiencing severe psychological distress. Each chapter in this section presents a new perspective on these different levels of prevention of women's mental health problems.

REFERENCES

Alberti, R. E. (Ed.), *Assertiveness: Innovations, applications, issues.* San Luis Obispo, Calif.: Impact Press, 1977.

[1]Although Caplan defined tertiary prevention as rehabilitation, he was referring to hospitalized psychiatric patients. For our purposes tertiary prevention is defined as longer term treatment, compared to secondary prevention which includes acute treatment.

Alberti, R. E., & Emmons, M. L. *Your perfect right.* San Luis Obispo, Calif.: Impact Press, 1974.

Brecher, R., & Brecher, E. *An analysis of human sexual response.* New York: The New American Library, 1966.

Brownell, K. D., Heckerman, C. L., & Westlake, R. J. Therapist contact as a variable in a behavioral weight control program. *Journal of Consulting and Clinical Psychology,* 1978, **46**, 593–594.

Burlin, F., & Guzetta, R. Existentialism: Towards a theory of psychotherapy for women. *Psychotherapy: Theory, Research and Practice,* 1977, **14**, 262–267.

Caplan, G. *Principles of preventive psychiatry.* New York: Basic Books, 1964.

Chesler, P. *Women and madness.* New York: Doubleday, 1972.

Cotler, S. B., & Guerra, J. *Assertion training: A humanistic-behavioral guide to self dignity.* Champaign, Ill.: Research Press, 1976.

Erikson, E. *Childhood and society.* New York: W. W. Norton, 1950.

Freud, S. Some psychial consequences of the anatomical distinctions between the sexes. In J. Strachey (Ed.), *Collected papers.* London: Hogarth Press, 1950. (Originally published 1925.)

Freud, S. Female sexuality. In J. Strachey (Ed.), *The complete psychological works of Sigmund Freud.* Vol. 21. London: Hogarth Press, 1974. (Originally published 1931.)

Galassi, J. P., Galassi, M. D., & Litz, M. C. Assertive training in groups using video feedback. *Journal of Counseling Psychology,* 1974, **21**, 390–394.

Glasgow, R. E., & Rosen, G. M. Behavioral bibliotherapy: A review of self-help behavior therapy manuals. *Psychological Bulletin,* 1978, **85**, 1–23.

Kline-Graber, G., & Graber, B. *Woman's orgasm: A guide to sexual satisfaction.* Indianapolis: Bobbs-Merrill, 1975.

Mahoney, M. J., & Thoreson, C. *Self-control: Power to the person.* Monterey, Calif.: Brooks/Cole, 1974.

Maslow, A. H. *Toward a psychology of being.* New York: Litton Educational Publishing, 1968.

Masters, W. H., & Johnson, V. E. *Human sexual inadequacy.* Boston: Little, Brown, 1970.

Masters, W. H., & Johnson, V. E. *Human sexual response.* Boston: Little, Brown, 1966.

May, R. (Ed.), *Existential psychology.* New York: Random House, 1961.

Miller, J. B. (Ed.), *Psychoanalysis and women: Contributions to new theory and therapy.* New York: Bruner Mazel, 1973.

Phelps, S., & Austin, N. *The assertive woman.* San Luis Obispo, Calif.: Impact Press, 1975.

Rogers, C. R. *On becoming a person.* Boston: Houghton Mifflin, 1961.

Rosen, G. M. The development and use of non-prescription behavior therapies. *American Psychologist,* 1976, **31**, 139–141.

Sherfey, M. J. *The nature and evolution of female sexuality.* New York: Random House, 1972.

Smith, M. J. *When I say no I feel guilty.* New York: Dial Press, 1975.

Strouse, J. *Women and analysis: Dialogues on psychoanalytic views of femininity.* New York: Dell, 1974.

Sugarman, A. Psychoanalysis as a humanistic psychology. *Psychotherapy: Theory, Research and Practice,* 1977, **14**, 204–211.

Weissman, M. M., & Klerman, G. Sex differences and epidemiology of depression. *Archives of General Psychiatry,* 1977, **34**, 98.

White, R. W. Motivation reconsidered: The concept of competence. *Psychological Review,* 1959, **66**, 297–333.

Williams, E. S. *Notes of a feminist therapist.* New York: Praeger, 1976.

7

A New Look at the Psychoanalytic View of the Female

Leon Salzman

*I*n the past two decades there has been a major revolution in the status of the female sociologically, politically, and psychologically. Although the change has not been sudden or explosive, it has, in view of the persistent mythology about the female, been advancing slowly toward the clarification that now demands a hearing from all directions. No longer is the female the second-class, deprived male for whom the absence of a penis meant a lifetime of longing, envy, frustration, and passive acceptance, to be remedied by the birth of a child that symbolically rectified the discrepancy by supplying the desired male genital.

It has suddenly been realized by the scientific and political community that women are not neurotic masochists

EDITOR'S NOTE: Portions of this paper are reprinted from *Archives of General Psychiatry,* 1967, **17** 195–203, by permission of the *Archives of General Psychiatry.* Copyright © 1967, by the American Medical Association.

incapable of assertive and productive initiative because their sexual systems supply the fetal environment and nurturing breast that forces them to remain dependent on dominant, aggressive males. Myths of creation, theological dogma supported by holy writ whose ultimate source was the sociological and anthropological viewpoints of these earliest religious writings, no longer dominate the cultural role and expectations of the female in many parts of the world. Political power rested in the patriarchy which, until recently, utilized a technology that required muscular force and strength. The psychology of the female was derived from these philosophical sources and dignified by the scholars and "wise" men who repeated historical gossip and proclaimed them scientific and biological facts. This was true well into the twentieth century, when our physical sciences had brilliantly conquered large pieces of nature—from the infinitesimally small particles and rays that comprise the atom to the expanse of the universe, providing visits to other planets. These explorations, which allowed us to understand the natural world, provided practically little insight into the nature of man. The how and why of human behavior, even the more observable aspects of human anatomy, still escaped our understanding. It is truly astonishing to realize that there was still a great deal of ignorance regarding the female orgasm and the details of the physiology of sex behavior in addition to our ignorance and continued distortion of the psychology of the female in general. It is less than three decades ago that we were able to describe with visual confirmation the female sexual response from its initiation to climax.

From the dawn of history the status of the female was dictated not only by her biological role, but also by the prevailing technological limitations and religious doctrines. Her role was presumed to be innate and determined exclusively by divine forces. When scientific observations were called on to support these notions, her behavior reinforced the prevailing conceptions of character structure. Her behavior, however, was also the result of the prescribed role and status that the culture assigned to her. Yet Freud's (1905) theories buttressed all the prevailing prejudices and promoted the notion that the female was a deficient male and a second-class citizen, lacking in muscular prowess, emotionally unstable, and devoid of creative potentialities except in limited areas. Her role was directed almost exclusively to childbearing, child rearing, and providing the atmosphere in which the man and the children could be served. It is sad to state that this view is not only widespread among contemporary cultures, but among many social scientists of great wisdom and repute and among psychologists and psychoanalysts.

The psychology of the female as elaborated by Freud (1905) was strongly influenced by the theological and cultural attitudes that prevailed throughout his lifetime as a student and as a researcher. He grew up in a patriarchal world in which the Christian myth of creation was the dominant notion of the female's status. Sociological theories and Darwinian views of evolution tended to support these notions. Freud's libido theory was male-centered, and the psychology of the female was forced to fit the male model by introducing a number of additional hypotheses to cover the discrepancies. Many a priori opinions based on cultural and historical prejudices were given scientific status in Freud's theory. He linked biology to psychology, and psychosexual development to character structure. This overemphasis on biology neglected many relevant factors that derived from the culture.

While indissolubly linked to that of the male both biologically and, therefore, sociologically, the psychology of the female must be viewed by studying her as a person in her own right; her role and function are partly determined by her gender and partly by the assigned limits that the culture imposes on her and that she accepts for a variety of reasons. The female has adaptive needs and security requirements identical to those of the male; the differences between them lie in the idiosyncratic ways these needs are expressed by biological roles and cultural definitions.

PSYCHOPHYSIOLOGICAL REAPPRAISAL

In an excellent anatomical, biochemical, and physiological review of the nature of the female sexuality, Sherfy (1966) has asserted that it is the female sex that is primal and not the male sex. This has been established by biologists for many years. One can no longer speak of a bisexual phase of embryonic development. While genetic sex is established at fertilization, the early embryo is female; the effect of the sex genes is not felt until the fifth or sixth week of fetal life. During this period, all embryos are morphologically female. However, if the genetic sex is male, primordial germ cells stimulate the production of a testicular inductor substance that in turn stimulates fetal androgens, suppressing the growth of ovaries. In this way androgens induce the male growth pattern. If the genetic sex is female, germ cells stimulate the production of follicles and estrogen. However, if estrogens are not produced by artificial removal of gonads before the seventh week, a normal female anatomy will develop. Therefore, no ovarian inductor is required, and female differentiation is the result of the innate, genetically determined morphology of all mammalian embryos. Thus, only the male embryo undergoes differentiation necessary for masculinization, while female development is autonomous. After the twelfth week sex reversals are impossible, since the masculine nature of the reproductive tract is fully established. Thus, it is more correct to say that the penis is an exaggerated clitoris and that the scrotum is derived from the labia. The original libido, if one wishes to assume such a concept, is clearly feminine, not masculine.

In addition, the extensive research of Masters and Johnson (1966) has illuminated many previously clouded and confused areas of female anatomy. The sequence and significance of the female orgasm has been clarified. Both the Kinsey report (1953) and the investigations of Masters and Johnson (1966) definitely affirm that, from a biological point of view, clitoral and vaginal organs are not separate entities. It is firmly established that the clitoral glans and the lower third of the vagina are the active participants in the female orgasm and are not separate sexual entities. The tendency to reduce clitoral eroticism to a level of psychopathology or immaturity because of this supposed masculine origin is a travesty of the facts and a misleading psychological deduction. Although the lower third of the vagina is an erotogenic zone with some sensitivity, it does not produce orgasmic contractions; therefore, there is no such thing as an orgasm in the vagina.

The stimulation of the clitoral glans is what initiates the orgasm, which then spreads to the outer third of the vagina. It is a total body response with marked variations in intensity and timing. Physiologically, it is a physical release from vasocongestive and myotonic increments developed in response to sexual stimuli.

The female is capable of multiple orgasm, while the male requires a refractory period before further orgasm is possible. However, there is a need for continuous stimulation until orgasm, since the sexual tension in the female can fall instantaneously if such stimulation is discontinued. This capacity for multiple orgasm and readiness to respond to sexual stimulation requires regular and consistent sexual activity in the female for her to respond more adequately. It is likely that the most common cause of frigidity and difficulty in achieving orgasm in the female is due to infrequent or insufficiently employed sexual intercourse.

There is no doubt that some aspects of the biological role of the female inevitably and invariably influence her psychology. First, the role of childbearing, which falls exclusively on the female, must be distinguished from child rearing, which may or may not be her lot, depending on the culture. Second, the distribution of muscle and fat and the capacity for physical exertion must be borne in mind in appraising her character development. In addition, the availability of the male genital for visual and tactile perception, in contrast to the largely hidden female genital, must also play a role in her sexual attitudes. The conventional gender attitude, which appears very early and influences dress, appearance, play habits, and playmates, seems to be largely a cultural phenomenon that differs from time to time and place to place.

DEVELOPMENT OF INDIVIDUAL SEXUALITY

To explain further the issue of femininity and the heretofore assigned roles and characteristic traits, we must distinguish between gender and sex, and between genitality and sexuality. Gender differentiation in the fetus and during early infancy merely indicates male or female, without any necessary implications of sexual capacity until a later time; it is only later that the male or female will have some knowledge and skill with regard to the genitals and their ultimate role in the sex act. This is particularly relevant in the male; throughout life the male genital shares the dual function of a sexual procreative organ as well as an excretory organ.

While it is clearly established in most instances at birth what the gender of the infant is, we must not assume that his early activities can be attributed specifically to his gender. Because a male infant is very active or very passive, we should not assume this to be a sexual factor. Only when the genital as a sexual organ is involved in an activity or influences behavior should it be considered to be part of a gender involvement. The play of infants or children cannot be considered sexual simply because the genitals are involved; otherwise, we presume a knowledge of sex which may be completely lacking, or we make the error of confusing genital and sexual, just as we sometimes fail to make a distinction between a tool and a particular activity carried on with it. The choice of playmates by children could be influenced by availability, similarity of play interest, concordance of energy output, and muscular prowess, and not necessarily by gender determination.

Many other factors come into operation, as the research of Money (Money, Hampson and Hampson, 1957), Hampson (Hampson and Hampson, 1961), and others have suggested. One's behavior as a male or female is strongly influenced by the cultural factors of maleness and femaleness, not by an appreciation of the sexual significance of one's gender. This can only occur later, when we are capable of understanding the complicated requirements of sexual rather than gender behavior. Being dressed as a boy or a girl means being identified with privileges or denials regarding gender and not sexual identity. The abundance of questions, confusion, ignorance, and curiosity about sex roles in both genders need not be the result of repression, but of ignorance. Although gender interest and genital manipulation are present in both sexes, it is largely an a priori assumption that sexual knowledge exists and that such interest and play have sexual origins and derivatives. A revision of some of the early notions of female deficits in terms of penis envy and a host of other presumed sexual privileges of the male child will have great influence in clarifying our views on the psychology of the female.

The efforts to study behavior in the framework of instinct, learning, concepts of maturation, or experience have not been illuminating, since they tend to become either-or dichotomies instead of a recognition of the essential role of all elements. Research in primates as well as in humans clearly indicates that the physiological mechanisms involved in coitus are functional before the individual is capable of reproduction. In addition, social experience clearly influences the capacity to perform the sex act.

The complex problem of gender role in contrast to morphology or sexual object in sex behavior has been illuminated by many physiological, biochemical, and chromosomal studies in recent years. There are a large number of variables that enter into the total sexual pattern. They are: (1) sex chromatin; (2) gonadal sex as indicated by morphology; (3) hormonal sex, which is correlated to secondary sex characteristics; (4) external genital morphology; (5) internal accessory reproductive structure; (6) psychological sex and rearing; and (7) psychological sex or gender role.

Psychological maleness or femaleness is not attributable to any single one of these variables and does not seem to have an innate performed instinctive basis. Rearing often plays the major factor in gender role. Thus, gender role and orientation in humans seem to depend on learned experience as well as somatic variables. Hampson and Hampson (1961) conclude: "Physiologic sex or gender role appears to be learned, that is to say it is differentiated through learning during the course of many experiences of growing up. In place of a theory of innate constitutional psychologic bisexuality we can substitute a concept of psycho-sexual neutrality in humans at birth."

Freud's (1905) views on the female centered around her desire to obtain the favored male organ. The hopeless striving to obtain a penis was finally abandoned at childbirth, when the woman could accept her child as a substitute for the penis. Freud believed that this struggle left the female with permanent psychological scars, such as insatiable envy and feelings of inferiority, vanity, passivity, and other so-called feminine traits. In addition, he assumed that certain character traits were linked with gender: passivity with femininity and activity with masculinity. After an elaborate anatomical, biochemical, and physiological appraisal, Sherfy (1966) states that: "It is also evidence for the concept that direct sexual aggressiveness or passivity in humans is largely culturally determined."

Freud's (1905) view was almost entirely the result of speculation and superficial observation, and the evidence used to support this hypothesis was derived from interpretations that grew from the original assumption. For example, the girl who was curious or admiring of the boy's penis, for whatever reasons and perhaps because of its urinary versatility, was presumed to be envying the genital for its symbolic and procreative capacities. With the assumption of the primacy of the genital, such curiosity would be interpreted as envy or desire to be boys because of an a priori assumption of male genital primacy instead of as other factors such as the possibility of special privileges and status related to the cultural mores and prejudices regarding the male.

The issue of penis envy is often singled out for criticism by women in the women's movement. Clearly no woman would want a penis. It's a nuisance. It is clear to me that Freud used a metaphor that was unfortunately viewed as literal. I personally do not believe that Freud really thought that women literally wanted the organ, the penis. I think it was a metaphor. What they wanted was the privileges that being a male represented—all the rights, the multitude of social privileges that went with it. But, unfortunately, in some psychological circles the metaphor also gets used literally—that penis envy exists when women do not want to accept their role as being passive.

Freud's (1905) attempts to document this portion of his psychological theory were very unconvincing. The major part of the evidence regarding his views on female psychology were derived from observations of the behavior of young girls in their awareness of sex differences and from the analyses of neurotic adults. In both instances interpretations of the data are heavily prejudiced by the libido theory, which forms the framework for such interpretations. The psychoanalytic literature on this subject is abundant and reaffirms Freud's views, since it begins with the same premise. In more recent years this notion has been shaken by biological studies and by psychoanalytic data. The female is hardly a poorly equipped specimen of manhood, biologically inferior to the male, permanently envious, and perpetually dissatisfied with having been given the less desirable biological role. In many ways the female is better equipped biologically to fulfill her role than the male is. She has a more labile nervous system and a more responsive autonomic system. These physiological findings are undoubtedly related to the need to handle the regularly recurring crises of menstruation and childbirth and the physiological trials of childbearing. In addition, the notion of a sex-linked character structure has been rudely shaken by recent investigations of the role of the female sexual apparatus. (Masters and Johnson, 1966) These studies indicate that the woman, far from being passive in the sex act, is an extremely active participant to the extent that vaginal contractions are more responsible than the sperm's own motile powers for sperm reaching the ovum. In almost every phase of Freud's views on the psychology of the female there have been many objections, revisions, and clarifications.

CHARACTER AND GENDER RECONSIDERED

The attempt to link character and gender overlooked the multicausal bases for character and the crucial significance of the role of the individual in a particular time and place. Character structure is the result of a multiple set of interactions, of which biology is only one factor, along with the cultural determinants of a social, political, economic, and philosophical nature. This is the view of the post-Freudian ego psychologists and cultural psychoanalysts who see character structure as the result of the cultural pressures on the libidinal development. This altered view of character development is particularly significant in elucidating the psychology of the female. The attitudes, characterological traits, and behavioral characteristics of the female may not be due exclusively to her given genital apparatus, but to the demands, restraints, expectations, and controls that the particular culture places on her. The biological and physiological differences, nevertheless, are significant. The marked difference in the size and bulk of the voluntary muscles would obviously produce some divergent attitudes regarding the male and female when the culture requires strength and endurance. This was the paramount need in primitive cultures, but the advent of mechanical contraptions and a modern technology capable of replacing muscular power have obviated this advantage. The major differences that revolve about the roles of the male and female in the procreative and child-rearing processes may produce distinctive characterological elements in each sex.

In earlier years the female was entirely divorced from political, economic, and sociological problems. The prevailing cultures limited her significance to the kitchen and bedchamber. Her role was determined by the combination of being a mother and being completely dependent on the male, both economically and physically. Freud stated that the dependency was biologically ordained due to the absence of the penis, and he thus maintained that the submissiveness and masochistic attitudes of the female were outgrowths of her gender. However, as greater opportunities opened up for women and they became less economically dependent on men, it is possible to see that the characteristics that Freud assumed to be ubiquitous could be culturally determined. The masochistic tendencies that are frequently evident in female behavior can be completely and sufficiently understood on cultural grounds. Being limited in her social and political influence, she had no other recourse but to swallow her needs, desires, and disappointments.

However, the gender enlightenment has produced growing evidence of woman as an outspoken and capable defender of her rights. It is no longer the picture of the masochist—the silent, long-suffering person—but of the participant who expects an equal share of the returns and makes it abundantly clear. This development has recently been reflected in the many women's groups actively engaged in politics and consciousness raising in order to force changes in the social and economic atmosphere of the women's world. It has generally involved women's rights and has culminated in the Equal Rights Amendment, which is having a hard time in spite of the evident justice and validity of their claim. The centuries of discrimination, inequality, and justification by faith and invalid science still plague efforts at liberation.

We have to recognize, however, that the biological role of the female involves her being the childbearer. If women choose to bear children, childbearing and the endocrine cycle between pregnancies demand great physiological flexibility and adaptability. The physiological changes that accompany menstruation and conception necessitate, at times, a more sedentary, less generally active existence. Although women have traditionally carried out practically every function of which men are capable, at certain times their procreative role necessitates some restriction of motion in order to deliver offspring; the care of the young further limits mobility. To this extent women are different from men. Childbearing and motherhood are the biological roles restricted to the female, and it is the special demands of these roles that determine the differences in the sexes, not the presence or absence of particular genital organs or conventional ideas of sexual activity.

Nowadays the issue of having children is a very personal choice; some women have decided to have no families or to have small families. This freedom of choice is important. Why should anyone assume that not using the equipment we have impairs us in some way? If women do not want to have children, it may eliminate a piece of living, but that's all. There is no maternal instinct, all you can demonstrate is a very strong attachment based on needs, but there are no true instincts in humans. Although it is necessary to recognize that the childbearing role cannot be eliminated as a biological role, women are free to do as they please with their biology.

We must recognize that what was considered to be the biological consequence of the absence of the male genital system may be more closely related to the cultural attitudes toward the female. The notion of the weak, helpless, and submissive female, which is not supported by any biological or psychological evidence, may also need to be abandoned, even though some women as well as men have come to accept this notion and to oppose its abolition actively. This observation requires a chapter in itself, and has great relevance to the notion of identifying with the aggressor. It is analogous to the prisoner, slave, or member of a minority group who comes to accept the derogatory view of his own status in order to achieve maximum security and advantage. As his status slowly changes, he reluctantly examines the realities of the situation. Thus, there is always a time lag in the recognition of one's power and privilege after a long period of subjugation.

A more enlightened attitude toward sex and sexuality should avoid assigning priorities to particular methods of achieving sexual satisfaction. The laws regarding sex behavior in many parts of the world still cling to the categories "normal" or "deviant," but psychological theory has avoided labeling the variations of sex behavior between male and female as deviant so long as they are not physiologically or psychologically injurious to either partner. This is particularly applicable to the variations as they involve the female in terms of activity or passivity in the sex act. There is no aggressive partner, the male, or passive partner, the female, in sexual intercourse. Each partner must be passive *and* aggressive and must participate mutually and cooperatively in a venture that calls for both activity and passivity. The unfortunate persistence of labels attributable to one sex as opposed to the other has led to untold misery in the form of feeling guilty, inferior, inadequate, or even homosexual when one's inclinations are somewhat different from the prevailing notions or prejudices of the role of one sex as opposed to the other. The female has been the major victim in this hangover from Victorian morality and scientific infantilism. Since the mantle of being submissive or passive falls on her, under this notion she is required to wait upon the desires and demands of the male and subject to his particular program for sexual activity. To encourage or direct this activity is to step outside the female role. To suggest or recommend some measures that might enhance her enjoyment would be aggressive or too masculine. Consequently, she must be patient and long-suffering, depending on the male's goodwill and competence to provide for her enjoyment. When she has refused to function in these prescribed ways, there still remain some misguided psychologists and psychoanalytic theorists who insist on calling it penis envy, masculine protest, latent homosexuality, or a refusal to accept her proper biological role. Such labels are remnants of outmoded conceptions of female psychology, and no longer serve to illuminate the conflicts and difficulties in her personal relationships.

Conclusion

The understanding of the psychology of the female has only just begun. We have yet to see the psychological effect of the marked technological changes that have reduced the need for the gross musculature of the male and favor the smaller, more discriminating musculature that characterizes the female. These machines will certainly alter the role and status of the female. As the demand for the equality of opportunity, education, and employment is met, the role of the female may radically enhance her status and view of herself beyond the boundaries of motherhood. Profound changes can be expected in her psychology as she moves out of the confines of a minority into an equal status with the male, economically as well as sociologically.

REFERENCES

Freud, S. *Three essays on the theory of sexuality.* London: Imago Press, 1905.

Freud, S. *New introductory letters on psychoanalysis.* New York: W. W. Norton, 1933.

Freud, S. Three contributions to the theory of sex. In A. A. Brill (Ed.), *Basic writings of S. Freud.* New York: Modern Library, 1938.

Hampson, J. L. and Hampson, J. G. The ontogenesis of sexual behavior in man in Young, W. C. (Ed.), *Sex and internal secretion's.* ed. 3, Baltimore: Williams and Wilkins, 1961.

Kinsey, A. C., Pomeroy, W. B., Martin, C. E. and Gebhard, P. H. *Sexual behavior in the Human Female.* Philadelphia: W. B. Saunders, 1953.

Masters, W. H., and Johnson, V. E. *Human sexual response.* Boston: Little, Brown, 1966.

Money, J., Hampson, J. G., and Hampson, J. L. Imprinting and the establishment of gender role. *Archives of Neurology and Psychiatry,* 1957, 77, 333–336.

Saltzman, L. Memory and psychoanalysis. *Journal of Medical Psychology,* 1966, **39,** 127.

Saltzman, L. Sexuality. In J. Marmor (Ed.), *Psychoanalytic frontiers.* New York: Basic Books, 1967.

Sherfy, M. J. The evolution and nature of female sexuality in relation to psychoanalytic theory. *Journal of the American Psychoanalysis Association,* 1966, **14,** 28–128.

8

Assertion Training
for Women

Eileen D. Gambrill
Cheryl A. Richey

An essential part of everyday life is made up of our interactions with other people. Whether at work, with family members, shopping, or enjoying leisure-time social activities, we interact with others, and we interact with different degrees of effectiveness. One aspect of social behavior that has received a great deal of attention is that of assertion. Assertion has been defined as the open expression of preferences by words or actions in a manner that causes others to take them into account (MacDonald, 1974). Assertive behaviors are the verbal and nonverbal responses that enable us to act in our own best interests, to stand up for our selves, and to express our opinions, feelings, and attitudes honestly without undue anxiety or the depreciation of others. Assertive persons exercise their rights without denying or violating the rights and feelings of others (Alberti & Emmons, 1974). Assertion does not guarantee "winning" in situations, but it does facilitate self-expression and increases the likelihood that a satisfactory resolution or compromise will occur and that one's

goals will be obtained. Examples of types of assertive behavior include refusing requests, requesting behavior
changes, complimenting others, disagreeing with others,
asking favors, giving and receiving criticism, initiating
and terminating conversations, arranging future meetings, stating opinions, requesting information, and introducing topics of conversation.

Assertion training is designed to increase the influence
people exert over their interpersonal environment by increasing the appropriate expression of both positive and
negative feelings. Thus, depending on a woman's interests, assertion training may help her to say "no" more
effectively to unfair demands such as working overtime, to
initiate conversations, or to express more of her own opinions when conversing with others. Implicit in assertion
training is the assumption that it is adaptive to express
oneself in appropriate ways, being able to distinguish situations in which restraint is required from those in which
assertion would be most adaptive, and acting accordingly.
It is considered nonadaptive and unjust to be taken advantage of, to allow oneself to be unduly imposed on, or to be
intimidated (Salter, 1949; Wolpe, 1958). In assertion training, the risks entailed in being more active in influencing
one's social environment are assumed, irrational and rational anticipated consequences are separated through
discussion, and the client is prepared for possible negative
ones through establishing positive self-instructions and
self-reinforcement patterns.

Emphasis has been placed on the limiting effects of a
failure to express one's preferences, that is, on submissive
reactions. The potential role of assertion as an inhibitor of
anxiety associated with submissive behavior has been
suggested (Salter, 1949; Wolpe, 1958). Submissive behavior
has been defined as "the act of allowing one's rights to be
ignored, as any act which yields humbly to the preference
of another person" (MacDonald, 1974). Nonassertive behaviors are those that are self-denying, restrained, and

inhibited. Nonassertive persons are passive in social situations and often experience a high degree of interpersonal anxiety and allow others to make decisions or choices for them. Nonassertiveness can be extremely self-depreciating and humiliating. Nonassertive people feel helpless, controlled, and bitter because they rarely express what they want and thus are unlikely to achieve their goals. Feelings of self-dislike and resentment toward others are not uncommon effects of a lack of assertive self-expression. Let us say that a woman does not understand why her doctor has asked her to complete certain tests. A submissive reaction would involve expression of her desire for more information in a way that is not readily noticeable. For example, she would not make a direct request for further information, but might look down at the ground and leave without saying anything; or she might say with a forced smile and in a low voice, "Well . . . I guess you know best. . . ."

A lack of assertive behavior may result in overly aggressive behavior; for example, a person may store up injustices and then "explode" inappropriately. Appropriate assertion of one's preferences should decrease the probability of inappropriate angry outbursts. Aggression has been defined as the "hostile expression of preferences by words or deeds in a manner that coerces others to give in to these preferences; an act which suppresses or takes away the rights of others" (MacDonald, 1974). Aggressive persons are interested in "winning," and they attempt to achieve this goal by any means possible, including putting others down, hurting or humiliating them. Although aggressive persons may not feel particularly anxious and may achieve their goal, the price for "winning" can be very high, indeed. The reactions of others to an aggressive person who has violated their rights is generally one of dislike, hostility, and counteraggression that may be expressed directly or indirectly. Also, the high level of emotion that may accompany and result from aggressive behavior may distract involved parties from what was wanted in the first place. An aggressive response in relation to the preceding example might be, "You doctors are so insensitive to patients' needs; you're just interested in making money. Well, you can't treat me that way, I demand that you tell me why you are ordering these tests or I will report you to the Board of Medical Examiners." An assertive alternative in this situation would consist of a direct request for information, such as "I would like to know the purpose of these tests and what they would entail. Could you tell me about this?" Here, personal attacks and threats are avoided and "owning of feelings" through the use of "I" statements is evident. A recent study has supported the suggestion that assertive responses occasion greater compliance and provoke less anger than aggressive statements (Hollandsworth & Cooley, 1979, in press).

Considering the ubiquity of social interaction, it is not surprising that a lack of effective social behavior has been found to be related to a wide variety of presenting problems, including depression (Lazarus, 1971), physical complaints (Gray, England, & Mahoney, 1965), marital discord (Eisler, Miller, Hersen, & Alford, 1974), sexual difficulties (Fensterheim, 1972), and aggressive behavior (Novaco, 1975; Wallace, Teigen, Liberman, & Baker, 1973). Either aggressive or submissive behavior may lead to lost opportunities for satisfaction and/or to the unnecessary toleration of punishing events. Ineffective social behavior places the person at a disadvantage to others. It interferes with achieving a high frequency of positive events in everyday life.

Assertion training has particular relevance for women for three reasons. First, it offers a way to help women equalize their positions in relation to a number of inequities, such as in the world of work (Bird & Briller, 1968). Second, women comprise the majority of people seeking outpatient mental health services (National Institute of Mental Health, 1973) and the largest percentage of clients with presenting problems that often relate directly to a lack of assertion, such as depression (National Institute of Mental Health, 1974). Third, many women have been socialized to be self-critical, fearful, and nonassertive (Fodor, 1974a, 1974b; Phelps & Austin, 1975; Richey, 1975b). Women's lack of assertion is suggested by a recent study in which 42% of a sample of 81 single women 25 to 64 years old reported that they rarely or never tell a friend at work when they do something that bothers them; 41% rarely or never ask a favor of anyone; and 37% rarely or never initiate a conversation with a stranger (Gambrill, 1975).

There is further evidence that women may have more of a problem with nonassertiveness than men. A review of the literature on female-male verbal interaction indicates that women are nonassertive when interacting with men in dyadic and group discussions (Richey, 1974). Women tend to talk less, offer fewer opinions and problem solutions, engage in shorter comments, and are more easily interrupted and less influential over the final decision reached (Hall, 1972; Kenkel, 1957; Strodbeck, James, & Hawkins, 1957; Whittaker, 1965).

THE COMPONENTS OF ASSERTIVE BEHAVIOR

Unfortunately, little information is available concerning what mix of behaviors is most effective in specific situations. People rated high in assertion tend to speak louder, respond more rapidly, give longer replies, evidence more profound affect, show less compliance, and request more changes in behavior than those rated low in assertion (Eisler, Miller, & Hersen, 1973). Nonverbal behaviors such as eye contact and body posture oriented toward the other person are also important (Serber, 1972). Subjects rated high in assertion expect more positive reactions from others and have less of a discrepancy between what they think they should do and what they actually do compared to subjects rated low in assertion (Eisler, Frederiksen, & Peterson, 1978).

Definitional problems concerning what is effective social behavior in specific situations are compounded by cultural and ethnic differences in what is considered appropriate behavior and by rules that arise within families. They are also complicated by sex differences in normative behavior and by unequal power relationships in which many people find themselves. Let us say that a woman wishes to increase her participation during staff meetings, which are attended mainly by male colleagues. The woman may feel that she has a "perfect right" (Alberti & Emmons, 1974) to participate more in group meetings. Her attempts, although judged appropriately assertive by outside observers, may be considered aggressive by her colleagues. Thus, judgments as to "how things should be" may enter into the decision as to what is appropriate social behavior.

These problems are of special concern to women, considering the socialization of many women to be dependent, passive, and submissive (Hoffman, 1972; Kagen, 1964). Not only may their attempts to increase their assertive behavior not be followed by positive events from significant others, it may also be actively discouraged by the mental health professionals from whom they seek help. The sex biases that have been found among psychotherapists (Broverman, Broverman, Clarkson, Rosenkrantz, & Vogel, 1970) should raise a cautionary note for women clients who consult mental health counselors.

THE SITUATIONAL NATURE OF ASSERTIVE BEHAVIOR

Ineffective social behavior is typically situational. A woman may have very effective skills in many areas but may lack skills in others. She may, for example, be able to refuse requests effectively from family members, but be unable to request favors effectively for them. She may be able to initiate conversations with other women, but have difficulty doing so with men. A variety of dimensions may affect social competence, including (1) the degree of intimacy involved; (2) whether the feeling to be expressed is positive or negative; (3) various characteristics of the people involved, such as their status, age, or sex; (4) perceived status of self in the situation; and (5) the number of people present (MacDonald, 1975; Nedelman, 1976).

Situational differences were found in two studies that utilized role-play situations in which women responded to a series of 12 taped situations, half of which involved a male and half of which involved a female (Gambrill, 1973; Richey, 1978). The situations required the women to initiate a conversation with a man or with a woman, terminate a conversation, change the topic of conversation, and disagree with someone. Twice as many "no responses" occured in situations involving a male. In contrast to these findings, other studies have found that women college students evaluate the consequences for refusing a female peer as more negative than refusing a male authority (Fiedler & Beach, 1978). Thus, women tended to comply more with unwarranted requests from other women students than from male "bosses." Another recent study, again with women college students, suggested that assertion with females was more difficult than with males (Nedelman, 1976). These apparently contradictory findings strengthen the importance of determining the situational nature of the client's assertive difficulties before training commences. This investigation can best be undertaken during assessment.

Interpersonal Situations that are Problematic for Women

A number of studies have attempted to describe specific situations that members of select population groups would like to handle more assertively or interpersonal situations in which they experience difficulty. MacDonald (1974) asked female college students to record "very specific descriptions of situations (she encountered) over the next week which (struck her) as situations in which standing up for (her) rights was or would have been the best course of action." Over 800 discrete situational descriptions were extracted from the diaries of the 107 undergraduate women who volunteered. These descriptions clustered into 10 classes of situations such as asking favors, saying no, and dealing with situations in which someone had been insulting or inconsiderate. A pool of responses was collected by requesting another sample of undergraduate women to record specific descriptions of what they would do or say if they encountered the situation. Goldfried and D'Zurilla (1969) consider identification of specific interpersonal situations of concern to selected populations and identification of appropriate and inappropriate reactions in each situation essential initial steps in the development of social skill training programs.

DeLange (1976) developed five categories of difficult situations experienced by women of various ages and backgrounds. These categories included: stating one's needs and initiating confrontation, handling criticism, making requests of others (asking for help, favors), interacting with authority figures, and initiating actions (giving opinions, making social contacts). Attempts have also been made to identify difficult interpersonal situations for older men and women (Berger & Rose, 1977; Edinberg, Karoly, & Gleser, 1977; Toseland & Rose, 1978). Other efforts have employed only males, for example, Goldsmith and McFall's (1975) isolation of difficult interpersonal situations experienced by male psychiatric patients. Clearly we need more information of this type for women to help us design more relevant training materials.

Items on the Assertion Inventory (Gambrill & Richey, 1975) circled by a group of 101 women 25 to 64 years old as situations they would like to handle more assertively related most often to situations requiring negative assertion; these items included refusing unwanted demands, requesting changes in negative behaviors, dealing with criticism, admitting fear, and requesting consideration. About 30% of the sample gave such items high anxiety ratings and a low response probability (Gambrill, 1975). Similar areas of difficulty were reported by Richey (1975a) for a group of 76 women who took the Assertion Inventory before training. The majority of group members wanted to work on four areas: disagreeing and basic conversation skills; saying "no" to unfair requests; handling criticism; and giving negative feedback.

Sex differences have been found in self-reported assertion. For example, women reported that they are less likely to question someone's criticism of their work (Gambrill & Richey, 1975). Men consider themselves more assertive with bosses and supervisors, more outspoken when stating opinions, and more ready to take the initiative in social contacts with members of the opposite sex. Women report themselves to be more assertive in expressing love, affection, and compliments (Hollandsworth & Wall, 1977).

A description of assessment and intervention procedures involved in assertion training, including assessment of the particular situational contexts in which assertion is difficult, follows. Examples of the use of assertion training with women are then presented; they focus especially on programs that have some empirical support.

Assessment

Many factors may be related to a lack of assertive behavior, including skill deficits (Glasgow & Arkowitz, 1975), anxiety (Greenwald, 1978), lack of practice (Martinson & Zerface, 1970), lack of discrimination among various response alternatives (Eisler, Frederiksen, & Peterson, 1978), and various types of dysfunctional cognitions such as too much attention to negative consequences (Fiedler & Beach, 1978; Glass, Gottman, & Shmurak, 1976). Women are particularly prone to such negative thoughts because of their socialization to be self-critical of their actions compared to men and because of their tendency, as compared with men, to place more importance on social approval than on self-approval (Richey, 1975b).

The variety of potential factors related to a lack of assertion highlights the need for an individual assessment. It cannot be assumed that women do not know how to perform certain assertive behaviors simply because they do not do so. In fact, with some groups of women, this is unlikely to be the case. For example, Brockway (1976) found that professional women usually did have assertive skills available but did not display these due to anxiety. Nor can it be routinely assumed that anxiety is the cause rather than a skill deficit. Only through a careful assessment can the possible contribution of behavior deficits, conditioned anxiety, faulty cognitions, and a lack of practice be determined. Also, assessment activities can identify the general context (e.g., home or work) and the specific situations in which assertive difficulties occur, who is involved, what the client's purpose is in the situations, and what moments are most difficult for her. Only when these factors are known can intervention procedures be judiciously selected based on the unique assessment pattern of each woman. Fortunately, a variety of sources of assessment information are available. These include self-report through behavioral interviews or paper and pencil inventories, self-monitoring, role playing, direct observation in the natural environment, and reports from significant others (Rich & Schroeder, 1976).

Self-report

The relevance of a lack of assertive behavior may be directly voiced by a woman, perhaps stimulated by the increased availability of popular books about assertion training (Alberti & Emmons, 1974; Bloom, Coburn, &

Pearlman, 1975; Butler, 1976; Fensterheim & Baer, 1975; Gambrill & Richey, 1976; Osborn & Harris, 1975; Phelps & Austin, 1975). Often it will emerge through examples of interactions offered by the woman related to a presenting concern, or through complaints that she is "depressed" or "exhausted from being torn in a hundred directions," or that "nobody listens to me" (Bower, 1976, p. 469). For example, a 67-year-old woman client who complained of chronic fatigue revealed on inquiry that she was forced to remain awake at night by her housemate, who "made her" watch TV, even the commercials, after she took her sleeping pill.

Paper and pencil inventories such as the Assertion Inventory may be employed to gain an overview of possible situations relevant to assertion. Unfortunately, most currently available inventories do not permit identification of possible aggressive reactions (DeGiovanni & Epstein, 1978). One self-report instrument that does identify assertive, aggressive, and submissive reactions is the "Discrimination Test on Assertive, Aggressive and Nonassertive Behavior," designed by Lange and Jakubowski (1976).

Self-Monitoring

Valuable information may be provided by data gathered by the client in real-life settings. Information collected can be carefully reviewed, noting possible relationships between a lack of effective social behavior and the presenting problem, the situations in which this occurs, and any positive behaviors that are noted. For example, a 34-year-old female client who was seen by Gambrill presented an initial complaint of depression. She discovered by keeping a log that she consistently failed to refuse unwanted requests and that this failure to assert herself had an impact on her self-esteem and mood.

Observation of the Client's Reactions

Indications of a lack of assertive behavior may reveal itself by interaction between two people, such as a husband and wife, during an interview. Direct observation by the counselor in relevant situations may also be employed to assess the client's social behaviors, as may the use of role playing, in which the client is asked to simulate how she usually acts in a given situation with the counselor or, if in a group situation, with some other group member. It is important to make the role play as realistic as possible, carefully describing the context so that both nonverbal and verbal behaviors can be accurately assessed. Films, videotapes, or audiotapes may be used to present situations so that the woman's responses to these can be observed. For example, DeLange (1976) developed an audiotaped, behavioral role play test consisting of 60 situations by having women keep a 7-day log of situations in which assertive responses would have been desirable. Stimulus films for women have also been prepared for use in assertion training (Jakubowski-Spector, Pearlman, & Coburn, 1973). If the woman is in a group, her interactions with others, such as giving and receiving feedback and engaging in small talk, can be noted.

The important task in assessment is to identify the factors related to ineffective social behavior. One woman may lack effective social skills, whereas another may possess these but have unrealistic standards of performance and so never reinforce herself for the display of these skills. An individual assessment should be made in each instance to identify the possible contributions of skills deficits, conditioned anxiety reactions, and faulty cognitions. The negative effects of a lack of assertive behavior are often made apparent through assessment. Specific situations are selected in which nonassertive behavior has occurred; these are carefully examined, pointing out negative consequences such as doing things she did not wish to do, aggravating others unnecessarily, lost opportunities for enjoyment, and unpleasant feelings such as anxiety and resentment. The losses incurred through ineffective behavior are highlighted together with the possible relationship of these to her presenting problem. Possible detrimental effects on others are also noted. Such detrimental effects are indeed quite likely, especially when submissive or aggressive behavior persistently occurs in ongoing relationships. This is likely to generate ill will and a lack of mutual respect, which may decrease when more appropriate behavior occurs. If negative consequences are likely to follow new behavior, the short- and long-term benefits and costs of engaging in more effective behavior should be discussed, and the woman must make a decision as to her preferred alternative (Fiedler & Beach, 1978; MacDonald, 1975).

Each woman must make the final choice herself in terms of the situations in which she wishes to be more assertive, if any. It is the counselor's ethical obligation to point out the potential advantages and disadvantages of increased assertion in specific situations and in remaining submissive or aggressive in these contexts. The woman must then make up her mind what she wants to do. Certainly in many situations there will be little conflict for a woman in deciding whether to become more assertive or not. It is when potential losses may follow increased assertive behavior, even of a temporary nature, that conflict may arise. For example, a woman may temporarily experience mild surprise or some rejection from fellow employees after she starts to speak up more during staff meetings. Our impression is that women tend to *underestimate* the potential losses from a failure to assert themselves and *overestimate* the likelihood of negative social consequences and disastrous outcomes. Our clinical experience indicates that more often than not, the reactions to increased assertion are, at worst, neutral and quite often are positive, to the great surprise of clients.

INTERVENTION

Addressing Misconceptions

An important initial intervention procedure for many women may be correcting any misconceptions that interfere with a woman's willingness to become more assertive. Various beliefs may have to be challenged, such as the beliefs that one should never hurt people's feelings, one must always please others, and one must be liked by everyone (Ellis, 1962). A woman may initially feel that to be assertive is to be aggressive; that she will hurt other people's feelings; that she will appear unfeminine; that others will not like her; and that she has no right to assert her preferences. Convincing the client of the irrationality of some of her concerns can be encouraged by asking her to observe appropriate models in the natural environment and to note what happens following their effective social behavior and what happens after her own successful behaviors. It is also important that the client weigh the importance of negative social consequences, if they occur, and balance these with self-reinforcement for increased assertion and self-actualization.

Many books and articles, especially those on assertion training for women, devote attention to "raising women's consciousness" about the ways in which their socialization may interfere with becoming more assertive and exercising more influence over the environment (Jakubowski-Spector, 1973). Phelps and Austin (1975) discuss the "compassion trap," which identifies "women who feel that they exist to serve others, and who believe that they must provide tenderness and compassion to all at all times"; they note that this is often a difficult barrier for women and that it often prevents them from acting assertively. Examination of this role involves the woman in reappraising the potential costs and benefits to herself and to others in continuing with this role versus rearranging it. She is encouraged to place more weight on the importance of her own rights. Continued discussion of the value stance involved in assertion training, that one has a "perfect right" (Alberti & Emmons, 1970) to express preferences in a manner that also considers other people's rights, may be necessary. Ironically, people often fail to accord to themselves the same rights that they extend to others.

Possible detrimental effects of submissive or aggressive reactions are noted; if significant others such as a spouse are involved in a counseling effort, they may be the first to affirm their unhappiness with their partner's lack of assertion. Highlighting the disadvantages of ineffective behaviors will help to secure their support. Many writers also point out that women are socialized to use indirect instead of direct methods to influence others (Phelps & Austin, 1975). Although such indirect methods may be ones of first choice for men or women in some instances, women would have greater options if they could use direct methods more frequently.

Misconceptions related to aggressive behavior should also be addressed. Not surprisingly, there have been far more reports of submissive behavior on the part of women in the literature on assertion training than reports concerning aggressive behavior. Reports concerning the use of assertion training to alter aggressive behavior have mainly concerned males so far. One possible cause of aggressive reactions is a persistent lack of assertive behavior and the resentment or frustration that may finally culminate in an overly intense reaction. Lange and Jakubowski (1976) mention that threat and a sense of powerlessness may lead to aggressive reactions. The learning of appropriate assertive behavior should decrease such reactions and convince the person that gains can be made without the use of aggression.

Unless misconceptions are removed, behavior change and appropriate self-reinforcement patterns may not develop. The equal effectiveness of intervention programs that focus on altering cognitions compared to those focusing exclusively on acquisition of social skills supports the important role of cognitions in assertion training (Glass, Gottman, & Schmurak, 1976; Linehan & Goldfried, 1975). However, there are some studies that show that simply practicing new behaviors is sufficient to increase specific social behaviors (Christensen, Arkowitz, & Anderson, 1975). Because these new behaviors are followed by positive consequences, one would expect that they would continue and perhaps be followed by cognitive changes rather than being proceeded by such changes. Some who write about assertion training for women assume that an attitudinal change is essential for a behavior. And, for some women, this may be necessary before they will even try out new behaviors. However, for women who are more experimental, attitude change may follow behavior change. Again, assessment information can help determine how much time in training must be devoted to discussions concerning attitudes and beliefs and how much time should be devoted to skill development and refinement.

Specific Training Procedures

Assertion training typically consists of a variety of procedures that include behavior rehearsal or role playing; feedback or social reinforcement; prompting, instructions, or verbal guidelines; model presentation or demonstration; programming of change or development of training goals; homework assignments; and self-reinforcement training. Model presentation, which involves the demonstration of behavioral alternatives or visible examples of what one might say or do in a difficult situation, has been found to be especially important when behavior deficits exist (Eisler, Hersen, & Miller, 1973). When behavior deficits are not significant, practice alone has been found to be just as effective as model presentation (Christensen, Arkowitz, & Anderson, 1975). As with any interpersonal helping endeavor, assessment is an ongoing process, since more detailed information is gathered during intervention, and assessment is a reactive process in that changes may occur during that stage as a result of learning to identify specific situations in which one would like to act differently. Assessment should sharpen a woman's observational skills in relation to her own behavior and discourage the use of global labels as she learns to recognize assets she possesses and to define more clearly areas in which she would like to act more effectively. During assessment, women also begin to learn to discriminate among submissive, assertive, and aggressive reactions in specific situations. This discrimination training is continued during intervention through model presentation, feedback, and prompting.

Selection of procedural mix depends on the nature of each woman's cognitive, emotional, and behavioral deficits, surfeits, and assets in relation to relevant situations. If appropriate behaviors exist but are not performed because of anxiety, the focus may be on developing anxiety management skills such as training her to relax (Bernstein & Borkovec, 1973) and on how to utilize cognitive coping statements such as, "Relax, you're in control. Take a slow, deep breath" (Meichenbaum, 1977, p. 155). However, even if a woman presents high anxiety as a major component of her assertive difficulties, skill training can still be effective in reducing discomfort and increasing assertive responses (DeLange, 1976).

If skills are absent, response acquisition procedures such as model presentation and behavior rehearsal are employed. Discrimination training is required when skills are available but are not performed at appropriate times. A careful search during assessment for available skills often reveals many appropriate social behaviors that simply have to be prompted in other situations. For example, available appropriate ways of making requests for assistance from a spouse may be of use in work situations but may not be employed there. Thus, the selection of procedures flows directly from assessment, which will reveal relevant cognitive, affective, and overt behaviors and specific situations of concern.

The use of the "minimal effective response" is focused on in assertion training (Rimm & Masters, 1974). This refers to responses that require a minimum of effort and negative emotion and that have a high probability of positive consequences. Potential negative consequences can often be avoided by taking the time to understand the relationships and interpersonal dynamics of the situations in which assertive behavior is proposed (Wolpe, 1958). In situations in which negative reactions are likely to occur, a woman should be prepared by having numerous assertive alternatives available before she tries out her new skills. She may also need to learn some skills for coping with anger and potential aggression. For example, she may need to develop self-statements such as, "I'm not going to get pushed around, but I'm not going haywire either" (Novaco, 1975). It may also be important for a woman who experiences negative consequences following assertive behavior to develop a support system with people who reinforce her attempts to express her preferences and stand up for her rights.

If negative consequences are anticipated and the costs of assertion outweigh potential benefits (e.g., a woman might lose her job or a good friend), she may decide not to assert herself in that situation. The issue of choice is important, and no one should feel obligated to assert themselves in any situation just to adhere to the doctrine of a therapist, a book, or another group member.

There may be situations in which the minimal response is not effective and persistence and escalation may be required. Again, a thoughtful analysis of the costs and benefits of persisting or withdrawing should be carried out by the individual herself.

Behavior Rehearsal

Behavior rehearsal provides an opportunity to practice new behaviors in a safe environment. It also allows others present, such as a counselor or other group members, to observe the woman's behavior carefully, noting appropriate nonverbal or verbal components and those that still need some work. The situational contexts focused on should be very specifically described and realistically arranged so that behavior will be practiced in a situation that is similar to the real-life context. Guidelines for rehearsing situations have been discussed by several trainers (Lange & Jakubowski, 1976; Richey, 1977). Clients can also be encouraged to rehearse difficult situations in their imaginations. Covert rehearsal has been found to be as effective as overt rehearsal in increasing assertive skills (Kazdin, 1973).

Feedback

Positive feedback is offered following each rehearsal; that is, positive aspects of performance are carefully noted and praised. Emphasis is on noting even small improvements. Critical comments such as "You can do better" or "That wasn't too good" are avoided. Feedback helps the woman to identify what she should do more and less of. Model presentation, rehearsal, and feedback are repeated until the requisite skill and comfort levels are attained. Clients can report their anxiety levels by using a Subjective Units of Discomfort Scale (SUDS) (Wolpe & Lazarus, 1966).

A structured format has been developed at the Oxnard Mental Health Center to promote systematic feedback and to encourage involvement of group members (Liberman, King, DeRisi, & McCann, 1975). Positive group feedback to members for assertive responses can also be provided by a group testimonial time before each training session; at this time each member has a chance to share with the group one or two assertions that she engaged in during the week (Richey, 1975a, 1977).

Prompting

Specific instructions or verbal guidelines given to the client before she rehearses a situation "prompts" her to engage in certain behaviors rather than others. The use of such guidelines offers the client specific suggestions for handling a difficult situation, so she does not have to depend on trial and error to discover effective techniques. Instead, she can learn from the experiences of others. Once guidelines have been offered, feedback and coaching are facilitated. For instance, perhaps a person was smiling and nodding while she was trying to say "no." She could be given this feedback following reinforcement for specific appropriate behaviors and then coached to try again without smiling and perhaps asked to try shaking her head instead of nodding.

It is important to give clear instructions in terms of identifying specific behaviors. It would be more helpful to point out lack of eye contact and lack of "I" statements than it would be to tell a client she was "evasive" or "hostile." In addition to prompts being offered verbally by the trainer or other group members, they can also be offered through hand gestures during rehearsal so as not to disrupt the role play. As the client's behaviors improve, guidelines and prompts should be gradually withdrawn.

Model Presentation

Model presentation and rehearsal are usually employed when a client lacks requisite behaviors. Effective behaviors may be modeled by the counselor, other group members, written scripts, audiotapes, videotapes, or films.

Nonverbal behaviors, which are so important in social interaction, are demonstrated, as are verbal behaviors, and the client's attention is drawn to those that are especially critical. Model presentation is more effective if the client's attention is directed toward desired response elements (Bandura, 1969). For example, the client may be requested to notice the model's eye contact and hand motions. The model may verbalize appropriate positive thoughts during the role play if effective social skills are hampered by negative thoughts.

Following model presentation, the client is requested to practice (rehearse) the modeled behavior. Praise is offered for effective behaviors or approximations of these, and coaching is given in relation to needed changes. Modeling effects can be enhanced by asking the women to identify important components of and general rules associated with the modeled behavior. Models are utilized as needed, and rehearsal, prompts, and feedback are continued until desired responses and comfort levels are attained.

The client may be instructed to watch people with effective behavior who are in similar situations and to write down in a log the context, what was done, and what happened. Observing people in real situations increases exposure to a variety of effective models, offers examples to use during rehearsal, increases discrimination as to when to employ certain behaviors, and permits observation of positive reactions following effective behavior. Client observations are carefully discussed, and other situations in which such behaviors may be usefully employed are noted.

Programming of Change

Specific goals should be established for each assertion training session. Perhaps only one or two behaviors will be focused on during a session (e.g., use of "I" statements and assertive posture). Or available skills might be such that all verbal and nonverbal behaviors involved in handling a given situation can be practiced (e.g., practicing handling criticism). Reinforcement for improvement should always be in relation to the woman's own past performance, not in relation to the behavior of others. Situation hierarchies, ranked in terms of the degree of anxiety or anger that situations induce, can be employed to increase and refine assertive behaviors gradually. Training procedures should start with situations that induce a small degree of anger or anxiety; as these are mastered, higher-level scenes can be introduced.

Homework Assignments

Much of the important work in assertion training is carried out by the woman herself in real-life settings. After needed skill and comfort levels are attained in training, new behaviors can be tried out in the natural environment through specific homework assignments. Initial assignments are selected that have a high probability of being followed by positive consequences and that entail minimal discomfort to the woman. If negative reactions are anticipated, the woman should be trained in appropriate coping skills to handle these before trying out new behaviors; that is, she should learn how to reevaluate her thoughts, develop her repertoire of positive self-instructions, and learn how to reinforce herself for trying out new behaviors (Gambrill & Richey, 1976). An example of a homework assignment related to increasing social contacts is to initiate two brief conversations (more than a greeting) with a stranger and with two acquaintances during the next week.

Self-Reinforcement Training

Self-reinforcement can be employed to facilitate the development of assertive behavior. For example, Richey (1974) employed self-reinforcement to increase the expression of elaborated opinion statements by women in mixed-sex groups. Women were trained to offer themselves praise statements and to award themselves points on "bead belts." Examples of praise statements might be "I really did a good job" and "Now that took a lot of courage" (Gambrill & Richey, 1976, p. 78). A woman may also offer herself some tangible item contingent on trying out new skills; for example, if she fulfills an assignment of initiating three conversations, she could buy a favorite magazine that night. Some overt form of reinforcement may temporarily be needed to encourage new behaviors, such as awarding herself points on a wrist counter while also engaging in covert self-praise. Different degrees of success could be awarded a different number of points. For example, DeLange (1976) encouraged women in her assertion skills training groups to give themselves one point for making a response, two points for improvement and being fairly satisfied with their performance, and three points for feeling very good about a response.

Self-reinforcement is important in maintaining new behaviors, particularly when these will sometimes be followed by punishing consequences. Women are instructed to reinforce themselves for trying to exert more effective influence over their social environment, even though their attempts are not always successful.

EXAMPLES OF ASSERTION TRAINING FOR WOMEN

Reports concerning assertion training for women include case reports, laboratory-based analog studies, and group experimental studies that employ a clinical population. Most of the experimental studies concern minimal dating (Arkowitz, 1977) and those involving psychiatric patients (Hersen & Bellack, 1976) include only men. Presented next are examples of the use of assertion training for women clustered in four major areas: the family, work contexts, social contexts, and dealing with professional and service personnel.

Assertion Training Related to Family Situations

Concerns about interactions with family members are often expressed in assertion training groups for women. One aspect of assertion training in such situations may be to increase the sharing of positive and negative feelings. For example, Fodor and Wolfe (1977), in their article "Assertion Training for Mothers and Daughters," report the conflict between a divorced woman in her mid-forties and her 18-year-old daughter. Neither the mother nor the daughter expressed their feelings to the other, and they were building up increasingly negative feelings about one another. For example, when the mother was rude to someone who telephoned to ask the daughter to babysit, the daughter did not tell her mother how angry she was that her mother was rude to this person, nor did the mother share with her daughter how upset she was that her daughter might babysit for someone else when she herself wanted to go out. As usual, dysfunctional beliefs were related to such behaviors. The daughter said "that she was afraid to upset her mother, while (the mother) reported feeling guilty because she felt she should take care of her daughter and might be robbing her of her 'teenagehood.' Each woman was denying her own feelings, taking emotional responsibility for the other's feelings, then feeling angry and resentful because her own goals 'were not met' " (Fodor & Wolfe, 1977, p. 180). Assertion training for these women centered on first teaching them how to share positive feelings and, when they became comfortable with this, working up to the expression of angry feelings. It is important in such training to encourage the participants to identify clearly the behavior that is involved, whether sharing positive or negative feelings. Thus, instead of saying "I like you," which is general and vague, they were encouraged to identify what the other person did to warrant this expression of feeling, such as "I really appreciate your doing the dishes tonight."

Some situations that women pose as problematic between themselves and another family member will require not only assertion training, but negotiation training as well. For example, Fodor and Wolfe (1977) present an example between a mother and her 16-year-old daughter; the mother complained that she had to nag her daugher to do her chores, and the daughter complained about being nagged. Certainly, expression of feelings is an aspect of assertion training. The additional steps of negotiation training, which are sometimes mislabeled as assertion training, are often necessary. Negotiation training includes learning to offer possible solutions, select compromises and solutions, and balance costs and benefits for each party (Kifer, Lewis, Green, & Phillips, 1974).

Shoemaker and Paulson (1976) employed assertion training in a group context with 16 mothers who reported child-rearing difficulties and who demonstrated an unassertive style of communication. The training group met twice a week for 5 weeks for 1½ hours each meeting. Assertive behaviors were encouraged through the use of tokens distributed by the trainer and by other group members. Tokens provide a source of immediate feedback for behavior in a manner that does not require interruption of ongoing conversation. White tokens were offered for assertive behaviors or reports about these. Red tokens were given for aggressive statements such as threatening or provoking comments, sarcasm, malicious joking, insults, blaming, name calling, and interruption of someone unless the other person had interrupted the speaker or was trying to change the topic. Blue tokens were given for submissive reactions such as overapologies, extreme or continuous self-criticism, inappropriate changing of the topic, interjected laughter or joking to release tension if this was avoiding a question, refusal to speak when spoken to, or curt answers to avoid issues, such as "I don't know."

The mothers significantly increased their assertive statements following assertion training and significantly decreased their aggressive statements and reported positive changes in their childrens' behavior. Husbands, although not participating in assertion training, also showed significant increases in assertive statements and decreases in aggressive statements.

Assertion training of husbands has been found to lead to interaction changes in the behavior of their wives (Eisler, Miller, Hersen, & Alford, 1974). Here, too, there was a decrease in the frequency of negative expression by both partners and an increase in the frequency of positive expressions after assertion training. Thus, an increase in the assertive behavior of one family member has been found to result in positive changes in other family members. Significant increases in assertive behaviors (e.g., nonattacking requests) and decreases in verbal behaviors coded as aggressive (e.g., disparagement) have also been found following conjoint assertion training with couples (Epstein, DeGiovanni, & Jayne-Lazarus, 1979, in press).

Landau and Paulson (1977) employed assertion training with 16 Spanish-speaking mothers referred by welfare or probation departments. Weekly 2-hour sessions were held for 12 weeks. The initial stage of the program was devoted to structuring expectancies toward change and to identifying the disadvantages of the women's present unassertive responses styles. For example, one of the mothers found all her days taken up with babysitting for two friends who insisted that she was "the only one their children would stay with," in spite of the fact that she did not need the money or want to babysit. Her inability to say "no" made it extremely difficult for this woman to find the time to pursue interests she had (Landau & Paulson, 1977, p. 122). Situations of interest to the mothers included giving positive messages, giving and receiving criticism, limiting what they agreed to do for others, and taking time out from an interaction with someone to obtain more information or to decide what to do or, if the situation involved an emotional confrontation, to get "breathing space." The next phase consisted of helping the participants to discriminate among aggressive, assertive, and submissive response styles and to identify the criteria and consequences associated with each.

Poker chips given out by the counselor and by group members were also employed in this study to offer immediate feedback to the women for specific behaviors during group meetings and for reports of assertive behaviors in real-life settings. Assertive behaviors that were followed by positive feedback included requests, statements of opinions or preferences, disagreeing with someone, and asking for clarification. Landau and Paulson (1977) reported that the mothers reacted very positively to the use of tokens and that attendance at group sessions was high.

Initial training sessions centered on positive assertions and giving compliments, and initial assignments were addressed to offering family members positive feedback. This emphasis was quite deliberate in anticipation of possible problems with husbands. "Many of the members reported that their husbands were enthusiastic about their attending the group—they liked the positive feedback they were getting and the benefits from wives who were becoming able to say 'no' to others, i.e., neighbors borrowing items, salesmen, and their children" (Landau & Paulson, 1977, p. 126). Emphasis was placed on the women making requests of their husbands instead of on saying "no" to their husbands.

Mothers in the assertion training program improved significantly compared to women in a wait-list group. The mothers evaluated the program positively; they, and significant others, noted many positive changes, including a decrease in somatic complaints such as headaches.

The Work Context

What is encouraged in men—initiative and highlighting one's good points in relation to securing and maintaining jobs—has often been discouraged in women's socialization. Situations of interest to women include how to "present themselves" in employment interviews, how to ask for raises and express interest in higher positions, how to express complaints, and how to speak up more frequently in group meetings. A recent study (Rosen & Jardee, 1975) showed that the women who demand redress of a wrong from an employer will get much further than one who assumes a "pleading" posture.

Being prepared with information concerning sexist objections raised by a prospective employer is helpful. Thus, when an employer says that he has a hesitation about hiring women because they are absent more frequently (untrue), being prepared with the facts and sharing those facts will bolster her position. Brockway's (1976) study, limited to professional women, illustrated the importance of eliminating dysfunctional beliefs and attitudes and decreasing anxiety in contrast to an emphasis on establishing social skills, which many of these women already possessed.

Social work (Rose, Cayner, & Edelson, 1977) and nursing (Herman, 1977) are two professional settings in which assertion training has received increasing attention. Some nursing schools have assertion training courses built into the curriculum. An anecdotal report by Herman (1977) offers examples of relevant situations, including those related to being overloaded with work, answering patients' questions, disagreeing with doctors, accepting criticism, asking for further information, dealing with pain, and setting helpful limits. Here, too, helping women to discriminate among assertive, submissive, and aggressive reactions is an important part of assertion training. Examples of different types of responses to a nurse who is recurrently late to shift report include: (1) during the report, the charge nurse states: "Well, I wonder if Mrs. X will even show this evening. She's late every day (submissive); (2) in a sweet voice while smiling, the charge nurse says to Mrs. X, "It must be convenient to make your own time schedule" (aggressive-sarcastic); and (3) in a firm, calm voice the charge nurse says, "You have been coming in 15 to 20 minutes late this week. I am frustrated as I have to repeat the patient report and many patients are asking for their medications. I would like you to be on time" (Herman, 1977, p. 288). The latter response is considered an assertive comment in that the charge nurse specifies the bothersome behavior, expresses her feelings of frustration, does not mix her negative message with diluting positive nonverbal behaviors such as smiles, directly asks for a specific behavior change, and avoids aggressive comments.

The Social Context

An interest in increasing the frequency of social contacts is frequently mentioned by women. The relationship between assertion and frequency of social contacts is suggested by Greenwald's (1978) finding of a positive relationship between these variables. Assertion training emphasizes taking more initiative in meeting people and offers skills for initiating and maintaining conversations, arranging future meetings, and being more active in conversations (Gambrill & Richey, 1976). Here, too, the degree of initiation required often diverges from women's accustomed roles, and some women are at first reluctant to take a more active stance in increasing their contacts, especially with men. Beliefs and attitudes are often more of an inhibiting factor than social constraints. Two reports investigated the effectiveness of training procedures to increase the frequency of social contacts among women

(Gambrill, 1973; Richey, 1978). In the Gambrill (1973) study, subjects were volunteers who were interested in increasing their frequency of social contacts with men, women, or both. The age range of the women was between 19 and 34 years of age. Three treatment groups were compared to a wait-list control group. Subjects in the "manual" group received a training manual that included information about general principles related to changing one's behavior, such as the importance of working in small steps, ways to assess one's behavior, how to initiate conversations, where to locate promising places to meet other people, how to terminate conversations, how to identify and handle troublesome thoughts, and so forth. A second group received self-reinforcement training in addition to the manual. Subjects in a "self-help group" discussed the same topics as the other groups and were encouraged to increase their social contacts, but they received neither the manual nor the self-reinforcement training. The former two groups were given weekly assignments, and all three groups monitored the frequency of their social contacts. Intervention took place during three weekly 1½-hour sessions that were structured with audiotaped instructions and minimal leader participation. Prepost measures included self-report inventories, self-monitored data, and behavioral measures based on responses to 12 audiotaped stimulus presentations.

Subjects receiving the manual were significantly more successful in increasing the frequency and range of their social contacts compared to the other groups. Subjects in the self-reinforcement group initiated a higher proportion of social contacts than subjects in either the self-help or wait-list control group. Significant increases from the baseline to a 3-month follow-up in the percentage of contacts initiated were found in both treatment groups. This study indicates that an assertion training program in which the counselor is relatively inactive can be helpful in increasing social contacts of women.

Richey (1978), in a recent attempt to replicate part of the Gambrill (1973) study, utilized an older, more clinical population. The 21 women ranged in age from 23 to 53 years (mean age 35.5 years). The women were randomly assigned to either a training group ($N = 10$), or a wait-list group ($N = 11$). Training was carried out in a community agency during five weekly 2½-hour sessions. The group utilized *It's Up To You: Developing Assertive Social Skills* (Gambrill & Richey, 1976) as a training manual. Information from the book, homework assignments, self-reinforcement, and group support for risk taking were the main treatment variables. Rehearsal was minimal, and there was no structured modeling within the group context.

Examination of prechange and postchange measures indicated that the training group improved significantly on self-report measures of self-esteem and self-confidence, decreased significantly in their Assertion Inventory discomfort scores, and improved significantly in the content of their responses during behavioral role-play tests. Many of the women were taking much more initiative in their daily contacts with friends, co-workers, and new acquaintances.

Dealing with Professional and Service People

Women are often socialized to accept what information they are given and not expected to ask for more. This places them at a disadvantage in their interactions with professionals and service people. Learning to request information and to persist with their requests is important. Women are also encouraged to be armed with relevant information. If a woman seems to know something about the malady from which her car is suffering, the mechanic may not be as likely to "snow her." Requesting reasonable service is another important behavior, for example, being able to ask for more information from one's physician regarding a particular medication or requesting that a plumber complete a job satisfactorily.

Assertion training has been employed with public welfare recipients, training these individuals to interact more effectively with social service workers in terms of stating their requests and asking for clarification (Galinsky, Schopler, Satier, & Gambrill, 1979, in press). The use of assertion training with the elderly both in institutional (Berger & Rose, 1977) and noninstitutional settings (Edinberg, Karoly & Gleser, 1977; Toseland & Rose, 1978) is also being explored.

THE EFFECTIVENESS OF ASSERTION TRAINING

Reports discussed in the last section indicate that assertion training is effective in changing behavior and that it encourages reciprocal positive changes in the behavior of significant others. Two recent studies employing women as subjects investigated the relative effectiveness of a rational restructuring approach and a skill-training approach. Linehan and Goldfried (1975) compared rational restructuring (RT) alone, behavior rehearsal (BT) alone, a combination of the two (RBT), a relationship control, and an assessment only condition. Women in both the RBT and BT groups were significantly more assertive during role-play tests compared to women in the RT group. All three treatment groups showed more assertion compared to the control groups.

Wolfe and Fodor (1977) compared three intervention programs (BT = model presentation and rehearsal; RBT = BT plus rational therapy; and CR = consciousness raising) with a wait-list control group. Subjects were recruited through notices at an outpatient psychotherapy clinic that called for women who were experiencing difficulty in asserting themselves. Women in the BT and RBT groups improved significantly on assertive content during a behavioral role-play test. Although more women in the CR group compared to the other groups reported that they benefited from the group experience, these women did not differ in any other measure from women in the wait-list group.

DeLange (1976) compared two behavioral approaches with a clinical population of women. Systematic desensitization and assertive skill training were compared to discussion and assessment only groups. One hundred and twenty women, ages 19 to 56 years, were divided into high and low anxiety and randomly assigned to one of the four conditions. Groups of six met for five weekly sessions. Women in the assertive skill training group showed greater gains on the role-play test than women in any of the other groups, with low-anxiety women showing more generalization of assertive behaviors to new situations than high-anxiety women. Women in both the desensitization and assertive skill training groups decreased significantly in reported anxiety as compared with the assessment-control group. These three studies indicate that skill training does enhance the quality of assertive behavior but that on many measures, intervention focused on alteration of cognitions and/or anxiety is just as effective.

Rathus (1972) compared results obtained with a group of women who observed videotaped assertive models and practiced assertive behavior with two other groups of women, one receiving a placebo intervention and another completing assessment measures only. Women in the former group reported more assertive behavior and were rated as significantly more assertive compared to women in the other two groups.

Many studies have attempted to isolate the relative importance of specific components of assertion training such as model presentation or rehearsal. Some studies have found that model presentation enhances effects (Eisler, Hersen, & Miller, 1973). Model presentation appears more necessary when behavior deficits are significant, such as with psychiatric patients. When such deficits exist, practice alone is unlikely to result in positive change.

The diverse results achieved in studies investigating the relative effectiveness of various components of assertion training is probably due to the failure to describe carefully and appropriately vary possible individual differences in terms of relevant assessment factors (Wolpe, 1977). One would expect a woman with a high frequency of negative self-evaluations to be more reluctant to try out new behaviors than a woman who does not have a high frequency of such thoughts. One would expect that if a woman did not know how to refuse requests effectively or had high anxiety in refusal situations, simply asking her to practice refusal responses would probably fail. There is no doubt that emphasis on altering negative self-evaluations can be effective; in fact, it may be more effective than skill training (Glass, Gottman, & Shumurak, 1976). Because negative self-evaluations are more outstanding in the assessment picture than behavior deficits, this would be expected.

Studies examining the extent to which the effects of assertion training generalize to other situations indicate that positive changes are usually confined to highly similar situations (McFall & Lillesand, 1971). Considering that different behavioral components are involved in different types of assertive reactions, this is not surprising. Many studies have failed to find significant effects on generalization measures (Hersen, Eisler, & Miller, 1974; McFall & Lillesand, 1971). Where effects have been found, positive changes are typically greater in laboratory-based tests, such as during role plays, than in naturalistic settings. Caution must clearly be exercised in terms of assuming generalization of change from analog situations to real-world situations (Lick & Unger, 1977).

To the extent that similar cognitive events interfere with the display of social skills, one would expect that a change in such cognitions might result in a wider range of assertive behavior changes. Richey (1974), for example, demonstrated that women who were trained to reinforce themselves for assertive discussion skills were more active in group discussions than women who received assertion training without the self-reinforcement component. Women who continued to reinforce themselves for assertive responses after an assertion training group experience reported that their skills generalized to new situations not practiced during training significantly more than those of women who reported less continued self-reinforcement for assertive successes (Richey, 1975a). Although cognitive factors such as self-reinforcement may play a role in generalization, other factors, such as opportunities to practice and receive feedback, may also influence the extent to which positive effects generalize to other situations. The brevity of intervention in many studies, such as 40 minutes (Kirchner, 1976), makes generalization of results unlikely.

How well are positive changes maintained? A number of case reports and clinical studies provide follow-up data. Piaget and Lazarus (1969) report the successful intervention with a 37-year-old housewife. Twenty-seven sessions were held. A 6-month follow-up revealed maintained improvement in assertive responses. MacPherson (1972) employed assertion training with a 45-year-old housewife who responded submissively to her mother and who was overly critical with her husband. A 2-year follow-up revealed that therapeutic gains were maintained. Assertion training together with a variety of other procedures was employed to decrease the self-mutilating behavior of a 19-year-old woman (Roback, Frayn, Gunby, & Tuters, 1972). During intervention this young woman learned how to express her anger in more appropriate ways. Intervention took place over a 44-day period, and self-burning incidents fell to zero during this time. Gains were maintained at a 4-month follow-up. Fensterheim (1972) employed assertion training to address the marital difficulties of a young couple who reported a deteriorating sexual relationship that seemed to be related to a failure by the couple to express feelings to each other about their sexual interaction. For example, the wife said that she was unable to tell her husband about his lack of tenderness when making sexual advances, and the husband never mentioned his anger concerning the remoteness of his wife during sexual activity. Intervention took place over 16 sessions. A 1-year follow-up indicated that gains had been maintained. Unfortunately, in each of these clinical reports, other procedures in addition to assertion training were also employed. Thus, we cannot isolate the relative contribution of assertion training per se.

Two recent clinical follow-up studies of group assertion training for women indicate that assertive gains were maintained or increased even with women who had been out of training for a year or more (Mayo, Bloom, & Pearlman, 1975; Richey, 1975a). Other clinical studies report follow-up results on assertion training at 10 months (Field & Test, 1975), 12 months (Galassi, Kostka, Galassi, 1975), and 24 months (Longin & Rooney, 1975).

Follow-up periods from analog studies in which nonclinical populations have been employed have been much more brief. However, overall, these results are also encouraging; see Curran and Gilbert (1975) for 6-month follow-up. A key factor related to the maintenance of new behaviors will be the extent to which they are reinforced by the person and by those with whom the person interacts. If possible, significant others should be involved in the assertion training program so they can assume a supportive function. This source of support together with self-reinforcement training should help to maintain gains. Additional reinforcement could be provided by a partner system or by a support group that meets regularly.

THE RELATIONSHIP BETWEEN ASSERTION AND SELF-ESTEEM

One would expect that there would be a positive relationship between assertion and self-evaluation, and such a relationship has been found (Percell, Berwick, & Beigel, 1974). One hundred clients (50 men and 50 women) either in treatment or seeking treatment at a community mental health center completed an assertion inventory and a self-acceptance questionnaire. The correlation between assertion and self-acceptance was significant at 0.51 for women and 0.49 for men. The self-evaluation of clients increased and anxiety decreased after assertion training. Shy women significantly increased their self-opinion, self-esteem, and self-confidence ratings on self-report inventories after a group assertion training experience. Women in a wait-list group remained unchanged on these measures (Richey, 1978). Greenwald (1978) found that high- and low-dating women differed in self-esteem and in perceived social adequacy.

THE USE OF A GROUP CONTEXT

Assertion training for women is often carried out in a group context. A group provides a variety of advantages for such training, including a greater number of available models, multiple sources of support, finding that other women have similar concerns, and the availability of many people to participate in role plays (Alberti & Emmons, 1974; Rimm & Masters, 1974; Rose, 1975). Assertion training in groups has been utilized with a variety of populations, including college students (Galassi, Galassi, & Litz, 1974; Rathus, 1972); mothers (Shoemaker & Paulson, 1976); clients in social agencies (Rose, 1975); and severely disturbed hospitalized patients (Field & Test, 1975).

Group training may be especially important for women who have problems being assertive (Osborn & Harris, 1975). Because of their socialization, women may require more social support and more opportunities to observe assertive women who are still seen as appropriately "feminine" in order for them to be direct and independent (Jakubowski-Spector, 1973; Richey, 1974). Assertion training may also be successfully combined with consciousness raising (CR) for women. Lange and Jakubowski (1976) discuss the benefits of utilizing both assertion exercises and CR experiences. First, they indicate that CR increases the members' awareness that their problems are not individual failures but, instead, are common problems experienced by most women because of their femininity training. Second, they stress the importance of CR as a way to help members view themselves and others differently; that is, beliefs and cognitions change, which facilitates generalization of new assertive skills to a variety of interpersonal situations. A detailed description of a 5- to 6-week assertion training group format for women is presented elsewhere (Richey, 1979, in press).

FUTURE RESEARCH NEEDS

Little is known concerning what reaction really works best in the natural environment in relation to specific situations. And very little is known about the assertion training needs of special populations such as older women, disabled women, and women of various ethnic and cultural groups. This is very relevant information, since what will be effective seems to be heavily influenced by the particular social context in which the reaction occurs. We also know little about what types of reactions might work when direct assertion would probably not be effective, although we have some interesting leads (Watzlawick, Weakland, & Fisch, 1974).

SUMMARY

Assertion training is uniquely suited to alter the roles of dependency and passivity to which women have often been socialized. It is a multifaceted endeavor in terms of considering beliefs, feelings, and behavior. This is especially important with women, since the limits they place on their behavior through internal constraints such as fear, worry, and guilt often outweigh the social constraints that may actually exist. It allows women to expand their influence on their social environment. It relates to inter-personal problems in the family and problems at work. A woman can learn to make requests for changes in her partner's behavior in such a way that these requests are likely to be followed by compliance and an increase in the mutual pleasure of the relationship. The woman who has been consistently refused a job promotion can learn more effective ways and times to request a promotion from her employer. The professional who wishes to make changes in an organization can learn to interact with supervisors and administrators in such a way as to maximize her probability of success and minimize the cost to herself. Assertion training can help women to reverse the current situation in which women are in the majority in the use of mental health services but are in the minority in their access to many of society's resources.

References

Alberti, R. E., & Emmons, M. L. *Your perfect right.* San Luis Obispo, Calif.: Impact Press, 1974.

Arkowitz, H. Measurement and modification of minimal dating behavior. In M. Hersen, R. M. Eisler, and P. M. Miller (Eds.), *Progress in behavior modification.* Vol. 5. New York: Academic Press, 1977.

Bandura, A. *Principles of behavior modification.* New York: Holt, Rinehart and Winston, 1969.

Berger, R. M., & Rose, S. D. Interpersonal skill training with institutionalized elderly patients. *Journal of Gerontology,* 1977, **32,** 346–353.

Bernstein, D. A., & Borkovec, T. D. *Progressive relaxation training. A manual for the helping professions.* Champaign, Ill.: Research Press, 1973.

Bird, C., & Briller, S. W. *Born female: The high cost of keeping women down.* New York: David McKay, 1968.

Bloom, L. Z., Coburn, K., & Pearlman, J. *The new assertive woman.* New York: Delacorte, 1975.

Bower, S. A. Assertiveness training for women. In J. P. Krumboltz and C. E. Thorensen (Eds.), *Counseling methods.* New York: Holt, Rinehart and Winston, 1976.

Brockway, B. S. Assertion training with professional women. *Social Work,* 1976, 21, 498–505.

Broverman, I. K., Broverman, D. M., Clarkson, F. E., Rosenkrantz, P. S., & Vogel, S. R. Sex role stereotypes and judgments of mental health. *Journal of Consulting and Clinical Psychology,* 1970, 34, 1–6.

Butler, P. *Self-assertion for women: A guide to becoming androgynous.* San Francisco: Canfield Press, 1976.

Christensen, A., Arkowitz, G. H., & Anderson, J. Practice dating as treatment for college dating inhibitions. *Behavior Research and Therapy,* 1975, 13, 321–331.

Curran, J. P., & Gilbert, F. S. A test of the relative effectiveness of a systematic desensitization program and an interpersonal skills training program with date anxious subjects. *Behavior Therapy,* 1975, 6, 510–521.

DeGiovanni, S., & Epstein, N. Unbinding assertion and aggression in research and clinical practice. *Behavior Modification,* 1978, 2, 173–192.

DeLange, J. M. Relative effectiveness of assertive skill training and desensitization for high and low anxiety women. Unpublished doctoral dissertation, University of Wisconsin, Madison, 1976.

Edinberg, M. A., Karoly, P., & Gleser, G. C. Assessing assertion in the elderly: An application of the behavioral-analytic model of competence. *Journal of Clinical Psychology,* 1977, 33, 869–874.

Eisler, R. M., Frederiksen, L. W., & Peterson, G. L. The relationship of cognitive variables to the expression of assertiveness. *Behavior Therapy,* 1978, 9, 419–427.

Eisler, R. M., Hersen, M., & Miller, P. M. Effects of modeling on components of assertive behavior. *Journal of Behavior Therapy and Experimental Psychiatry,* 1973, 4, 1–6.

Eisler, R. M., Hersen, M., Miller, P. M., & Blanchard, B. Situational determinants of assertive behavior. *Journal of Consulting and Clinical Psychology,* 1975, 43, 330–340.

Eisler, R. M., Miller, P. M., & Hersen, M. Components of assertive behavior. *Journal of Clinical Psychology,* 1973, 29, 295–299.

Eisler, R. M., Miller, P. M., Hersen, M., & Alford, H. Effects of assertive training on marital interaction. *Archives of General Psychiatry,* 1974, **30,** 643–649.

Ellis, A. *Reason and emotion in psychotherapy.* New York: Lyle Stuart, 1962.

Epstein, N., DeGiovanni, I. S., & Jayne-Lazarus, C. Assertion training for couples. *Journal of Behavior Therapy and Experimental Psychiatry,* 1978, **9,** 149–157.

Fensterheim, H. Assertive methods and marital problems. In R. D. Rubin, H. Fensterheim, J. D. Henderson, and L. P. Ullman (Eds.), *Advances in behavior therapy.* New York: Academic Press, 1972.

Fensterheim, H., & Baer, J. *Don't say yes when you want to say no.* New York: Dial Press, 1975.

Fiedler, D., & Beach, L. R. On the decision to be assertive. *Journal of Consulting and Clinical Psychology,* 1978, **46,** 537–546.

Field, G. D., & Test, M. A. Group assertive training for severely disturbed patients. *Journal of Behavior Therapy and Experimental Psychiatry,* 1975, **6,** 129–134.

Fodor, I. G. The phobic syndrome in women: Implications for treatment. In V. Franks and V. Burtle (Eds.), *Women in therapy: New psychotherapies for a changing society.* New York: Brunner/Mazel, 1974. (a)

Fodor, I. G. Sex role conflict and symptom formation in women: Can behavior therapy help. *Psychotherapy: Theory, Research and Practice,* 1974, **11,** 22–29. (b)

Fodor, I. G., & Wolfe, J. L. Assertiveness training for mothers and daughters. In R. Alberti (Ed.), *Assertiveness: Innovations, applications, and issues.* San Luis Obispo, Calif.: Impact Press, 1977.

Galassi, J. P., Galassi, M. D., & Litz, M. C. Assertive training in groups using video feedback. *Journal of Counseling Psychology,* 1974, **21,** 390–394.

Galassi, J. P., Kostka, M. P., & Galassi, M. D. Assertive training: A one-year follow-up. *Journal of Counseling Psychology,* 1975, **22,** 451–452.

Galinsky, M. J., Schopler, J. H., Satier, E. J., & Gambrill, E. D. Assertion training for public welfare clients. *Social Work with Groups,* 1979, in press.

Gambrill, E. D. A behavioral program to increase social interaction. A paper presented at the Seventh Annual Convention of the Association for Advancement of Behavior Therapy, Miami, December 1973.

Gambrill, E. D. Assertion training for single women. Paper presented at the Ninth Annual Convention of the Association for Advancement of Behavior Therapy, San Francisco, December 1975.

Gambrill, E. D., & Richey, C. A. An assertion inventory for use in assessment and research. *Behavior Therapy*, 1975, **6**, 550–561.

Gambrill, E. D., & Richey, C. A. *It's up to you: Developing assertive social skills*. Millbrac, Calif.: LesFemmes, 1976.

Glasgow, R., & Arkowitz, H. The behavioral assessment of male and female social competence in dyadic heterosexual interactions. *Behavior Therapy*, 1975, **6**, 488–408.

Glass, C. R., Gottman, J. M., Shmurak, S. H. Response acquisition and cognitive self-statement modification approaches to dating skills training. *Journal of Counseling Psychology*, 1976, **23**, 520–526.

Goldfried, M. R., & D'Zurilla, T. J. A behavior-analytic model for assessing competence. In C. D. Spielberger (Ed.), *Current topics in clinical and community psychology*. Vol. 1. New York: Academic Press, 1969.

Goldsmith, J. B., & McFall, R. M. Development and evaluation of an interpersonal skill-training program for psychiatric patients. *Journal of Abnormal Psychology*, 1975, **84**, 51–58.

Gray, B., England, G., & Mahoney, J. Treatment of benign vocal nodules by reciprocal inhibition. *Behavior Research and Therapy*, 1965, **3**, 187–193.

Greenwald, D. P. Self-report assessment in high- and low-dating women. *Behavior Therapy*, 1978, **9**, 297–299.

Hall, K. Sex differences in initiation and influence in decision-making groups of prospective teachers. Unpublished doctoral dissertation, Stanford University, 1972.

Herman, S. J. Assertiveness: One answer to job dissatisfaction for nurses. In R. E. Alberti (Ed.), *Assertiveness: Innovations, applications, issues*. San Luis Obispo, Calif.: Impact Press, 1977.

Hersen, M., & Bellack, A. S. Social skills training for chronic psychiatric patients: Rationale, research findings and future directions. *Comprehensive Psychiatry*, 1976, **17**, 559–580.

Hersen, M., Eisler, R. M., & Miller, P. M. An experimental analysis of generalization in assertive training. *Behavior Research and Therapy*, 1974, **12**, 295–310.

Hoffman, L. W. Early childhood experiences and women's achievement motives. *Journal of Social Issues,* 1972, **28,** 129–155.

Hollandsworth, J. G., Jr., & Cooley, M. L. Provoking anger and gaining compliance with assertive versus aggressive responses. *Behavior Therapy,* 1979, in press.

Hollandsworth, J. G., Jr., & Wall, K. E. Sex differences in assertive behavior: An empirical investigation. *Journal of Counseling Psychology,* 1977, **24,** 217–222.

Jakubowski-Spector, P. Facilitating the growth of women through assertive training. *The Counseling Psychologist,* 1973, **4,** 75–86.

Jakubowski-Spector, P., Pearlman, J., & Coburn, K. Assertive training for women: A stimulus film. Washington, D.C.: American Personnel and Guidance Association, 1973.

Kagen, J. Acquisition and significance of sex typing and sex role identity. In M. L. Hoffman and L. W. Hoffman (Eds.), *Review of child development research.* Vol. 1. New York: Russell Sage Foundation, 1964.

Kazdin, A. E. Covert modeling and the reduction of avoidance behavior. *Journal of Abnormal Psychology,* 1973, **81,** 87–95.

Kenkel, W. Differentiation in family decision-making. *Sociology and Social Research,* 1957, **42,** 18–25.

Kifer, R. E., Lewis, M. A., Green, D. R., & Phillips, E. L. Training predelinquent youths and their parents to negotiate conflict situations. *Journal of Applied Behavior Analysis,* 1974, **7,** 357–364.

Kirchner, N. M. Generalization of behaviorally oriented assertive training. *The Psychological Record,* 1976, **26,** 117–125.

Landau, P., & Paulson, T. Group assertion training for Spanish speaking Mexican-American mothers. In R. E. Alberti (Ed.), *Assertiveness: Innovations, applications, and issues.* San Luis Obispo, Calif.: Impact Press, 1977.

Lange, A., & Jakubowski, P. *Responsible assertive behavior.* Champaign, Ill.: Research Press, 1976.

Lazarus, A. A. *Behavior therapy and beyond.* New York: McGraw-Hill, 1971.

Liberman, R. P., King, L. W., DeRisi, W. T., & McCann, M. *Personal effectiveness: Guiding people to assert themselves and improve their social skills.* Champaign, Ill.: Research Press, 1975.

Lick, J. R., & Unger, T. E. The external validity of behavioral fear assessment. *Behavior Modification,* 1977, **1,** 283–306.

Linehan, M. M., & Goldfried, M. R. Assertion training for women: A comparison of behavior rehearsal and cognitive restructuring. Paper presented at the Ninth Annual Convention of the Association for Advancement of Behavior Therapy, San Francisco, December 1975.

Longin, H. E., & Rooney, W. M. Teaching denial assertion to chronic hospitalized patients. *Journal of Behavior Therapy and Experimental Psychiatry,* 1975, **6,** 219–222.

MacDonald, M. A behavioral assessment methodology as applied to the measurement of assertion. Unpublished doctoral dissertation, University of Illinois, 1974.

MacDonald, M. Teaching assertion: A paradigm for therapeutic intervention. *Psychotherapy: Theory, Research and Practice,* 1975, **12,** 60–67.

MacPherson, E. L. R. Selective operant conditioning and deconditioning of assertive modes of behavior. *Journal of Behavior Therapy and Experimental Psychiatry,* 1972, **3,** 99–102.

Martinson, W., & Zerface, J. Comparison of individual counseling and social program with non-daters. *Journal of Counseling Psychology,* 1970, **17,** 36–40.

Mayo, M., Bloom, M., & Pearlman, J. Effectiveness of assertive training for women: A report of a questionnaire study. In L. Z. Bloom, K. Coburn, and J. Pearlman (Eds.), *The new assertive woman.* New York: Delacorte, 1975, pp. 227–228.

McFall, R. M., & Lillesand, D. B. Behavior rehearsal with modeling and coaching in assertion training. *Journal of Abnormal Psychology,* 1971, **77,** 313–323.

Meichenbaum, D. *Cognitive-behavior modification: An integrative approach.* New York: Plenum Press, 1977.

National Institute of Mental Health, Utilization of Mental Health Facilities, 1971, DHEW, Pub. No. NIH 74–657, 1973.

National Institute of Mental Health, Utilization of Psychiatric Facilities by Persons Diagnosed with Depressive Disorders, DHEW, Pub. No. ADM 74–6, 1974.

Nedelman, D. An experimental analysis of the dimensions of generalization of assertive training. Doctoral dissertation, University of Washington, 1976. Dissertation Abstracts International, 1977, **37,** 1444B, University Microfilms No. 76–20, 728.

Novaco, R. W. *Anger control: The development and evaluation of an experimental treatment.* Lexington, Mass.: Heath, 1975.

Osborn, S. M., & Harris, G. G. *Group assertive training for women.* Springfield, Ill.: Charles C Thomas, 1975.

Percell, L. P., Berwick, P. T., & Beigel, A. The effects of assertive training on self concept and anxiety. *Archives of General Psychiatry,* 1974, **31**, 502–504.

Phelps, S., & Austin, N. *The assertive woman.* San Luis Obispo, Calif.: Impact Press, 1975.

Piaget, G. W., & Lazarus, A. The use of rehearsal-desensitization. *Psychotherapy: Theory, Research and Practice,* 1969, **6**, 264–266.

Rathus, S. An experimental investigation of assertive training in a group setting. *Journal of Behavior Therapy and Experimental Psychiatry,* 1972, **3**, 81–86.

Rich, A. R., & Schroeder, H. E. Research issues in assertiveness training. *Psychological Bulletin,* 1976, **83**, 1081–1096.

Richey, C. A. Increased female assertiveness through self-reinforcement. Unpublished dissertation, University of California, Berkeley, 1974.

Richey, C. A. Utilizing self-reinforcement in group assertion training for women: A follow-up report. Paper presented at the Ninth Annual Convention of the Association for Advancement of Behavior Therapy, San Francisco, December 1975. (a)

Richey, C. A. Women as a special target group: An exploration of the mental health concerns of female clientele. Paper presented at the Twentieth Anniversary NASW Symposium, Miami, October 1975. (b)

Richey, C. A. How to conduct an assertion training group: A workshop manual for trainers. Unpublished manuscript, University of Washington, Seattle, 1977.

Richey, C. A. Relative effectiveness of a group training program to increase social interaction skills among shy women. Unpublished manuscript, University of Washington, Seattle, 1978.

Richey, C. A. Group assertion training for women. In S. P. Shinke (Ed.), *Community application of behavior therapy: A sourcebook for social workers.* Chicago: Aldine, 1979, in press.

Rimm, D. C., & Masters, J. C. *Behavior therapy: Techniques and empirical findings.* New York: John Wiley, 1974.

Roback, H., Frayn, D., Gunby, L., & Tuters, K. A multifactorial approach to the treatment and management of a self-mutilating patient. *Journal of Behavior Therapy and Experimental Psychiatry,* 1972, **3**, 189–193.

Rose, S. D. In pursuit of social competence. *Social Work,* 1975, **20,** 33–39.

Rose, S. D., Cayner, J. J., & Edelson, J. L. Measuring interpersonal competence. *Social Work,* 1977, **22,** 125–129.

Rosen, B., & Jardee, T. H. Effects of employee's sex and threatening versus pleading appeals on managerial evaluations of grievances. *Journal of Applied Psychology,* 1975, **60,** 442–445.

Salter, A. *Conditioned reflex therapy.* New York: Capricorn, 1949.

Serber, M. Teaching and nonverbal components of assertive training. *Journal of Behavior Therapy and Experimental Psychiatry,* 1972, **3,** 179–183.

Shoemaker, M. E., & Paulson, T. L. Group assertion training for mothers: A family intervention strategy. In E. J. Mash, L. C. Handy, and L. A. Hamerlynck (Eds.), *Behavior modification approaches to parenting.* New York: Brunner/Mazel, 1976.

Strodbeck, F. L., James, R., & Hawkins, C. Social status in jury deliberations. *American Sociological Review,* 1957, **22,** 713–719.

Toseland, R., & Rose, S. D. Evaluating social skills training for older adults in groups. *Social Work Research and Abstracts,* 1978, **14,** 25–33.

Wallace, C. J., Teigen, J. R., Liberman, R. P., & Baker, V. Destructive behavior treated by contingency contracts and assertive training: A case study. *Journal of Behavior Therapy and Experimental Psychiatry,* 1973, **4,** 273–274.

Watzlawick, P., Weakland, J., & Fisch, R. *Change: Principles of problem formulation and problem resolution.* New York: W. W. Norton, 1974.

Whittaker, J. Sex differences and susceptibility to interpersonal persuasion. *Journal of Social Psychology,* 1965, **66,** 91–94.

Wolfe, J. L., & Fodor, I. G. Modifying assertive behavior in women: A comparison of three approaches. *Behavior Therapy,* 1977, **8,** 567–574.

Wolpe, J. *Psychotherapy by reciprocal inhibition.* Stanford, Calif.: Stanford University, 1958.

Wolpe, J. Inadequate behavior analysis: The achilles heel of outcome research in behavior therapy. *Journal of Behavior Therapy and Experimental Psychiatry,* 1977, **8,** 1–3.

Wolpe, J., & Lazarus, A. *Behavior therapy techniques.* New York: Pergamon, 1966.

9

The Role and Function of Women's Consciousness Raising

Self-Help, Psychotherapy, or Political Activation?

Gary R. Bond
Morton A. Lieberman

One important consequence of the women's movement has been to direct society's attention to widespread dissatisfaction with traditional sex role structures and attitudes toward women. As an early outgrowth of the movement, consciousness-raising (CR) groups provided a setting where women could convert personal experiences into commonalities for understanding what hitherto was private discontent. Women's Liberation, the branch of the feminist movement that developed the consciousness-raising group format, originated with women active in the

The studies cited in this chapter were supported in part by an N.I.D.A. postdoctoral research fellowship (#F22 DA 00791–01) to Dr. Bond and a Research Scientist Award (PHS 5-KO5-MH20342–04) to Dr. Lieberman.

1960s antiwar and civil rights movements (Carden, 1974; Freeman, 1973; Hole and Levine, 1971). Carden (1974) viewed Women's Liberation as a network of "social action-oriented" women with CR groups as a secondary network of "relatively short-lived groups (providing) a constant supply of recruits to the movement's social activist core" (p. 73).

Most CR groups are organized by women's organizations or from friendship networks. Typically, 6 to 15 women meet weekly to discuss topics related to their shared experiences as women: femininity, motherhood, self-image, relationships with men and with women, and sex. Ordinarily, the membership of a group does not expand after the group has begun meeting. Participants are urged to speak from personal experience. A turn-taking format is often followed, providing each woman with a chance to speak on the chosen topic for that specific meeting. Members are expected to listen nonjudgmentally and without interrupting.

But just what exactly are CR groups and why do women join them? Our inquiry began with a simple curiosity to understand this new social phenomenon that attracted thousands of women in the early 1970s. What was it about these groups that women found useful? Has the nature of CR changed over time? What factors have influenced the particular group working style that is now standard? It soon became clear to us that a single model for viewing CR groups was inadequate because of the multiplicity of purposes that CR has served and the evolution of CR over the decade since the emergence of the original groups. The ambiguity and complexity of CR as a social form has led to misunderstanding and confusion. We have found it heuristic to view CR from three different contexts: political-social action, psychotherapeutic, and self-help.

The political viewpoint derives its rationale from the historical context and the objectives of feminists in forming such groups. A full understanding of CR requires knowledge both of the women's movement and of the emergence of feminism in the United States. Although we believe that CR activities have evolved to a point of functional autonomy from the original recruiting objectives of Women's Liberation, ignoring all ties to the movement would seriously misrepresent the goals and concerns of CR groups. The term "consciousness raising" describes the purpose of the groups, which is to offer an alternative world view or ideology in order to change perceptions and attitudes about social roles. A pivotal issue concerns the way feminist teachings are communicated in CR groups and how, subsequently, women are mobilized to become involved in political-social action. The connections between exploration of personal experiences, feminist ideology, and social action are seldom spelled out in the feminist literature. So, for example, Sarachild (1970) suggests: "In our groups, let's share our feelings and pool them. . . . Our feelings will lead us to ideas and then to actions. Our feelings will lead us to our theory. . . ." Allen's (1970) personal account suggested that CR groups move from sharing of experiences to analysis of the reasons for oppression and eventually to abstract theorizing. Many early proponents believed that the group discussions would lead to social action and surely to greater identification with feminist objectives.

A second perspective on CR is to view it as a kind of "do-it-yourself" psychotherapy. Strong parallels between CR and group therapy have been noted in the processes of expressing feelings, reviewing personal histories, and mutual identification and support (Warren, 1976). More important, there is a clear precedent for the co-optation of a movement in the case of the encounter group movement. Lieberman and Gardner (1976) found that people go to encounter groups for much the same reasons that they would enter psychotherapy, and that in fact for some this choice was a disguised form of help-seeking. These considerations led us to examine CR as an alternative to professional psychotherapy (Lieberman & Bond, 1976; Lieberman, Solow, Bond, & Reibstein, 1979, in press).

A third perspective for understanding CR is to view it as an example of self-help. Katz and Bender (1976) have described self-help groups as

> voluntary, small group structures for mutual aid and the accomplishment of a special purpose. They are usually formed by peers who have come together for mutual assistance in satisfying a common need, overcoming a handicap, or life-disrupting problem, and bringing about desired social and/or personal change. (p. 278)

Although there are many kinds of self-help organizations (Borman, 1975; Levy, 1976; Riessman & Gartner, 1977), over the past few years our particular interest has been in groups serving people who find themselves in a life crisis such as a major illness, the death of a child, widowhood, or the birth of a first child.

These groups are conducted by persons having the problem and not professionals. Their activities vary; some groups engage in face-to-face sharing of their circumstances; others view as their primary mission the preparation or comfort of others who are about to undergo a crisis or a major transition; and others serve their clients by offering a social context.

Central to all such groups is the fact that members share a common plight. Mutual identification and empathy are core therapeutic mechanisms. Dealing with stigma and the frequent societal taboos associated with the affliction is another theme. Make Today Count, a group for cancer patients, permits free and open discussion of a highly charged topic that, in the experience of the patient, is taboo in their ordinary social network. But while self-help organizations share with professional helping systems the concern for helping individuals cope, the underlying philosophies of helping people differ. In psychotherapy the focus is on finding individual solutions to problems, and the therapist draws on general techniques and strategies grounded in general theories of human development, behavior, or functioning. The unique constellation often associated with a particular trauma may be reconceptualized to fit the psychological language system of the therapist. So, for example, the depression experienced after heart surgery would be considered as only one of the infinite variety of ways in which a person could arrive in that condition. Similarly, the social isolation of a widow might be examined in terms of her life history. Self-help groups may ignore the person-specific antecedents to the life condition and focus instead on the problem and its consequences as they usually occur. Self-help groups evolve highly codified systems of belief, rituals, and ideologies tailored to respond to the particular problems of their members (Antze, 1976).

The motifs of feminism, alternative psychotherapy, and self-help appear throughout this chapter as we seek to describe this new phenomenon, which does not fit neatly into any existing models. We will be summarizing two recent studies of CR (Lieberman & Bond, 1976; Lieberman et al., 1979, in press). The first was a national survey of 1669 women who joined CR groups between 1969 and 1975; the second was a study of the therapeutic impact on 32 women who participated in CR. The studies address the following questions. Who joins CR? What are their reasons for joining? What kinds of problems and life circumstances are they facing? We next consider the CR group. What is a typical CR experience? What are the norms? How do the group characteristics found in typical CR groups articulate the problem of being a woman? What experiences that women encounter in such groups provide the most meaningful help?

Finally, we consider the issue of impact. What are the

effects of membership? What aspects of the person seem most affected? And how does CR interact with other help-providing settings used by participants?

METHOD OF DATA COLLECTION

The Survey

From 1973 to 1974, Drs. Lieberman and Diane Kravetz of the University of Wisconsin developed a 26-page survey instrument for CR participants that examined issues such as their reasons for joining, life stresses, symptoms, impressions of their group processes, and helpful group experiences. Table 9–1 summarizes the major survey variables.

The sampling plan was to make the survey known widely throughout the country through announcements at women's centers and in various feminist publications. Distribution of questionnaires involved contacts with a diversity of individuals, groups, and organizations. Forty percent of the questionnaires distributed were returned. In all, women from 41 different states participated in the survey, with 1669 respondents in the final sample. All regions of the country were represented (Northeast—35%; Midwest—26%; West—25%; and South—14%). Although a majority of the respondents (55%) were from groups sponsored by women's organizations, 22% had joined groups started by friends. The remainder indicated some other source of formation. Membership status included 66% current, 31% former, and 4% prospective members. About one-third had been in more than one group. The amount of time spent in CR was as follows: 17%—over 2 years; 25%—between 1 and 2 years; 28%—6 to 12 months; and 30%—less than 6 months. The year joining their first CR group was distributed as follows (based on 1398 respondents):

Table 9–1

Major Survey Measures

Name of Instrument	Chief Reference	Format	Content
1. Source of knowledge about CR	New	12 items (check 3)	Friends, media, women's movement, etc.
2. Precipitating life events	Paykel et al. (1971)	65 items (checklist)	Major life transitions and stressors in year preceding joining group
3. Attitudes of social network	New	5 target persons, 3 scales each	Husband, parents, children, and friends
4. Reasons for joining	Lieberman and Bond (1976)	33 items (4-point scale)	Interest in women's issues, help-seeking, social needs, political activation, sexual awareness, curiosity
5. Hopkins Symptom Checklist	Derogatis, Lipman, Rickels, Uhlenhuth, and Covi (1974)	35 items (4-point scale)	Symptom distress in year preceding joining group
6. Fears about CR	New	8 items (5-point scale)	Group pressure to change politics, roles, relationships
7. Image of typical member	New	17 items (3-point scale)	Positive adjectives (independent, self-confident) and negative adjectives (hostile, depressed)

8. How group got started	New	7 items (checklist)	See Table 9–5
9. Norms	Modeled after Lieberman et al. (1973)	34 items (5-point scale)	See Table 9–6
10. Reasons for dropping out	New	18 items (checklist)	Psychological, political, and external reasons, individual versus group decisions
11. Significant group experience	Lieberman and Bond (1976)	22 items (4-point scale)	Sharing commonalities, involvement, risk-taking, insight, role analysis
12. Testimony	Modeled after Lieberman et al. (1973)	4 items (7-point scale)	Met goals, constructive, personally learned, enjoyed
13. Recommended similarity among members	New	10 items (3-point scale)	Demographic factors
14. Who would benefit	Lieberman and Bond (1976)	16 items (4-point scale)	Perceived satisfaction or dissatisfaction in various role areas
15. Discrimination Index	Lieberman et al. (1979, in press)	6 items (3-point scale)	Perception of personal discrimination
16. Feminist orientation scale	Lieberman et al. (1979, in press)	7 items (4-point scale)	Attitudes on feminist issues

prior to 1971: 89 (6%); 1971: 113 (8%); 1972: 217 (16%); 1973: 356 (26%); 1974: 593 (42%); and early 1975: 29 (2%). (The year of joining CR was not asked in earlier versions of the questionnaire.) While we cannot, of course, determine how representative the survey was of women joining CR during this time, the extensive range of CR participants and groups probably reduces some of the biases in this nonrandom sample.

The Outcome Study

Lieberman, Solow, Bond, and Reibstein (1979, in press) initiated the outcome study in 1976.

Two women's centers located in an eastern metropolitan area were contacted. Both held open meetings during which CR "starters" (women who help coordinate and advise CR groups) organized a number of smaller CR groups.

The research was presented to women attending a large organizational meeting and at several smaller meetings. Packets containing self-administered questionnaires were distributed to about 150 women in attendance. Seventy-three questionnaires were returned.

Six months later, respondents were mailed a follow-up questionnaire. Eighteen respondents who did not provide addresses were lost from the sample. In all, 43 women (76% of those contacted at follow-up) completed the second questionnaire. We found no systematic bias on any of the demographic variables in this reduced sample; women completing both questionnaires seemed to be similar to those completing only the first questionnaire. Of the 43 returning follow-up questionnaires, 32 had participated for 4 months or more. The evaluation of changes was based on this subsample. In addition to the self-administered questionnaires, we conducted phone interviews with 24 of the respondents.

Outcome measures listed in Table 9–2 reflect the hypothesized areas of change in CR. Measures of psychological functioning, personal value systems, and quality of marital relationships were drawn from the psychotherapy and encounter group literature, while the feminist attitudes scales were used in the aforementioned CR survey. In the follow-up questionnaires we included measures of marital stress, strain, and coping.

FINDINGS

Who Joins CR?

Most observers of Women's Liberation have commented on the selective appeal to young, white, well-educated women. The survey demographics support these impressions. Ninety-nine percent of the survey sample were white. The median age was 31, with 2% in their teens, 41% in their twenties, 39% in their thirties, 12% in their forties, 6% in their fifties, and less than 1% over 60. Ninety percent had attended college, and two-thirds had received a bachelor's degree. Occupational levels were executive or major professional (11%), lesser professional (31%), administrative (20%), skilled, semiskilled, or unskilled (4%), unemployed (3%), housewife (14%), and student (16%). Forty-eight percent of the husbands' occupations were major professionals or executives.

The sample consisted of 401 single women (24%), 919 married women (56%), 103 separated women (6%), 211 divorced women (13%), and 17 widowed women (1%). Altogether 880 women had children. Thus, the widespread appeal of CR does not extend to women who are not young, white, or well educated. This finding is consistent with the finding so frequently noted in surveys of the use of psychotherapy and mental health facilities: "YAVIS" (young, attractive, verbal, intelligent, successful—see Schofield 1964) clients are more likely to seek formal help-providing systems than the deprived segments of the society. To date, there is scant data on self-selection into self-help

Table 9–2
Outcome Battery

	Name of Instrument	Chief Reference	Format	Content
I. Mental health status and psychological functioning	A. Target problems	Battle, Imber, Hoehn-Saric, Stone, Nash, and Frank (1966)	3 items (open-ended)	Ideographic problems and goals in group
	B. Self-esteem	Rosenberg (1965)	10 items (scale)	Feelings about self
	C. Hopkins Symptom Checklist	Derogatis et al. (1974)	35 items (checklist)	Symptom distress (e.g., depression, anxiety)
	D. Coping strategies	Lieberman et al. (1973)	19-point Likert scale	Coping styles: defensive, adequate subscales
	E. Personal resources	New	8 items (open-ended)	Source of social support for stressful events; self-reliance subscale
II. Personal value systems	A. Life space	Lieberman et al. (1973)	12 items (open-ended)	Personal values; life-style goals and decisions; orientation toward growth

III. Marital relationship	A. Marital satisfaction	Landau (1976)	6 items (checklist)	Extent of satisfaction
	B. Marital communication	New, adapted from Jourard (1961)	15 items (checklist)	Degree of disclosure to spouse
	C. Marital discord	Landau (1976)	17 items (checklist)	Frequency and areas of disagreements
	D. Decision making	Landau (1976)	6 items (checklist)	Actual and ideal ratings
IV. Feminist attitudes and orientation	A. Feminist identification	New	7-point Likert scale	Identification with women's movement
	B. Discrimination Index	Lieberman and Bond (1976)	6 items (checklist)	Perception of personal discrimination
	C. Feminist Orientation Scale	Lieberman and Bond (1976)	7 items (scale)	Attitudes on feminist issues: ERA, day care, abortion
	D. Feminist affiliations	Lieberman and Bond (1976)	9 items (checklist)	Membership in women's groups

groups, although the existing evidence points toward the samepatternoftheoverutilizationbythemiddleclass.

Why Do They Join?

Guiding our survey investigation were two major hypotheses. The first states that women would join CR because of political motives and a desire to effect external changes in society by organized means. The rationale for this "political orientation" hypothesis was grounded in the historical context in which CR emerged and the intentions of the originators of CR.

An alternative hypothesis was that CR participants were distinguished by their psychological distress and need for help in dealing with personal problems. This "help-seeking" hypothesis stated that women joined CR to seek relief for the stresses and anxieties experienced in day-to-day living. Participants expressing these reasons would be expecting CR to be a psychotherapeutic experience.

In addition, we were interested in the possibility that the kinds of women attracted to CR may have changed over time. Such changes would suggest a view that the purposes of CR groups have shifted from the original goals.

Using a Reasons for Joining Checklist (see Table 9-1), we derived six motivational factors for joining CR, as described elsewhere (Lieberman & Bond, 1976).[1] Political

[1]The factors were as follows. *Interest in women's issues* (to share thoughts and feelings about being a women, to learn about other women and their experiences, to examine problems women have with their traditional roles—mother, wife); *help-seeking* (to get relief from things or feelings troubling me, to solve personal problems, to get help, to deal with current life problems, to solve long-term problems, to bring about some change in myself); *social needs* (to make friends, loneliness, to find community); *political activation* (to expand political awareness, to obtain political information, to be more active in the women's movement); *sexual awareness* (to explore my sexual feelings toward men, to explore my sexual feelings toward women, to increase my understanding of how I feel about my body); *curiosity* (to do something different, curiosity).

activation and help-seeking correspond to the two contrasting motives just described. Lieberman and Gardner
(1976) independently derived the help-seeking factor, employing the same factor analytic technique, and they
showed help-seeking to be the basic motive for patients
entering psychotherapy. In fact, 91% of the women in
their psychotherapy sample rated these items, on average,
"extremely important" or "important." Supporting the interpretation of the political activation factor were significant positive relationships with prior involvement in
political organizations and a self-ascribed label of "radical" on the political spectrum. Help-seeking and political
activation were statistically independent ($r = 0.001$), thus
providing two distinct alternative explanations for joining.

Using factor scores, we examined trends by year of joining for the six motives (Table 9–3). Political activation is
at best a minor motive for joining, and the temporal decline is highly significant. Help-seeking is a moderately
important motive with no change over time. Overt expression among CR participants of help-seeking is substantially less than for women entering psychotherapy or
entering a growth center. Only 15% of the CR participants,
compared with 37% of the women entering a growth center and 91% of the women entering psychotherapy, rated
the help-seeking items in the extremely important quad-
rant. Even so, help-seeking was an important motive for
about half of the CR sample (Lieberman & Bond, 1976.)

Moreover, help-seeking orientations were indicated by
the high percentage of women (54%) who had been in
psychotherapy at some time during the 5 years preceding
the survey, including 34% of the sample whose psychotherapy was concurrent with (24%) or following (10%)
their CR experience. Furthermore, symptom distress
(from the Hopkins Symptom Checklist) for women in the
CR survey was significantly higher than a demographically similar normative sample of women, although significantly lower than a demographically similar sample of

Table 9–3

Motives of CR Participants by Year of Initial Involvement

Motive	Year						1976 Outcome Sample	Total Survey	Trend Analysis (survey data only)	
	Pre-1971	1971	1972	1973	1974	1975			Linear F	Nonlinear F
Interest in women's issues	1.52	1.54	1.54	1.54	1.55	1.52	(1.56)	1.54	<1	<1
Help-seeking	2.54	2.52	2.41	2.44	2.44	2.22	(2.43)	2.44	1.8	<1
Social needs	2.61	2.57	2.60	2.46	2.60	2.36	(2.77)	2.56	<1	2.2
Political activation	2.23	2.54	2.63	2.72	2.77	2.72	(3.22)	2.68	31.9[a]	1.6
Sexual awareness	2.95	2.96	3.03	2.95	2.87	2.80	(2.92)	2.93	4.0	<1
Curiosity	3.06	3.06	3.18	3.16	3.05	3.28	(3.04)	3.10	<1	1.7
N	89	113	217	357	593	29	41	1398		

Note: Scores are mean ratings for items loading on each factor: 1 = very important, 2 = important, 3 = somewhat important, 4 = not important.
[a]$p < 0.001$.

women in psychotherapy (Lieberman & Bond, 1976). Women joining CR were experiencing more subjective distress than was typical of women in their age range and educational level.

The findings do not suggest that political activation as a motive for joining was completely absent in the sample, but that its importance rapidly declined. Some women may have used CR as a personal outlet or learning experience, channeling their political energies into task-oriented groups. Indications of prior political involvement were given by the percentage of women formerly involved in the civil rights movement (19%), the antiwar movement (27%), a "politically radical" women's liberation organization (7%), professional women's organizations (10%), League of Women Voters (11%), and women's political organizations (e.g., NOW) (25%). Altogether, 4 out of 10 women were affiliated with a women's political group prior to joining CR.

The great majority of women (89%) did consider themselves identified with Women's Liberation, although the percentage not identified rose from 2% among those joining prior to 1971 to 16% among those joining in 1974 to 1975. There is no doubt that identification with feminism and the women's movement is very common among CR participants. Being identified with the movement, however, bore little relationship for most participants to the objectives of political and social change.

Neither help-seeking, with its emphasis on anxiety reduction, nor political activation, with its emphasis on external change, accurately portrays the motives of women entering CR. The fact that virtually every woman indicated an interest in women's issues offers little insight into the motivational issue. We observe that the three items loading on this latter factor have a distinctively cognitive flavor and are consistent with the notion that CR offers an alternative world view. Still we ask, why do women join? For what kinds of life circumstances are they seeking a changed perspective? Are there common themes in the issues and problems they are facing?

What Problems Bring Women to CR?

What kinds of life problems and circumstances bring women to CR? Are there role conflicts—the competing demands of career, marriage, and motherhood? Are relationship issues the predominating factor? Do economic reasons provide the common denominator? We have found it difficult to pinpoint this elusive issue because no concise constellation of problems summarize the plight of women. This contrasts sharply with other self-help groups, such as the striking similarity of stories given by gamblers at GA meetings: the financial devastation, the humiliation, the pattern of lying, and the desperation gamblers feel about their addiction. New mothers in groups sponsored by LaMaze are all faced with a clearly defined set of tasks common to all new mothers. New widows all share many of the same feelings of loneliness, isolation, helplessness, and vulnerability. In all of these, personal idiosyncrasies are secondary to the problem. Regardless of the individual personality inadequacies and strengths of gamblers, mothers, or widows, their identities as these kinds of people make it highly probable that they will experience certain kinds of shared difficulties. The individual differences that do exist among members are minimized to fit the stereotypic circumstances around which the ideology of the self-help group is built.

In terms of feminist ideology, the problem of "being a woman" should be experienced in a similar fashion. Since womanhood is a shared problem, we should be able to identify a set of shared experiences. Our initial examination of the "common" basis was to examine convergence in the 65 life events (item 2 in Table 9-1). The following events had occurred for at least 20% of the participants in the 12 months preceding their CR experience: a lot of arguments with a man (45%), minor financial difficulties (28%), move to a new city (27%), move within a city (25%), separation from a close friend or relative (24%), arguments with husband (24%), change to a different line of work (23%), and start of school (20%). With the exception of conflicts with men, it is difficult to identify a central issue.

Thus the common denominator of this self-help movement—if CR is to be considered a self-help system—is a great deal more abstract than being widowed, being a compulsive gambler, or being a mother. Life events that are part of the life cycle for men and women alike were most frequent. Emotionally loaded events that dramatize feminist issues, such as abortion (4%), rape (1%), and forming lesbian relationships (3%), were relatively infrequent.

Although all these life events, since they are involved in the socialization process, are seen within the feminist ideology as illustrating sexism, it is not obvious that a woman faced with job discrimination readily identifies with another woman who is working through her feelings after a divorce. The feminist doctrine that the male oppressor who prevents a job advancement is a product of the same system as the man who made a bad marriage partner may or may not be helpful in enabling these women to find similarity. What we can say is that the kind of explanation necessary to find parallels in the lives of women is more abstract than the explanations offered by the ideologies and teachings of the self-help groups mentioned previously. The life concerns of CR participants are heterogeneous and resemble the problem of heterogeneity that is encountered in psychotherapy. The question is if their "sisterhood" is a strong enough bond to allow for immediate acceptance and empathy.

Forty-one of the life events were combined to create a cumulative index measuring objective stress (Paykel, Prusoff, Uhlenhuth, 1971). The CR sample was not statistically different than a demographically similar normative sample (Lieberman & Bond, 1976). Apparently, it is not the sheer quantity of life stressors that lead women to join CR. Women entering psychotherapy, on the other hand, have been found to have significantly higher levels of stress than the CR sample or the normative samples (Lieberman & Bond, 1976).

More direct evidence of the undifferentiated and heterogeneous problem set of CR participants came from the outcome study. We asked women to "describe briefly three problems or difficulties you currently have that you hope your CR experience will help." The classification of problems is shown in Table 9–4. Problems related to self-concept ("to discover who I am"; "to explore my identity as a woman"; "to find direction in my life") were most common, as were relationships with specific others and with interpersonal relationships in general. These problems are relatively amphorous. Lacking is the sharp convergence of shared concerns typical of self-help participants. The problem lists reflect a vague dissatisfaction, uneasiness, and lack of fulfillment in unfocused existential concerns. The problems, although more akin to issues brought to psychotherapy, depart from the problem lists generated by clients entering psychotherapy (Bond, Bloch, Yalom, Zimmerman, & Qualls, 1979, in press; Sloane, Staples, Cristol, Yorkston, & Whipple, 1975) in one major way. CR participants do not mention feelings of depression or anxiety as problems that they think their CR group will help. Compared with a demographically similar normative sample, however, CR participants had significantly higher levels of distress on the Hopkins Symptom Checklist. Their elevated scores suggest that a majority are mildly or moderately depressed and anxious. Although depressed, they do not see the CR group as a place to obtain relief from such affects. Perhaps the feminist framework leads women to reinterpret these inner feelings of distress to fit their anticipation of how the group works.

Table 9–4

Target Problems

Category	Percent of Women Mentioning Problem (N = 73)
Self-concept	
Self-esteem	38
Role dissatisfaction	23
Identity	27
Autonomy	15
Interpersonal	
With women	22
With men	11
Family	16
Marital	15
Loneliness	10
Isolation	8
General skills	16
Symptoms-Affective	
Anxiety	11
Handling of feelings	8
Depression	0
Other	
Career	16
Women's movement	8
Weight reduction	8
Sexuality	6
Growth experience	7
Physical complaints	1

Problems of Participants and CR Ideology

The women's movement perceives all women sharing a common plight. Participants, when asked in the survey who they thought would benefit from a CR group, reflected this ideology. The overwhelming majority of respondents (76%) felt that "all" or "three-fourths" of the women they knew would benefit. None of 16 possible inclusion and

exclusion criteria for benefiting were seen by CR participants as preventing a woman from benefiting (Lieberman
& Bond, 1976). Neither successful careers, happy or unhappy marriages, nor presence or absence of role conflict
were seen as roadblocks to joining. Nor were sexual conflicts, depression, or being in therapy seen as reasons that
would prevent a woman from benefiting. Neither a lack of
political awareness nor involvement in political activities
was seen as a disadvantage.

We can contrast this universal invitation with that of
many successful self-help organizations. Mended Hearts
requires that active members have had open heart surgery. People who have had related surgeries are not allowed to become active members. Even pacemakers are
disallowed. Naim, a large widowed person's group, ex-
cludes nonwidowed singles (e.g., separated and divorced)
and non-Catholics. Compassionate Friends is restricted to
bereaved parents whose children were under age 25 at the
time of death. Membership in various cancer groups tend
to be determined by the site of the cancer. These restrictions, some of which seem arbitrary to an outsider, pre-
serve what we believe to be a crucial principle of
successful self-help groups, a common affliction aiding
rapid identification. Specified boundaries are probably
quite reassuring to often stigmatized groups who feel that
they are outside conventional society.

In contrast, for psychotherapy the ticket of admission is
some sense of dissatisfaction with relationships and self-
image.

One practical implication of universal sisterhood
within CR is that groups are composed with little regard
to differences in life-style and developmental stage. A list
of 10 compositional criteria was given to respondents in
the survey (marital status, age, race, being a mother, etc.).
Only two (educational background and previous CR experience) were viewed as important considerations by more
than a quarter of the respondents. Differences in life-style

orientations and life stage do make it difficult for mutual identification and empathy to occur. In interviews we often heard the complaint that participants felt distant and alienated from women who were not like them. Younger women felt distant from the older women, while one subgroup of divorced women considered breaking off to form their own group. These differences were overcome in many instances, often in creative ways, but the immediate bonding that occurs in self-help groups was missing.

Our hypothesis that successful self-help movements develop ideologies that are responsive to the needs of its participants takes on an interesting form in CR. It is as if the *goal* of consciousness raising is to awaken women to their shared plight; in most self-help movements this is the *principle* for joining together. The goal of CR is to *discover* that the disparate problems and life circumstances are inherently related; in most self-help groups this commonality is a *given.*

We believe that the highly abstract level of feminist teachings is responsive to the nonspecific dissatisfaction and disappointment that many prospective CR participants felt about the way their lives turned out. In contrast, the Twelve Steps of Alcoholics' Anonymous contain specific and practical tenets of belief to counteract eventualities such as backsliding, public scorn, and rejections by one's immediate social network. There is no direct analogy in CR to this articulate ideology; it is to be discovered anew by each CR group.

The feminist ideology as evidenced within the CR groups studied stresses the belief that a negative self-image may not be linked to any dramatic rejections, injustices, or maltreatment. Instead, participants are encouraged to look at relatively small injustices as symbolic of larger issues. This abstract ideology permits participants to identify their own individualized problems with the common framework. Such an ideology may be successful because it avoids becoming overly identified with any specific life concern. Although most self-help groups prescribe a course of action to ameliorate a condition or set of circumstances, in CR the attempt is made to avoid direct advice giving or problem solving, partly because such prescriptions would tend to heighten differences among lifestyles, developmental stages, and problem definition instead of strengthening bonds of mutual support.

Group Processes

CR groups have been formed in three main ways: (1) a group may be sponsored by a women's organization (either one of the local women's centers that have sprung up in major cities around the country or a large national organization such as NOW); (2) a group may be an outgrowth of friendship networks, or (3) a group may be a "spin-off" of a group begun for other purposes. During the decade since their inception, there has been a rapid increase in groups sponsored by formal organizations. The percentage of organizationally sponsored groups based on the survey was: 1971 and prior: 40%; 1972: 53%; 1973: 69%; and 1974 to 1975: 75%.[2] This section examines the implications of the move away from a grass roots organization for the functioning of CR groups.

Groups formed by women's organizations usually have an experienced leader or "starter" who meets with the group to set its initial work style. Sixty-eight percent of the survey respondents in the organized groups said their group started in this way, compared with only 20% of the friendship groups and 28% of the spin-off groups (Table 9–5). The centrally organized groups were more likely to

[2]Percentages are based on 801 respondents for whom the method of formation of their first group is known. For the 19 women in the subsample who joined before 1971, 56% joined an organizationally sponsored group and, for the 21 women joining in 1975, 89% did.

Table 9–5

Initial Group Activities by Method of Group Formation

Activity[a]	Method of Group Formation				Chi-square (2 d.f.)
	Women's Organization (N = 917)	Friends (N = 380)	Spin-off from Another Group (N = 155)	Total (N = 1443)[b]	
Members talked about their lives	68.6%	66.3%	62.6%	67.4%	2.4
Scheduled general topics for each meeting	68.3%	44.4%	45.2%	59.6%	32.4[c]
Talked about whatever members wanted to bring up	49.4%	63.4%	63.9%	54.6%	27.3[c]
Person with experience in CR group came to get the group started	67.8%	19.7%	28.4%	51.0%	284.2[c]
Scheduled specific personal issues to discuss each meeting	40.6%	25.8%	25.8%	35.1%	78.1[c]
Discussed reading on women's issues	22.0%	28.4%	25.8%	24.1%	6.3
Debated whether the focus should be personal or political	18.6%	26.3%	22.6%	21.1%	9.7

a "What did your group do in the first month or two?"
b The remaining 226 either had not yet joined a group or listed some other specific method of group formation.
c $p < 0.001$.

schedule general topics. In all three types of groups, members began by talking about their lives. The friendship groups and spin-offs were more spontaneous and less structured, as indicated by a greater percentage of respondents whose groups began by talking about whatever members wanted to bring up.

The trend in CR, with the dominance of organizationally sponsored groups, is toward greater format standardization and a schedule of critical issues for examination and away from free-floating discussion. The period of experimentation with group process in the early CR groups, with unstructured, spontaneous sharing of personal experiences, may be drawing to an end. Such a change resembles the progression of many successful self-help movements, which develop a common format in order to stabilize and retain coherence. However, unlike other self-help movements, CR groups do not rally around a "bible" or the teachings of a charismatic leader.

Examination of the normative environments of CR groups involved the use of a 34-item behavioral checklist modeled after Lieberman, Yalom, and Miles (1973). Participants were asked to imagine describing their group to a prospective member. Ratings of acceptability of behaviors are made on a 5-point scale. A five-factor solution emerged, using a principle components factor analysis with various rotations (Table 9–6). The first factor, *self-disclosure*, consists of items such as "talking about feeling lonely," "talking about feeling inadequate," "sharing good things," "describing fantasies," and "pleading for help." All of these were rated as highly appropriate. Within very broad boundaries, it is permissible to discuss any personal experiences, as is true for psychotherapy groups (Bond, 1975).

The degree of personal disclosure in CR groups exceeds most self-help groups. For example, Mended Hearts and Naim actually discourage personal disclosure surrounding the central event that brings members together, and many other self-help groups delimit the kinds of disclosure to problems directly related to the trauma. In Gamblers Anonymous, the "therapies," as they are called, take on a ritual quality of confession, replete with aphorisms and slogans from the teachings of G.A. The stories of gamblers are rehearsed week after week, with old-timers correcting the initiates until their stories no longer conflict with the official ideology. In CR, some structuring of what might otherwise be rambling, unfocused personal accounts is achieved in the organizationally sponsored groups by the scheduling of general topics.[3] Within these broad issue areas, women are free to share any experience.

CR groups are sometimes used for first disclosures about shameful past events that participants have had difficulty sharing with others. Using a critical incident technique (Lieberman et al., 1973) in the outcome study, we found instances of women sharing experiences concerning abortions, lesbian relationships, and other sensitive topics. Current life concerns in their marriages and in raising children were also frequent. The range of legitimate topics is far greater than in most self-help groups, consistent with the absence of the single predicament characteristic of other self-help groups.

The norm factor, *affective relationships,* consists of items reflecting the expression of intense feelings toward other members. These include both negatively toned behaviors (shouting with anger, saying who one dislikes) and positively toned (saying who one likes). These behaviors are generally acceptable in groups operating on a "social microcosm" principle, that is, groups encouraging the expression and analysis of here-and-now feelings, such as

[3] For example, one set of CR guidelines suggested this sequence of topics: (1) Why did I join a consciousness-raising group?; (2) childhood; (3) fathers; (4) mothers; (5) puberty; (6) feelings; (7) self-image, personality; (8) self-image; body; (9) siblings; (10) independence-dependence; (11) marriage; (12) divorce-separation; (13) motherhood; and (14) sex.

Table 9-6
Normative Dimensions of CR Groups

	Method of Group Formation			
	Women's Organizations (N = 917)	Friends (N = 380)	Spin-off (N = 155)	F-Value
Factor I: self-disclosure[a] (12.0% of variance)				
Talked about feeling very lonely	4.81[b]	4.85	4.76	n.s.
Talked about feeling inadequate	4.80	4.83	4.74	n.s.
Cried	4.61	4.65	4.65	n.s.
Shared good things about herself	4.87	4.90	4.83	n.s.
Described her dreams and private fantasies	4.35	4.46	4.29	n.s.
Defended another who was being put on the spot	4.40	4.49	4.58	n.s.
Hugged someone when she felt like it	4.42	4.60	4.55	6.1
Brought up a current problem in her life	4.41	4.57	4.53	n.s.
Pleaded for help	4.02	4.19	4.20	n.s.
Factor II: affective relationships within group (10.8% of variance)				
Said which members she really disliked	2.27	2.51	2.71	10.5[d]
Shouted with anger at another member	2.56	3.09	3.08	27.3[d]
Said which members she really liked	2.80	3.20	3.13	14.4[d]
Told the group off	2.94	3.27	3.50	14.1[d]
Showed sexual attraction to another member	2.64	2.83	2.78	n.s.
Screamed	3.64	3.66	3.45	n.s.

Refused to go along with what the rest of the group wanted	3.16	3.40	3.40	6.4
Factor III: turn-taking (6.3% of variance)				
Dominated the group's discussion for more than one session	1.87	2.19	2.14	15.4[d]
Talked a lot without showing her real feelings	2.19	2.13	2.22	n.s.
Tried to manipulate the group to get her own way	1.38	1.41	1.39	n.s.
Tried to take over the leadership of the group	1.81	1.88	1.81	n.s.
Interrupted a dialog going on between two people	2.19	2.32	2.34	n.s.
Showed she had no intention of changing her behavior	2.89	2.86	2.75	n.s.
Factor IV: membership criteria (5.8% of variance)				
Left in the middle of the session without explanation	1.97	2.04	2.11	n.s.
Absent frequently	1.71	1.79	2.02	7.3[e]
Said nothing for an entire meeting	2.97	3.10	3.14	n.s.
Brought a friend to the group session	2.00	2.43	2.48	15.6[d]
Factor V: judgmental behavior (5.6% of variance)				
Gave advice to other members about what to do	2.78	3.43	3.38	44.2[d]
Said another member's behavior was wrong	2.17	2.49	2.59	14.6[d]
Disclosed information about the group on the outside	1.40	1.58	1.64	7.8[d]
Tried to convince people of the rightness of a point of view	2.47	2.85	2.70	14.4[d]

[a] Principle components factor analysis with varimax rotations. All loadings ≥ 0.40 are reported in the order of their magnitude

[b] Mean rating on 5-point scale: 5 = definitely acceptable, 4 = somewhat acceptable, 3 = mixed reaction, 2 = somewhat unacceptable, and 1 = definitely unacceptable.

[c] n.s. = not significant

[d] $p < 0.0001$

[e] $p < 0.001$

encounter groups (Lieberman et al., 1973) and therapy groups (Bond, 1975). These kinds of feelings are not openly expressed in CR groups, especially organizationally sponsored groups, which explicitly discourage affective interchanges. The model for learning in CR is not based on gaining insight into how one interacts with others in the group. In this regard CR resembles other self-help groups. What is unusual is that CR's structure of closed membership and weekly meetings would be expected to foster intimacy and the exchange of interpersonal feelings over a period of time. The organizationally sponsored groups apparently have sought to counteract this tendency (see Table 9-6).

Turn-taking, the third factor, consists of group rules for monitoring participation and leadership. CR guidelines address the tendency in unstructured groups of unequal sharing of the group's time by systematically assigning speaking turns for each member. Some groups actually time the turn that each person speaks. In this way members are prevented from dominating sessions. The fourth factor, *membership criteria,* also relates to rules for belonging to the group.

The fifth norm factor, *judgmental behavior,* regulates aggressive and competitive behavior. In contrast to the efforts of Synanon, G. A., and self-help groups for addictions, CR groups avoid such confrontation. Organizationally sponsored groups especially discourage active persuasion and pressuring. From the feminist perspective, criticism of the individual is more properly directed toward society.

Despite differences between organizationally sponsored, friendship, and spin-off groups in the mode of beginning the group and normative environments, participants in the different kinds of groups did not differ in their evaluation of the experience. Overall, 71% felt that CR "met their goals," 80% felt that they "learned a great deal," 89% felt that it was "a constructive experience," and 89% "enjoyed" their experience.

Change Mechanisms

We examined the events and experiences that participants found personally significant in their CR group. Factor analysis of the Significant Group Process Instrument (Lieberman & Bond, 1976) yielded a five-factor solution, shown in Table 9–7. *Sharing commonalities* was viewed as the most important factor. The processes of learning that one's problems are not unique, learning from others in a similar situation, and "sharing thoughts and feelings" about a member of the afflicted group aptly describe processes that are universals of self-help groups. In this regard CR is prototypical of self-help groups. A second factor, *involvement,* is probably important in all volunteer groups and is conceptually related to cohesiveness, which Yalom and Rand (1966) have suggested to be a central curative factor in group psychotherapy. *Risk-taking* consists of a cluster of experiences associated with encounter groups (revealing secrets, experimenting with behavior, experiencing feelings). *Insight* includes several processes commonly reported in psychotherapy (seeing undesirable things about oneself, being confronted, experiencing strong negative feelings). Finally, *role analysis* approximates activities that would be typical in a political discussion group.

These five change induction dimensions are representative of the different streams of influence on CR groups: self-help *(sharing commonalities);* psychotherapy *(Insight* and *risk-taking*), and political activation *(role analysis).* Among the factors, only *role analysis* was seen by the vast majority of CR participants as unimportant. Otherwise, unlike most self-help groups, which narrowly define the ways in which they give help, CR is noteworthy for its use of a wide range of help-providing mechanisms.

Another method for determining the importance of various mechanisms in CR was to examine their correlations with member evaluations of the benefit of their experience. Sharing commonalities correlated 0.29 with such

Table 9-7
Significant Group Processes in CR Groups (N = 1603)

Processes[a]	Percent "Definately Important"
Sharing commonalities	
Learning that my problems, feelings, and fears are not unique	63.0
Women in the group gave me hope	45.2
Seeing how others approach problems gave me ideas	48.7
Sharing thoughts and feelings about being a woman	76.1
Learning more about my positive strengths	63.3
Involvement	
Being an involved member of a group	47.6
Helping others, being important to others	40.4
Risk-taking	
Revealing things about myself I had kept secret	39.0
Discussing sexuality	37.3
Experimenting in group by doing things I had not previously done	45.2
Experiencing feelings of excitement and joy	45.1
Insight	
Seeing undesirable or unacceptable things about myself	36.7
Being confronted and challenged	24.5
Getting insight into causes and sources of problems	51.6
Experiencing and expressing strong negative feelings	30.2
Role analysis	
Examining problems of discrimination	28.1
Examining political issues	14.4
Examining problems women have with traditional roles	50.9

[a] "Which of these do you consider important for you in helping you achieve your goals?" 1 = definitely important, 2 = important, 3 = somewhat important, 4 = not important.

evaluations; role analysis, by contrast, correlated 0.07. The correlations for the remaining factors were: involvement (0.13), insight (0.11), and risk-taking (0.24).

The origin (social network, women's organizations or spin-off group) of the CR group was generally not an important influence on the relative salience of different change induction mechanisms. Analysis of variance on the 22 items yielded four significant differences: "being confronted and challenged" (less important in organizationally sponsored groups); "receiving advice and suggestions" (also less important), "examining problems women have with traditional roles" (more important); and "examining political issues" (more important). The latter two items characterize the role analysis factor and are linked to political-feminist objectives. Paradoxically, despite the increased sponsorship of CR groups by women's organizations (and its implied emphasis on political interests), women who are attracted to such groups enter with expectations about how such change will take place that do not mirror this political view.

Impact of CR on Participants

Finally, we turn to the question of impact. How is a woman affected by her participation in a CR group? To answer this question, we conducted a pre- and postoutcome study (Lieberman et al., 1979, in press). The outcome sample was a group of suburban women who were demographically similar to the survey sample. The findings, summarized in Table 9–8, were noteworthy both for the changes that did occur and for those that did not.

The primary change was increased self-esteem and self-reliance. Anecdotal information from interviews amply illustrated the theme that women felt greater self-respect, autonomy, and a sense of who they were. Such an outcome seems plausible in light of the highly supportive, low-confrontive environment typical of CR.

Table 9–8
Prechanges-Postchanges After
6-Months Participation in a CR Group (N = 32 Women)

Areas of Significant Change	Areas of Nonsignificant Change
Target problem distress (decreased)	Symptom distress
Self-esteem (increased)	Adequate coping[a]
Self-reliance (statistical trend toward increasing)	Defensive coping[a]
	Marital satisfaction[b]
Growth orientation in value domain (decreased)	Marital discord[b]
	Marital communication[b]
Feminist identification (increased)	Marital decision making[b]
Perceived discrimination (increased)	Feminist attitudes
	Feminist affiliations

[a] N = 19.
[b] N = 21.

Participants, however, did not become less anxious or depressed, even though initial symptom scores indicated that they were significantly higher in distress than a normative sample. Absence of improvement in this area could not be explained away by the "conversion" of these symptoms into an "alternative ideological based framework," as some have proposed (Kirsh, 1974; Klein, 1976). Women who felt generally distressed on entering a CR group usually did not receive much help for these feelings. They did not adopt new perspectives that minimized these painful effects. Women, however, as indicated earlier, did not come into CR expecting help for their depression or anxiety. Instead, as we will discuss, about one-third of them dealt with symptom distress in concurrent psychotherapy.

Change in personal value systems was minimal; the importance of major life-style changes seems to have decreased in the majority of women we studied. By and large, CR did not politically radicalize women, but it led them to reaffirm traditional values, such as the priority of the family.

The marital relationship was also generally unchanged. Marital satisfaction did not increase or decrease, nor did marital discord, communication, or decision making. Comparison with a demographically similar normative sample suggested that levels of marital strain among CR participants were significantly above average. Thus the lack of change in the marital area was not a result of our studying a group of women whose marriages were fundamentally satisfactory. Marital behavior was unchanged, aside from some symbolic acts of assertion (taking separate vacations, refusing to cook dinner when tired).

The CR experience did have an impact on feminist attitudes. Significant increase was noted in identification with the women's movement. Perception of personal discrimination in the vocational and economic sphere increased dramatically. On the other hand, attitudes toward issues such as abortion on demand, the Equal Rights Amendment, and transformation of the institution of marriage were unaltered. A few women joined NOW during the 6-month study period.

To say the least, the changes attributable to the CR experience were not dramatic. Furthermore, possibly some of the changes noted might be a product of measurement error, an assessment made difficult because we lacked an adequate control group. However, several conclusions are in order. First, the finding of increased self-esteem appears to be most substantial. Sustained involvement in a supportive, nonjudgmental environment might be expected to have this effect. The "high," or euphoria, from the feeling of belonging may, however, not be permanent, if we are to judge from the encounter group literature (Lieberman et al., 1973).

Second, it is our impression that CR groups are noncasualty inducing, especially if encounter group experiences are used as a basis of comparison (Lieberman et al., 1973).

The absence of confrontation and charismatic leadership reduces the possibility of the accelerated feeling of failure and self-blaming to which high-pressure environments are prone.

Third (and the most speculative of our interpretations), we detect in these women an acceptance of the status quo, quite contrary to feminist ideology.

Relationship of CR to Psychotherapy

The notion that CR serves as an alternative helping system for women who have not been helped by psychotherapy was not borne out. In the survey data, we found over half the women had been in psychotherapy at some time, and about two-thirds of these had found psychotherapy helpful. CR attracts the same segment of the female population who are also attracted to professional helping systems. We have therefore focused our attention in our second study on understanding how CR and therapy, representing ostensibly contradictory systems of belief, can be seen as helpful to the same women.

Even if psychotherapists experience dissonance as they try to integrate the processes and belief systems of CR with professional models, participants themselves do not. The evidence is mounting that clients often move back and forth, with no apparent conflict in loyalty, between change induction systems with radically differing ideologies about the causes and solutions for problems. For example, Yalom, Bloch, Bond, Qualls and Zimmerman (1978) found that alcoholics were helped, not hindered, by dual involvement in intensive group therapy and A.A. Although professional mental health services and peer-led self-help groups are often viewed as antagonistic helping networks, in actuality, about one-third of the participants in the outcome study were receiving professional psychotherapeutic treatment concurrent with their participation in

CR. Their satisfaction with this arrangement lends support to the potential for a synergistic relationship between professional services and self-help services. In fact, those in concurrent psychotherapy changed more (Lieberman et al., 1979, in press).

Another benefit of the dual involvement concerned the catalytic effects of CR discussions on psychotherapy. Several women found that the CR group provided important focus for later therapy sessions. One woman became aware of a tendency to compete with other women, a problem that her therapist had discussed with her but that she did not recognize until she participated in CR. For another woman, a CR discussion of childhood sexuality stimulated material for "a major breakthrough in therapy."

In addition to opening up new areas and providing new insights into old problem areas, the CR group seemed to play an important role in bolstering changes that had already been initiated in therapy. One women commented:

> My CR group gives very strong reinforcement of the self-confidence that gets built up in therapy. Every week I always get a compliment from someone; someone in the group will comment how I've thought something out well. The group really reaffirms my therapist who always tells me, "You can do it."

SUMMARY

CR groups, as a new social phenomenon, share some common attributes with each of the three types of change induction groups. In terms of who is attracted to CR, the participants have a help-seeking orientation, although not nearly to the degree seen in ether psychotherapy or encounter group participants. Despite a fair degree of prior political involvements, CR groups have little in common with political protest groups, nor are participants seeking out those experiences. Participants identify a common interest in understanding their traditional roles as women as the common bond that draws them to the group, but it is doubtful that they achieve the immediate mutual identification as readily as in most self-help groups.

CR has evolved and achieved a functional autonomy apart from the original goal of feminist proponents to recruit women into action groups. CR is used primarily for personal exploration and reflection on one's own life circumstances. The increasing use of organizationally sponsored CR groups, with experienced "starters" and written guidelines, however, has shaped CR in distinctive ways that differentiate it from psychotherapy, despite the small face-to-face group format, which fosters therapylike processes.

The impact of CR has yet to be fully explicated. Traditional measures of anxiety reduction do not represent the central arena for change. Nor does CR emphasize lifestyle changes. The major impact is on the development of a new sense of self, a heightened appreciation of one's own potentialities. However, it is not apparent how these transformations of self are translated into behavioral changes.

It is becoming increasingly clear to us that the relationships between professional systems of help and novel social phenomena such as CR need rethinking. CR groups offer an innovative social form that does not quite fit any of the available models. We have only just begun to understand how these groups work and what benefits accrue to those joining.

REFERENCES

Allen, P. *Free space: A perspective on the small group in women's liberation.* Washington, D.C.: Times Change Press, 1970.

Antze, P. The role of ideologies in peer psychotherapy organizations: Some theoretical considerations and three case studies. *Journal of Applied Behavioral Science,* 1976, **12,** 323–346.

Battle, C. C., Imber, S. D., Hoehn-Saric, R., Stowe, A. R., Nash, E. R., & Frank, J. D. Target complaints as criteria of improvement. *American Journal of Psychotherapy,* 1966, **20**, 184–192.

Bond, G. R. Norm formation in therapy groups. Unpublished doctoral dissertation, University of Chicago, 1975.

Bond, G. R., Bloch, S. T., Yalom, I. D., Zimmerman, E., & Qualls, C. B. The evaluation of a target complaint approach to outcome measurement. *Psychotherapy: Theory Research and Practice,* 1979, in press.

Borman, L. D. *Explorations in self help and mutual aid.* Chicago: Center for Urban Affairs, Northwestern University, 1975.

Carden, M. L. *The new feminist movement.* New York: Russell Sage Foundation, 1974.

Derogatis, L. R., Lipman, R. S., Rickels, K., Uhlenhuth, E. H., & Covi, L. The Hopkins Symptom Checklist (HSCL): A self-report symptom inventory. *Behavioral Science,* 1974, **19**, 1–15.

Freeman, J. The origins of the women's liberation movement. In J. Huber (Ed.), *Changing women in a changing society.* Chicago: University of Chicago Press, 1973.

Hole, J., & Levine, E. *Rebirth of feminism.* New York: Quadrangle Books, 1971.

Jourard, S. Self disclosure patterns in British and American college females. *Journal of Social Psychology,* 1961, **54**, 315–320.

Katz, A. H., & Bender, E. I. Self-help groups in western society: History and prospects. *Journal of Applied Behavioral Science,* 1976, **12**, 265–282.

Kirsh, B. Consciousness-raising groups as therapy for women. In V. Franks and V. Burtle (Eds.), *Women in therapy.* New York: Brunner/Mazel, 1974.

Klein, M. H. Feminist concepts of therapy outcome. *Psychotherapy Theory, Research and Practice,* 1976, **13**, 89–95.

Landau, I. Sex-role concepts and marital happiness in middle-aged couples. Unpublished doctoral dissertation, University of Chicago, 1976.

Levy, L. Self-help groups: Types and psychological processes. *Journal of Applied Behavioral Science,* 1976, **12**, 310–322.

Lieberman, M. A., & Bond, G. R. The problem of being a woman: A survey of 1700 women in consciousness-raising groups. *Journal of Applied Behavioral Science,* 1976, **12**, 363–380.

Lieberman, M. A., & Gardner, J. Institutional alternatives to psychotherapy: A study of growth center users. *Archives of General Psychiatry,* 1976, **33,** 157–162.

Lieberman, M. A., Solow, N., Bond, G. R., & Reibstein, J. The psychotherapeutic impact of women's consciousness-raising groups. *Archives of General Psychiatry,* 1979, in press.

Lieberman, M. A., Yalom, I. D., & Miles, M. B. *Encounter Groups: First facts.* New York: Basic Books, 1973.

Paykel, E. S., Prusoff, B. A., and Uhlenhuth, E. H. Scaling of life events. *Archives of General Psychiatry,* 1971, **25,** 340–347.

Riessman, F., & Gartner, A. *Self-help in the human services.* San Francisco: Jossey-Bass, 1977.

Rosenberg, M. *Society and the adolescent self-image.* Princeton, N.J.: Princeton University Press, 1965.

Sarachild, K. A program for feminist consciousness raising. In S. Firestone (Ed.), *Notes from the second year: major writings of the radical feminists.* New York: Notes, 1970, pp. 73–80.

Schofield, W. *Psychotherapy: The purchase of friendship.* Englewood Cliffs, N.J.: Prentice-Hall, 1964.

Sloane, R. B., Staples, R. F., Cristol, A. H., Yorkston, N. J., & Whipple, K. *Psychotherapy versus behavior therapy.* Cambridge, Mass.: Harvard University Press, 1975.

Warren, L. W. The therapeutic status of consciousness-raising groups. *Professional Psychology,* 1976, **7,** 132–140.

Yalom, I. D., Bloch, S. T., Bond, G. R., Qualls, B., & Zimmerman, E. Alcoholics in interactional group therapy: An outcome study. *Archives in General Psychiatry,* 1978, **35,** 419–425.

Yalom, I. D., & Rand, K. Compatibility and cohesiveness in therapy groups. *Archives in General Psychiatry,* 1966, **13,** 267–276.

10

The Treatment of Depressed Women
The Efficacy of Psychotherapy

Myrna M. Weissman

Depression is a psychiatric disorder of relatively high prevalence. According to recent community surveys, the current point prevalence rate of major depression is 3% (Weissman, Myers & Harding, 1978, in press) and of depressive symptoms is 15 to 18% (Weissman & Myers, 1978). Depression is a disorder of women. The sex ratios are 2 or 3 to 1. This sex ratio is found in every time period and in all Western countries, with few exceptions (Weissman & Klerman, 1977). Depressed patients are usually young women who are married and have children. Depression decreases with age in women. The peak ages for depression in women are 20 to 44.

[1]This work was supported in part by US PHS grant #1RO1MH26466 from the Clinical Research Branch, National Institute of Mental Health, ADAMHA, Rockville, Maryland.

Many different reasons have been proposed for the preponderance of females among depressives; some argue that the trends are spurious due to artifacts produced by methods of reporting symptoms or of differing modes of help-seeking between the sexes. Others argue that the differences are real because of biological susceptibility (possible genetic or female endocrine) or psychosocial factors such as social discrimination or female learned helplessness.

Among those holding a psychosocial explanation for the increased rates of depression among women, there has been controversy as to whether women should be treated for depression at all, and whether the only proper treatment is to change those conditions in society that contribute to the development of depression (Chesler, 1972; Weissman, 1976).

Alternately, there are those who, recognizing the psychosocial contribution to depression in women, argue that even if depression is the result of an oppressive sexist society, women internalize these conflicts and still need help in dealing with the consequence of the internalization.

This chapter will:

1. Review the evidence for the efficacy of consciousness-raising groups, which are oriented toward identifying and changing the conditions in society that presumably oppress women and contribute to their helplessness and depression.
2. Review research evidence for the efficacy of the traditional psychotherapies for the treatment of depression.

The Nature of Depression

The term depression covers a broad spectrum of moods and behaviors that range from the disappointment and sadness of normal life to the suicidal acts of the severe melancholic. There are at least three meanings to the term depression: a mood, a symptom, or a syndrome. Depression as a normal mood is a universal phenomenon familiar to everyone, and one that none of us escapes. It is produced by situations of loss and is a signal that something is not right in our lives.

As a symptom or abnormal mood, depression is also common. Here it is difficult to draw the line between the normal and the pathological. Depressions of mood that are unduly persistent, severe, or inappropriate are usually considered pathological. The symptom of depression is, again, a common one experienced by many psychiatric patients, including many who may not be regarded as primarily suffering from depression.

Beyond the symptom, a more specific and limited psychiatric meaning, that of a syndrome, can be distinguished. The term syndrome refers to a cluster of symptoms and is the clinical depression with which we will be concerned.

DETECTING THE ACUTE DEPRESSIVE SYNDROME

A typically depressed woman will talk of feeling sad, hopeless, and empty, will complain of a loss of interest and pleasure in activities, and will report crying spells. She will look sad, speak in a sad voice, appear to be slowed down, and will lack energy.

Typical symptoms of depression include: depressed mood; changes in appetite; disturbed sleep; loss of pleasure; loss of interest in work; decreased sexual interest; decreased ability to concentrate; feelings of helplessness; anxiety; feelings of guilt and shame; pessimism and hopelessness; bodily complaints; and thoughts of death. There are many other symptoms, and not all depressed patients exhibit all of these features. Because of the diversity of symptoms there have been many attempts to find subtypes of depression with specific symptomatology, age of onset, or family patterns. As a result, several classification schemes have been proposed. These attempts are of considerable research interest, but none is completely satisfactory as yet.

CONSCIOUSNESS RAISING FOR DEPRESSION: THE RATIONALE AND EFFICACY

Employment of consciousness-raising groups as an alternate to traditional treatment for dealing with female depression rest partially on the premise that the traditional feminine role leads to helplessness and that depression is a state of helplessness. In this view, traditional therapies are seen as encouraging women to adjust to situations in which they are helpless and that are in reality depressing. Helplessness and depression can occur by at least two pathways: by real social inequities; or by learned helplessness, which is part of the stereotypical female role.

The social inequity theory of female depression reviewed recently by Weissman and Klerman (1977) is embodied in theories that emphasize the discrimination against women in work, education, and marriage. This discrimination, it is noted, leads to chronic low self-esteem, low aspirations, real helplessness, dependency on others, and clinical depression. These real social inequities make it difficult for women to achieve mastery by direct action and assertion. The implied "treatment" for social inequities on a societal level is political, legal, and social change; on a personal level it is the development of technical skills.

The learned helplessness model emphasizes that the stereotypical ideas of femininity create in women a cognitive and emotional attitude against assertion and independence. This helplessness, which is learned early and is reinforced by society, is the prototype of depression (Seligman, 1975). Part of this view is the belief that women are trained not to be aggressive but are devalued for being passive and dependent. The treatment for learned helplessness is the development of emotional awareness of the condition (i.e., "raising one's consciousness").

Consciousness-raising (CR) groups began to sprout during the early 1970s and are concerned with the social roots of women's helplessness. Bond and Lieberman, as described in Chapter 9, have studied these groups in detail. In theory, the traditional CR group is small (6 to 10 members), leaderless, and has the goal of examining each member's social condition and its ramification on her personal life. Members encourage one another to become aware, to challenge and intervene in the conditions that limit their personal freedom and action. The CR groups were adopted by persons involved in the women's movement because of dissatisfaction with traditional therapies that encouraged women to accept a submissive role.

CR groups have some similarities to traditional therapies. There is opening up, sharing of feelings and opinions in a supportive and confidential relationship. Improvement of morale and self-esteem is the overall goal. However, there are also important differences. The CR group is leaderless, emphasizes peer equality, and relates the woman's problems to social, economic, and political problems of women's minority status. Most important, the CR group starts with the assumption that environmental and not intrapsychic dynamics play the major role in the person's difficulties. Moreover, the consumers of CR groups are not usually seeking therapy.

Women who attend these groups have reported more independence and confidence, higher ambition, and general well-being. Consciousness-raising groups could be alternative mental health resources for preventing the portion of depression that may be associated with women's roles. However, only two studies have systematically studied the CR groups: one completed recently by Lieberman, Kravetz, and Bond (1976), and one underway by Rose Weitz, a doctoral student at Yale University. Neither study has used the technique of a randomized, controlled clinical trial, which is necessary to determine the efficacy of the program as compared to some alternative control treatment. Lieberman et al. (1976) surveyed 1700 women (a sample of convenience) in CR groups in over 41 states. They found that the majority of respondents were white, upper middle class, educated women. These women were dissatisfied with their personal lives and had experienced significantly more symptoms of depression and anxiety than a normative sample (although they may not necessarily have had the diagnosis of a major depression). Relief of personal problems was not the major reason that women attended CR groups. The majority were or had been in psychotherapy and were users of multiple systems of help. Therefore, they did not see CR as an alternative to psychotherapy. They were not undergoing crises and were not seeking help for serious depression, but for loneliness, nonassertiveness, and identity problems. Lieberman et al. (1976) concluded that CR was a misnomer and that they should more appropriately be labeled support groups.

Preliminary results in Weitz's research have shown essentially the same patterns. The groups are largely attended by white, upper middle-class women and, while depressive symptoms were common, that was not the chief reason for attendance. Moreover, many women attending the CR groups were also in traditional treatments, usually psychotherapy.

CR groups in the research conducted thus far may be an adjunct to traditional psychotherapy for some women but do not seem to be used as an alternative for traditional psychotherapy.

EFFICACY OF TRADITIONAL TREATMENTS FOR DEPRESSION

What about the traditional treatment for depression—tricyclic antidepressants and psychotherapy?

The Efficacy of Psychotherapy Alone

There is considerable clinical testimony about the value of psychotherapy as the sole treatment for depression, and it is a treatment that is widely used in practice. However, Lieberman (1975), in an extensive survey of the 1967 to 1974 literature on the psychotherapy of depression, which generated over 200 published articles, did not find any completed controlled trials of psychotherapy that specifically included a homogenous sample of depressed patients, used minimum scientific standards for clinical trials, and had a reasonable sample size (more than 10 patients). These conclusions were also reached in independent reviews by Luborsky, Singer, and Luborsky (1975) and Cristol (1972). Some depressed patients undoubtedly have been included in efficacy studies of psychotherapy. However, Lieberman (1975) found that most of the studies reporting on the effects of psychotherapy in depression generally included unselected populations of troubled people.

Within the next 5 years the situation regarding evidence for the efficacy of the psychotherapies, particularly those based on behavioral principles as the sole treatment in depression, will change dramatically. A number of controlled clinical trials specifically including depressed patients are currently underway, although the samples included are still too small to draw conclusions. Table 10–1 reviews the available studies. Rehm (1976) has tested a self-control program versus social skills therapy and a

Table 10-1
The Efficacy of Psychotherapy Alone in Depression

Time (weeks)	Treatments	Outcome	Reference
6	Self-control/ social skills — Self-control/ group waiting list (*N* = 24)	Self-control Better	Rehm, 1976
4	Cognitive behavior/ attention by rating/ waiting list (*N* = 32)	Cognitive Best	Shaw, 1979, in press
8	Social learning/ doctor's choice (*N* = 20)	Social learning Better	McLean, 1975
10	Time limited/ time unlimited/ minimal contact/ waiting list (*N* = 120)	In process	Klein et al, 1976

self-control program versus group therapy control and waiting-list control groups. In general, his studies showed that the self-control program was the most efficacious in reducing self-reported symptoms of depression. Shaw (1979, in press) tested cognitive versus behavior therapy and used various control groups, including an attention-by-rating assessment and a waiting-list-no-treatment control group. He found that cognitive treatment was the most effective in alleviating symptoms of depression and that behavior therapy and the attention groups were better than no treatment. McLean (1975) has recently examined behavior therapy in depressed patients. Klein, Greist, Gurman, and Van Aura (1976) are testing time limited focused versus traditional time unlimited psychotherapy for depression. Controls will include minimal contact and waiting-list groups.

Although studies testing psychotherapeutic approaches without drugs in the treatment of depression are still in the initial phases, their precision in design and execution provide important paradigms for the conduct of future research (Fiske, Hunt, Luborsky, Orne, Parloff, Reiser, & Tuma, 1970). They include randomized assignment, homogenous and defined samples, uniform entrance criteria, and standardized assessments. Most important, these studies are highly specific as to the nature of the psychotherapeutic procedures, which should help considerably in replicating results in future studies and in clinical practice. These studies will ultimately provide information on the efficacy of specific psychotherapies, particularly behavioral approaches in depression, which can then be tested in comparison and in combination with pharmacotherapy.

The Efficacy of Combined Treatments (Drugs and Psychotherapy)

Although for this discussion we are interested in the efficacy of psychotherapies, it is important to review the evidence for psychotherapy in conjunction with drugs (usually tricyclic antidepressants) since, in practice, both treatments are employed separately, alternately, or combined. Although there is good evidence for the efficacy of antidepressants in reducing the symptoms of depression, those involved in women's issues have been concerned that women may be overmedicated in order to encourage them to adjust to intolerable situations that, in fact, might require social and political change. Therefore, clarity as to what condition and on what outcomes we can expect the different treatments to be effective may help us to understand their utility. For this discussion we will examine acute and maintenance therapies separately.

Drugs and Psychotherapy for Acute Treatments

The research evidence for the efficacy of psychotherapy in comparison or in combination with drugs for the acute treatment of depression, and for psychotherapy alone, is only now becoming available. To date, there are only two completed randomly assigned treatment trials using psychotherapy and drugs in acutely depressed patients (Table 10-2).

One recently completed study was reported by Rush, Beck, Kovacs, and Hallon (1977); it included 41 acutely ill, unipolar, depressed outpatients randomly assigned to twice-a-week cognitive behavioral therapy as opposed to imipramine up to 250 milligrams per day for a maximum of 12 weeks. Both treatment groups showed statistically significant decreases in depressive symptomatology. Cognitive therapy resulted in significantly greater improvement than did pharmacotherapy on both self-reported measures of depression and clinical ratings. Moreover, 79% of the patients in cognitive therapy, as compared to 23% of the pharmacotherapy patients, showed marked

Table 10-2

The Efficacy of Psychotherapy and Drugs in Acute Depression

Time (weeks)	Treatments	Outcome	Reference
12	Cognitive/drugs ($N = 41$)	Cognitive therapy better	Fiske et al, 1970
16	Interpersonal psychotherapy/drugs/both/ nonscheduled control ($N = 86$)	Combined treatment best	Weissman et al, 1977
12	Social skills/drugs/both ($N = 150$)	In process	Hersen, 1976
12	Cognitive/drugs/both ($N = 180$)	In process	Rush et al, 1977

improvement or complete remission of symptoms, and the dropout rate was substantially lower in the cognitive therapy group. This important work is being continued in larger samples and will also include a comparison of the effects of combined treatment.

In regard to studies that are under way, the New Haven-Boston Collaborative Depression Study group (DiMascio, Klerman, Neu, Prusoff, & Weissman) has completed a 16-week study of the acute treatment of depression using a four-cell design: individual interpersonal psychotherapy alone; amitriptyline alone; combined treatment; and no planned treatment (Weissman, Prusoff, DiMascio, Neu, Goklaney & Klerman, 1977). This study showed that all treatments were better than no planned treatment, that drugs and psychotherapy were about equal in symptom reduction and prevention of relapse, and that the combined treatment was the most efficacious and better than either treatment alone.

Hersen (1976) has undertaken a randomly assigned treatment trial that will also give information on psychotherapy (social skills training) in comparison and in combination with drugs (amitriptyline) for 12 weeks in unipolar, nonpsychotic female depressives. A 6-month maintenance treatment phase will be included with similar treatment as initially assigned, but at a reduced rate.

Rush et al. (1977) are testing cognitive behavioral therapy in comparison and in combination with amitriptyline among ambulatory depressed patients.

Drugs and Psychotherapy for Maintenance Treatment

By 1967 there was reasonable evidence for the efficacy of antidepressants on symptom reduction in acute depression, and the most pressing questions were how to prevent relapse and how to enhance social functioning. It was unclear how long patients should be maintained on drugs and if psychotherapy should be added. Three independent maintenance trials using both pharmacotherapy and psychotherapy were funded by the Psychopharmacology Research Branch, National Institute of Mental Health. Maintenance treatment is the treatment of recovered patients in an effort to prevent recurrence of illness. Table 10–3 lists the maintenance treatment studies.

The New Haven-Boston study examined 8 months of maintenance treatment, amitriptyline, placebo/no pill, with and without individual interpersonal psychotherapy, in 150 partially recovered depressed women (Klerman, DiMascio, Weissman, Prusoff & Paykel, 1974). The Baltimore study compared 16 months of maintenance treatment, imipramine, diazepam and placebo, with or without 4 months of group therapy, in 149 partially recovered depressed women (Covi, Lipman, Derogatis, Smith and Pattison, 1974). The Philadelphia study compared 3 months of amitriptyline or placebo, with or without marital therapy, in 196 married depressed men and women (80% of the sample was female) (Friedman, 1975).

There was a remarkable similarity in findings. All the studies showed an effect for tricyclic antidepressants in preventing relapse and reducing symptoms and either minimal or no effect on social and interpersonal functioning.

The New Haven-Boston study found no difference between amitriptyline, placebo, or no pill on the patient's social adjustment. The Philadelphia study found a small effect on participation and performance in family roles, and the Baltimore study also noted a small effect on the patient's interpersonal perceptions.

In summary, the findings in the three studies indicated that maintenance antidepressants, as compared to a placebo or to psychotherapy, were more efficacious in preventing relapse and symptom return. Although some recovery of social performance occurred as a result of the

Table 10-3

The Efficacy of Maintenance Psychotherapy and Drugs for Depression

Time (months)	Treatments	Effect of Antidepressants	Effect of Psychotherapy	Reference
8 8	Amitriptyline/placebo/no pill Individual psychotherapy ($N = 150$)	Reduced relapse, no effect on social functioning	Improved social functioning, no effect on relapse	Klerman et al, 1974
16 4	Imipramine/Diazepam/placebo Group therapy ($N = 149$)	Reduced relapse	Improved empathy, reduced sensitivity, no effect on relapse	Covi et al, 1974
4 3	Amitriptyline/placebo Marital therapy ($N = 196$)	Reduced symptoms, no effect on marriage	Improved family and marriage, slight symptom relief	Friedman, 1975

reduction of symptoms, medications themselves had only a limited impact on problems in living.

The results for the maintenance psychotherapies were also similar between studies. The New Haven-Boston trial showed a positive effect for psychotherapy on social and interpersonal functioning, but only in patients who completed the trial without relapsing. This effect was not apparent on symptoms or relapse rate and took 6 to 8 weeks to develop. Patients who became symptomatic and did not complete the trial showed no benefit from psychotherapy.

The Baltimore study showed a weak effect for group therapy on areas related to interpersonal functioning, empathy, sensitivity, and hostility, but no effect on symptoms. The group therapy effect was evident at 4 months, earlier than noted in the New Haven-Boston study.

The Philadelphia study, which was the briefest (3 months) and used marital therapy, showed an early effect. It was strongest on social functioning and family participation and on attitudes and behavior in marriage. There was also an effect on symptom relief, but this was not as great as on social adjustment or as shown overall for drugs.

All three studies show a positive effect for psychotherapy compared to low contact or to drugs, which was strongest on areas related to problems in living (interpersonal relationships) and less strong or absent on the symptoms of depression per se.

These studies allow us to answer partially some of the hypotheses proposed by Klerman (1976) about the possible negative interactive effects of combined treatments. The New Haven-Boston study results, which found a psychotherapy effect only in patients who remained free of symptoms, best support the hypothesis that drugs have a positive effect on psychotherapy in that the symptom relief, produced more readily by drugs, rendered the patient more accessible to psychotherapy. There was no evidence in any of the studies for a negative interaction between drugs and psychotherapy. Therefore, there was no evidence for the hypothesis that drugs have a negative effect on patients who had experienced symptom relief. Drugs did not make patients less interested in psychotherapy and did not lead to early termination or to poor response to psychotherapy, nor was there any evidence for a negative effect of psychotherapy on drug response. Patients receiving psychotherapy were not symptomatically disrupted.

Our interpretation of the findings from the three studies is that for depressives there is a strong argument for combination maintenance treatments (drugs and psychotherapy). The effects of both treatments seems to be largely independent, operating on different outcomes, and there are no reported negative interactions. Generalization of these results must be limited. They were for maintenance, not for acute treatments, and they did not cover the spectrum of depressive disorders.

CONCLUSION

There is little doubt that women have more depression, both treated and untreated, than men. There is good evidence that traditional treatments, both pharmacotherapy and psychotherapy, have value in the treatment of depression. Drugs essentially reduce the acute symptoms of depression and prevent their return; psychotherapy enhances interpersonal satisfaction and adjustment in the major roles. Contrary to the concerns a decade ago, no negative interactions have been found (Klerman, 1976); that is, drugs do not make the patient less interested in psychotherapy, and psychotherapy does not undo the positive effects of the drugs by making the patient more anxious and symptomatic. The advantage for combined treatment is striking and represents a possible additive effect of two treatments.

Clearer answers about the treatment of acute disorders

will not be available for several years. Preliminary evidence from one study comparing drugs to psychotherapy (cognitive therapy) suggests that cognitive therapy may have some advantage, but there is evidence as shown in the recently completed New Haven-Boston Collaborative Depression Study (Weissman, et al., 1977), that the combination could be more effective than either treatment alone. These promising findings will undoubtedly stimulate further research in the area over the next decade.

WHAT ABOUT THE EFFICACY OF CONSCIOUSNESS-RAISING GROUPS FOR DEPRESSION?

The concept of self-help for learned helplessness has a certain intuitive appeal. I suspect that CR groups, as the sole therapy, probably would not be too helpful and certainly would not work as rapidly as antidepressants for the full-blown syndrome of depression. In fact, self-help groups are now used as a supplement and not an alternative to traditional therapies. These groups require more energy, engagement, and optimism than someone with a moderate clinical depression can muster. Many women attending these groups may have mild depressive symptoms, but few have the full-blown depressive syndrome. Moreover, these groups appeal to a limited subsample of women—the educated, white, upper middle class. I would speculate that self-help groups may help prevent more serious symptoms in many dissatisfied, unhappy, and lonely women and may be useful as an adjunct to therapy following symptom reduction. Self-help groups are certainly as difficult to evaluate as the traditional psychotherapies, probably even more so, since women in the movement share a distrust of behavioral scientists. A deeper understanding of nontraditional therapies such as women's CR groups and an evaluation of their role in preventing mental disorders and in delivering mental health services are both timely and warranted. In the absence of such data, the research evidence strongly suggests that depressed women can rely on the traditional treatments, drugs and psychotherapy, for the alleviation of their suffering.

REFERENCES

Chesler, P. *Women and madness.* New York: Doubleday, 1972.
Covi, L., Lipman, R. J., Derogatis, L. R., Smith III, J. E. and Pattison, J. H. Drugs and group psychotherapy in neurotic depression. *American Journal of Psychiatry,* 1974, **131,** 191-198.
Cristol, A. H. Studies of outcome psychotherapy. *Comprehensive Psychiatry,* 1972, **13,** 189–200.
Fiske, D., Hunt, H., Luborsky, L., Orne, M., Parloff, M., Reiser, M., and Tuma, H. Planning of research on effectiveness of psychotherapy. *Archives of General Psychiatry,* 1970, **22,** 22–32.
Friedman, A. S. Interaction of drug therapy with marital therapy in depressive patients. *Archives of General Psychiatry,* 1975, **32,** 619–637.
Hersen, M. Pharmacological and social skill treatment for unipolar (nonpsychotic) depression. Unpublished protocol, personal communication, 1976.
Klein, M., Greist, J., Gurman, A., and Van Aura, L. Psychotherapy of depression: Computer outcome measures. Unpublished protocol, personal communication, 1976.
Klerman, G. L. Psychoneurosis: Integrating pharmacotherapy and psychotherapy. In J. L. Claghorn (Ed.), *Successful psychotherapy.* New York: Brunner/Mazel, 1976.
Klerman, G. L., DiMascio, A., Weissman, M. M., Prusoff, B. and Paykel, E. S. Treatment of depression by drugs and psychotherapy. *American Journal of Psychiatry,* 1974, **131,** 186–191.
Lieberman, M. Survey and evaluation of the literature on verbal psychotherapy of depressive disorders. Report prepared for the Clinical Research Branch, National Institute of Mental Health, 1975.
Lieberman, M., and Bond, G. R. The problem of being a woman: A survey of 1700 women in consciousness raising groups. *Journal of Applied Behavioral Science,* 1976, **12,** 363–379.

Luborsky, L., Singer, B., and Luborsky, L. Comparative studies of psychotherapies. *Archives of General Psychiatry,* 1975, **32**, 995–1013.

McLean, P. Depression as a specific response to stress. Paper presented at Conference on Dimensions of Anxiety and Stress, Oslo, Norway, 1975.

Rehm, L. P. Studies in self control treatment of depression. Paper presented at session, Behavior Assessment and Treatment of Depression (N. B. Lub, Chairman), American Psychological Association, Washington, D.C., 1976.

Rush, A. J., Beck, A., Kovacs, M., and Hallon, S. Comparative efficacy of cognitive therapy and pharmacotherapy in the treatment of depressed outpatients. *Cognitive Therapy & Research,* 1977, **1**, 17–37.

Seligman, E. P. *Helplessness: On depression, development and death.* San Francisco: W. H. Freeman, 1975.

Shaw, B. A comparison of cognitive therapy and behavior therapy in the treatment of depression. *Journal of Consulting and Clinical Psychology,* 1979, in press.

Weissman, M. M. Depressed women: Traditional and non-traditional therapies. In J. L. Claghorn (Ed.), *Successful psychotherapy.* New York: Brunner/Mazel, 1976.

Weissman, M. M., and Klerman, G. L. Sex differences and the epidemiology of depression. *Archives of General Psychiatry,* 1977, **34**, 98–111.

Weissman, M. M., and Myers, J. K. Rates and risks of depressive symptoms in a United States urban community. *Acta Psychiatry Scandinavia,* 1979, in press.

Weissman, M. M., Myers, J. K., and Harding, P. S. Psychiatric disorders in a United States urban community: 1975–76. *American Journal of Psychiatry,* 1978, in press.

Weissman, M. M., Prusoff, B. A., DiMascio, A., Neu, C., Goklaney, M., and Klerman, G. L. The efficacy of drugs and psychotherapy in the treatment of acute depressive episodes. Paper presented at the Annual Meeting of the American College of Neuropsychopharmacology, Puerto Rico, 1977.

11

Math Anxiety and Female Mental Health
Some Unexpected Links

Bonnie Donady
Stanley Kogelman
Sheila Tobias

𝒜iken (1976), in a recent review of the literature on attitudes toward mathematics, notes that "at the elementary and junior high levels, attitudes toward mathematics and achievement in the subject are significantly related to a number of personality variables indicative of good adjustment.... a high sense of personal worth, a greater sense of responsibility, high social standards, high academic motivation, and greater freedom from withdrawing tendencies" (p. 297). We are not yet in a position to state that the converse of this statement is also true: that failure at mathematics has a correlation with poor self-image, low motivation, and the like. However, we are beginning to become aware of the degree to which anxiety at approaching a mathematical task is appropriate and the degree to which it represents an incapacity to mobilize and direct energies in a positive direction.

The Wesleyan University Math Anxiety Project was not initially concerned with mental health. It was designed first and foremost to tackle the growing phenomenon of math avoidance in college-age and young adult women. Sells (1973), a Berkeley sociologist concerned about the clustering of females in self-stereotyped fields of study at the University of California's best campus, in 1972 undertook a simple survey of freshmen's math preparation in high school. She discovered that 57% of the men came to Berkeley with 4 years of high school math; only 8% of the women had the equivalent background. This meant that 92% of Berkeley's incoming freshmen women were ineligible for the calculus sequence, advanced statistics, and most physics and chemistry courses. No amount of affirmative action, she hypothesized, would successfully integrate women into all fields of study and all occupations until and unless women stopped avoiding math and science. Mathematics in particular, she concluded, is the critical vocational filter.

At about the same time that Sells was studying freshmen and women at Berkeley, Ernest (1976), a mathematician and teacher of statistics at the University of California at Santa Barbara, was noting that his women students suffered real mental blocks in learning statistics. When, in 1973, he was given an opportunity to lead a freshman seminar on the subject of "Women and Mathematics," he sent his students out into neighboring schools to probe pupil and teacher attitudes. The results of 1324 questionnaires are reported in *Mathematics and Sex* (Ernest, 1976), which has been distributed to school districts and feminist educators around the country.

Ernest's (1976) team discovered some interesting facts, many of which flew in the face of traditional literature on sex differences in mathematics. Girls in his elementary and high school sample showed no greater liking or disliking of arithmetic and mathematics than boys, although when asked which subject they liked best, girls were more likely to name English and boys, science. However, when mathematics became optional in the higher grades, fewer girls than boys elected to take mathematics. Ernest (1976) concluded that it was role expectation and not native ability that made the difference.

> ... men take more mathematics not for the superficial reason that they like mathematics more than women, but because ... they are aware that such courses are necessary prerequisites to the kinds of future occupations ... they envision for themselves. (p. 4)

Thus, an upgrading of the counseling program in high schools and colleges, designed to show young women the applications of mathematics, "could have a very significant effect" (Ernest, 1976, p. 4).

Ernest (1976) found even more interesting developments affecting the etiology of female underachievement in mathematics. From the sixth grade on, the fathers in his sample became the family authorities in mathematics, and it was to them that children normally went for homework help in math. Thus, the degree of interest that a father takes in his daughter's intellectual development may be the crucial variable in determining her attitude toward math and her success in overcoming negative peer pressure. Finally, his research documented the fact that whatever the contradictory evidence, both teachers and pupils believe that boys do better in math. Even bright girls presume this to be so. Indeed, as another study at Stanford University revealed, when boys do poorly in math in high school or in college, they explain their failure by asserting that they did not work hard enough; girls who fail are three times more likely to attribute their failure to a belief that they simply cannot do math (Ernest, 1976).

The issue of sex differences in math ability has been studied by psychologists for some years, and the literature reflects a spectrum of explanations, ranging from brain variance (verbal versus spatial ability) to teacher prejudice. Yet, in our opinion, the issue has been treated too globally. Few researchers are able to explain why females fail at different points in math and why some women, despite all obstacles, become exceedingly creative mathematicians.

Kogelman (1975), a mathematician and psychiatric social worker, has also been investigating the dynamics and etiology of math anxiety in women. His initial study was based on group and individual interviews with women graduate students and women mental health professionals. Although the women interviewed were all high achievers in other areas, Kogelman (1975) found that in math-related activities they exhibited many of the symptoms that would usually be associated with a phobia or inhibition of ego function. These symptoms were found to stem from conflicts over feminine indentification or from ambivalence about "detail" (looking at things they did not want to see).

In New York City, Kogelman and Warren (1978), another mathematician who has specialized in working individually with the math anxious, have founded Mind Over Math, a consulting service for the purpose of developing programs to deal with math anxiety in high school and college students and in professional men and women. Recently, they have reported success in alleviating math anxiety in professional women through the use of group therapy techniques.

Not everyone agrees that math avoidance is necessarily the result of math anxiety and that it is psychological in origin. The issue for some educators is simply poor or unimaginative teaching. Consciousness raising, availability of role models, and precalculus training increase the confidence and achievement of many women college students. Blum, chairman of the Department of Mathematics at Mills College, a women's college in Oakland, California, has doubled the enrollment of women in beginning calculus during the past few years by establishing a precalculus course that emphasizes graphing and functions, provides peer tutors, and organizes a program of visiting women scientists, mathematicians, and engineers. MacDonald, of the University of Missouri at Kansas City, created a special section of precalculus mathematics courses in 1975 for women only, and she reported some change in attitude. Hallett has been having some success with women students at Harvard through a newly designed precalculus course for men and women. Wellesley College offered an experimental math curriculum in the 1976 to 1977 year in which math applications to music and design will be incorporated into the syllabus. Brush, Assistant Professor of Psychology at Wesleyan and consulting psychologist to the Wellesley College and Wesleyan University math project, is investigating seven hypotheses to account for math avoidance.

1. Lack of math ability
2. Inappropriate style of thinking
3. Attitude that math is not useful or significant to society
4. Self-concept differing radically from stereotype of mathematician
5. Great anxiety in the face of quantitative situations
6. Perception that parents and teachers have low expectations for performance in math
7. Low career aspirations

It is her hope that once "an understanding of the seven parameters is reached, specific recommendations can be made as to how to halt the frequent and early defection of women from the sciences."

If, however, as Horner (1968) has concluded from her studies of high-achieving college women, anxiety about success is increased when females enter fields where they must compete with men, some therapy and counseling may also be necessary to help those women students for whom consciousness raising and remediation do not suffice. Indeed, in examining the attitude of women toward competence in general, we may see math avoidance as only one of many expressions of a conflict between seeking success and remaining passive and dependent. In a study of several hundred seventh- and eighth-grade girls in a German school, Schildkamp-Kündiger (1974), a German pedagogue, discovered that the only variable that consistently predicted high or low achievement in math ("high" and "low" achievement being defined in relation to native ability) was the pupil's score on a TAT test, indicating conformity or nonconformity with female role expectations. Of the high achievers, by far the majority were rebellious about female role expectations; low achievers were conforming to those expectations.

The "I can't do it" syndrome is precisely what the program at Wesleyan University was designed to combat. Starting with the establishment of a Math Clinic on the Connecticut campus, the project advertised itself as a place where students (and, for short special sessions, adult women) could come, not only to do remedial work in math, but also to discuss their problems in dealing with themselves as they learn mathematics. Thus, in addition to a precalculus course and special short-term modules on word problems, fractions, graphing, and elementary functions, the clinic encourages students to write or tell their "math autobiography," beginning with their earliest school years, including a discussion of the last math concept they *really* understood, and ending with a description of how they feel (or would feel) walking into a mathematics classroom today.

The presence of counselors and instructors trained in psychology is an important element in the clinic's design. For one thing, anxious students are comforted by such persons (see the transcript of typical interviews conducted by Donady, the project coordinator, later in this chapter).

Even more important, discussion of learners' problems from a psychological and emotional point of view among the clinic staff encourages the math instructors to consider seriously the affective climate in the classroom. As Skemp (1971) says, the explicit goal is not to teach mathematics, but to teach students how to learn mathematics. At Wesleyan, an optional psychology laboratory under the direction of Donady is being offered in conjunction with the precalculus course. Using techniques of group and individual therapy (Gestalt and others), the counselors aim to bring to the surface the latent associations that students have built up about mathematics, and eventually to exorcize those that are dysfunctional.

If ambivalence about its "appropriateness" is one major cause of low female achievement in math and science, attention to the issue of math anxiety may offer the counselor a clue to other conflicts in the late adolescent woman. Asking the client how she feels about mathematics may provide insight into other mental and emotional dysfunctions, such as fears of machines, the exercise of power and influence, rigorous or independent behavior, self-sufficiency, or purposefulness.

To illustrate both the dimensions of the problem and some of the techniques being used with students who are psychologically blocked, we present a selection of case examples in the next section. For a substantial number of students, the proportion still unknown, simple counseling, encouragement, and an opportunity to catch up may be all that is required. We have insufficient evidence to claim at this point that math avoidance in women is *always* a profound psychological problem. Yet the case studies that follow indicate that where a psychological block does exist, psychological methods can be employed to deal with it.

These examples come from three sources: (1) women interviewed by Kogelman (1975); (2) a five-session group therapy program for math-anxious professional women run by Kogelman and Warren (1978) of Mind Over Math in June and July of 1976 and; (3) counseling sessions using Gestalt techniques at the Wesleyan Math Clinic done by Donady (1975–1976).

In a final section, we consider policy implications and recommendations.

TREATING THE MATH ANXIOUS

Mary B:
I can't stand to add my check book. I hate it. I get anxious as hell. I avoid it ... it's crazy. I get nauseous.... There was something about math—about numbers. My thinking would get clouded. The anxiety would overwhelm me and I would get terrified that it wouldn't come out right. If someone told me that I got the wrong answer, I would feel horrible, crushed.... I can memorize other things, but when it came to math I couldn't memorize if I didn't understand it.

These statements were made by a 33-year-old female social worker whose academic performance in all other areas had always been outstanding. Her choice of such words and expressions as "hate," "anxious as hell," "nauseous," "terrified," "crushed," "thinking would get clouded," and "horrible" indicate a remarkable intensity of feeling. We may already begin to ask ourselves what it can be about math that is capable of producing such a reaction. We find a similar intensity in the remarks of Alice P. and Peggy L.

Alice P:
If someone was tutoring me in inorganic chemistry (which I associate with math), I would get so upset that I could hardly hear them explaining.... I would block as if there were an internal mechanism going in my mind which said, "I can't do it, I can't understand it." I was no longer hearing.... I felt like I have an intellectual weakness of the brain tissue.

Peggy L:
Mathematics or science are the ultimate test of intelligence. Not being able to do it leads me to feel that I'm really not so bright. Just surface. I must really be stupid. In the beginning of a physics course (which I see as the same as math), I experienced panic. . . . I panicked as I never had done in any course before. I was paranoid. I thought everyone in the class could see how stupid I was. . . . The hate I experienced toward that course was vicious. There is clearly something about the subject matter which is upsetting to me. There is difficulty absorbing it and concentrating on it. My mind wanders.

Again we note the choice of words and phrases such as "get so upset," "could hardly hear," "panic," "paranoid," and "vicious hate." Also noteworthy is the reported inability to hear, to concentrate, and to memorize. People who otherwise have excellent memories cannot learn simple rules because of the intensity of their anxiety. It is probable that concentration on the subject matter is for them virtually impossible.

When memory, attention, and concentration are so seriously impaired, we must begin to ask ourselves whether math has come to represent something else. Is math really just an innocuous set of words, symbols, and numbers on a page? Or is it like a sudden threat to one's safety? These issues need to be considered in more detail. Before doing that, however, it is important to note that all three women believed that there was something wrong with *them*. Almost every math-anxious person to whom we have spoken at length reports similar feelings of personal defectiveness compounded by a fear of having one's defects known to others.

In the presence of feelings of anxiety, fear, stupidity, embarrassment, and defectiveness, conventional teaching methods may be inadequate. If the learner cannot listen to what the teacher is saying or concentrate, he or she cannot learn. Nor need these disabilities be confined to the classroom. They extend to any life task that is seen by the individual as math-related: balancing a checkbook, figuring taxes, understanding statistics, or filling out forms. When faced with such tasks, the same phobic reaction appears and inhibits normal functioning. The task must be avoided; if this is not possible, there may be panic. Thus, a severe restriction of life choices may result. This is the problem as it particularly applies to young women.

We now turn back to the question of why mathematics should evoke such intense reactions. Although the reasons vary from individual to individual, two themes emerge that are particularly apparent in comments made by Betty N. and Diane S. Betty N. recalled:

> I learned from childhood that, in a restaurant, the man checks the check. ... I'm sure that part is a cultural thing that men have careers and are smartest. ... Women stayed home and raised children while men were career men. ... With my peers I had to make up for my performance by being the most popular, the prettiest, "in" with the right group. This was always the most important thing for me until I got to college. ... There was some satisfaction in not being able to do math because it's feminine and girlish not to do it well. It's okay if you don't do well in math and science—it's the boys that have to. ... I'm insecure. I have a conflict about what it means to be a woman.

Betty N. was brought up feeling that men have careers, check the checks, and do well in math. She felt conflicted about what girls do and do not do and even derived some feeling of satisfaction from her own inability to do math. Mary B. had similar feelings.

> In the fourth grade the teacher announced to the class that she hated math. ... I loved my teacher. She was terrific. She was a woman too. ... There was something about being a woman and interested in English and history. ... She was very sweet and kind and understanding. I remember thinking during that year that "I don't like it either—these numbers. I would

rather not have to deal with them. I wish they would go away...." I was embarrassed, ashamed of failing trig. I was this good student and everybody knew. Everybody just had to know.... Now it seems almost willful.

Obviously Mary B. identified with her teacher's dislike of math. A girl or a woman struggling with her feminine identity may see math as a masculine pursuit and reject it. Later exposure to math-related tasks may also reawaken earlier conflicts and result in a new round of fear and rejection. This possibility must be considered in treating math-anxious females.

There is another aspect to mathematics that may also evoke an intense reaction. This is illustrated by Diane S. as she speaks of her problems with math.

I have a tendency not to see things in the world clearly. I have to make myself more aware of detail. I block out a lot of what I see.... It is associated with not wanting to see details of my family life—with not wanting to take a clear look at my mother's problems or my father's distance from me. It has to do with not wanting to take a clear look at their relationship with each other—not really wanting to see that.... My tendency is to distance myself from things emotionally. That's manifested in my distancing myself from really looking at parts of math....

To Diane S. "focusing on detail" means looking at things she does not want to see. Doing mathematics requires a great deal of concentration and focusing on what, to the hostile learner, may appear to be detail. What is this "detail" really, and why does it evoke such frequent mention? For an answer to this question, consider another frequently proposed explanation for avoidance of mathematics: the fact that there are right and wrong answers in math. For example, Peggy L. states:

I don't like the idea of having an answer. I like abstract things where there is no right and wrong. The specificness, the exactness, disturbs me.... I don't like subjects that I can't utilize. I'm very interested in things I can apply to myself. When being tutored, I wanted to move faster and pass over things.... Anything that has a *logic* to it, where there are *steps* involved and a *process* that I have to *know* gets difficult.... I *hate* formulas. I *hate* everything being defined in terms of letters and numbers. (emphasis ours)

It is altogether unclear what Peggy L. means by "abstract things," but it is certain that she, too, would be more comfortable with a learning task that is less specific and permits a more free-floating, divergent approach. The system and, above all, the requirement that the system be followed evoke the most intense reaction. Peggy says, "I hate everything being defined in terms of letters and numbers," but what she really hates is discipline being imposed from without.

Good mathematical performance is enhanced by the learner's ability to separate herself or himself emotionally and intellectually from his or her own thoughts long enough to critically examine them, test them, and either feel confident with them or reject them. Anyone who cannot (or does not wish to) do this will perceive the "logic" of mathematics as exterior and an imposition. For this reason mathematics is perceived as an authoritarian subject by poor learners, but not by mathematicians. In rejecting the "logical thinking" that they associate with mathematics, women, we believe, are rejecting a part of themselves, the part that they associate with being masculine. Thus, Gestalt techniques that expose parts of the self that are in conflict may be used effectively in treating math anxiety. Donady's use of these techniques in counseling sessions at the Wesleyan Math Clinic will be discussed later in this section.

In a series of five workshops with a group of math-anxious professional women, Kogelman and Warren (1978) witnessed the surfacing of many of these issues. One participant felt that she was an "overachiever" and had experienced a "paralysis in algebra" that was "a function I could not deal with." Another woman who had skipped second grade felt that in geometry class "everyone seemed to know, to understand. I felt mocked. . . . I was passed out of pity." One member, a lawyer, said that she couldn't add: "I get crazy if I see numbers." Seeing that their problems were shared, the group members began to feel some relief.

At first, attention was directed toward the anxieties that math problems evoked. Later, the emphasis was on learning to concentrate and to analyze the problems. The members came to realize that their anxieties directed them away from what they knew how to do and toward what they could not do, from competence to incompetence. For example, when offered a choice of problems and instructed to choose the easiest, one member insisted on doing something that was difficult because she firmly believed that "you don't learn unless you are challenged." She would inevitably repeat the common pattern of trying to do too much, failing, being discouraged, feeling defective, and losing confidence in herself.

The next stage of treatment was to demystify mathematics. Throughout the five sessions, the leaders, who have earned Ph.D.s in mathematics and regularly do mathematical research, emphasized that they, too, had experienced difficulties and frustration when faced with new and complicated research problems. This disclosure was intended to enable the participants to feel more comfortable with their own difficulties and to see math as a more human, creative endeavor. The goal was to get them to relate the process of doing mathematics to activities in which they feel comfortable, such as painting and writing. In the last session, members were assisted in reacting less emotionally to math problems; in doing so they were able to tackle the problems with a greater degree of casualness. After the five sessions, all members reported considerable reduction of their anxieties and made comments such as

"I don't feel like I'm being tested anymore," and "I feel more freedom to do math-related things now." The woman who had initially confessed an inability to add said, "I went out to lunch. There was a complicated check. I figured it out in only a few seconds." Another woman found it easier to do everyday things. She reported, "In a cab the other day, I was figuring out royalties and advances more quickly and easily than I ever have before." All the women expressed a strong desire to learn more math. They requested another five sessions in which to learn the basic concepts of algebra, which they had either never studied or never mastered.

Part of the function of the Math Clinic at Wesleyan University has been to diagnose the degree of math anxiety in each client. The mildly anxious respond well to support, tutoring, and guidance while enrolled in regular or remedial math courses. For the severely anxious, the clinic's task is to diagnose the problem, confront the patient with it, and recommend more intensive treatment. In some cases, such as that of Michele S., which follows, an interview exposed the intensity of her conflicts about math that had not been evident at first.

Michele S. came in apprehensive and skeptical. She talked easily about her background and noted that her difficulties with math began in third grade.

Michele: I was always told that everyone knows how to do that, and that I was just not applying myself.

Donady: Did you think you weren't applying yourself?

Michele: I knew I just couldn't get it and I did badly in math in sixth, seventh, and eighth grade. I took just one general math class in high school and did badly in that too. Then I went into the service and did really well (A's) in everything except medical math.

Donady:	What happened then?
Michele:	Well, I was publicly ridiculed repeatedly and I just felt awful so I began avoiding anything that looked like it was vaguely associated with math.
Donady:	How is it in your present math class?
Michele:	Well, the teacher is better. She tries so hard and really wants me to get it.
Donady:	You don't want to disappoint her?
Michele:	Right. That's why I even came here, but I just can't do it. But I know if I can't do math I just never will be able to own my own business.
Donady:	Do you know enough math now to do what you need to do?
Michele:	I doubt it, but maybe I can do my art.
Donady:	Is it worth it to take math or should you focus on your art?
Michele:	I don't know. I just feel so terrible when I'm in math class.
Donady:	How?
Michele:	Stupid. Like I'm a moron, no good at anything. I just hate myself.
Donady:	What should you do then?
Michele:	I'm not sure.
Donady:	How about trying a kind of game? When you sit in the blue chair you'll be taking math. When you sit in the red chair you won't. In each chair talk about how you feel. Let it flow.
Michele:	Okay. I'll sit in the red chair—I just don't want to sit over there yet. I know I'm okay. I can do art, I know a lot about good health. Why should I make myself miserable about taking math?
Donady:	Come over here and answer that.
Michele:	[in blue chair] I should take math so I can own the farm. Everyone should be able to

do basic math. Only idiots can't handle numbers.

At this point she broke into tears and was unable to talk. Once composed, we quickly got back into the red chair. When asked where she felt more comfortable, she said it was in the red chair, not doing math, but she was not sure she could allow herself that freedom.

We continue talking; occasionally she would sit in the blue chair (doing math). She would repeatedly start sentences with "I should." In the red chair her posture was different. She sat up and felt more sure of herself, but she was sad.

Michele: I guess I won't do any math now. I'll drop this course and see how I feel about it in a while.
Donady: How do you feel now that you've decided?
Michele: Relieved a little, lighter, sad. Maybe I'll change in some months.

Michele S.'s choice of words like "stupid," "moron," "no good at anything," and "hate myself" indicates how defective she really feels. To enroll (or to continue to take) a course at this point would almost certainly result in failure and an intensification of her conflicts. On the other hand, since some of her conflicts have been made conscious, she may be receptive to a recommendation for further treatment.

This interview was not only diagnostic. It seemed to have had some therapeutic effect in that her decision not to take math was more assertive than helpless, and she had gained some insight into her multiplicity of motives for trying math. To some degree, taking math has a punitive dimension for Michele S.

At the end of the interview Michele concluded that she is not ready to take math, not that she cannot do it. This is a healthier reaction. The counselor suggested that Michele call again, but thus far she has not. Michele S. may never take math again. Or she may try one course. If she does, she will need support to clear up old feelings and thereby release energy to concentrate on the work.

Math anxiety is not limited to females. Many males find mathematics difficult and even frightening. But when a male has math anxiety, he presents his problem differently. There is more bravado in his presentation and more of an assumption that if he worked hard enough, he could surely do it. The following interview is with a young male transfer student to Wesleyan from a nearby junior college.

Donady: How do you feel about math now?

Eric: Math is not such a big deal. I'm not so impressed with people who can do math. And I'm definitely more confident because I can do word problems now.

Donady: What are your plans?

Eric: Well, I'd like to take self-paced calculus, but I have to pass every course I take next year, since I had to drop economics this year. I didn't have the algebra to do the economics. I'd like to take that same teacher and show him that I can do it.

Donady: What about calculus?

Eric: It sure would be terrific if I could do it, but when the teacher gave me a problem to do, he said I'd have difficulty because of the way I worked the problem.

Donady: How did that make you feel?

Eric: Just like in high school—inadequate, really not sure I could do calculus.

Donady: Let's try a game. When you sit in this blue chair you are the person who can and will take calculus. When you sit in the red chair, you don't take it. Okay?

Eric: [in blue chair] I want to take calculus. I
                 could really use it, I'll be proud of myself
                 and I'll feel so great when I finish it. It'll
                 allow me to do more things. [in red chair;
                 posture is slouching] But what if I don't
                 finish it, I have to pass every course. If I
                 take it and fail or have to drop it I won't
                 graduate.

Donady: Come over here and answer that.

Eric: [in blue chair] I can finish it. Steve said I
                 can do it and I finished the algebra and
                 can now do economics and really feel
                 good. Besides, I can start it this summer.
                 [in red chair] I just don't know. Algebra is
                 one thing, but calculus—that's really
                 hard stuff. What if the instructor is right
                 and I can't do it?
                 [in blue chair] I'll get tutoring. I'll work at
                 it and I'll do it.

Donady: How are you beginning to feel? Do you
                 notice you sit and talk differently in each
                 chair?

Eric: Yes, I guess so—I'm really more comfort-
                 able in the blue chair.

Donady: What is your decision then?

Eric: I'm going to take it. I'll start it this sum-
                 mer and I'll sign up in the fall.

Eric D. also reflects feelings of inadequacy, but these
alternate with a strong sense of ego. It may be that math
anxiety in males is the mirror image of mach anxiety in
females, reflecting their need not to admit to failing in a
man's field. But research on this must be done.

In summary, math anxiety in women first has to be recognized; then its intensity and particular manifestations
must be diagnosed and an appropriate treatment strategy
selected. The treatment may range from counseling to in-

dividual and group therapy. The results may vary from a simple decision to take a math course to a major change in one's personality and self-image. Such a transformation would surely contribute to greater mental health.

Sawyer (1949), a noted mathematician, wrote: "The ideal of mental health is to be ready to face any problem which life may bring—not to rush hastily with averted eyes past places where difficulties are found" (p. 1). We agree. To deal comprehensively with female mental health problems, we should look not only at where women are, but where they are not.

Policy Implications

It would be foolhardy to expect this nation to undertake yet another redesign of the elementary and secondary school math curriculum. Teachers, students, and parents have barely recovered from the introduction of the New Math 15 years ago, and a final assessment of that innovation is yet to be made. Nor can one reasonably expect that in less than a generation one could replace all "sexist" math teachers with new ones who expect equal performance from boys and girls. Instead, we must put our efforts realistically into consciousness raising and the building of support systems such as math clinics in the schools and in the communities to assist women who are ready to be helped.

One institutional change that might be introduced at low cost into the schools would be the provision of specialized teaching of mathematics as early as the fifth grade instead of waiting until the seventh, when it is usually begun. Fifth- and sixth-grade arithmetic, particularly fractions and word problems, where so many of our clients report that their problems in math started, should be taught by a teacher who has at least an undergraduate major in mathematics. Many European countries introduce specialized teaching (i.e., changing of classes) in the fifth grade precisely because they believe it vital that science and math be effectively presented. The rationale for postponing such changing of classes in this country is that the 10- and 11-year-old child is still presumed to need a mother substitute in the form of a single, all-purpose homeroom teacher.

Math anxiety, like so many other female disabilities, can be thought of as institutionalized intimidation of women and girls. Women tell us they did not ask questions in math class because they were afraid of appearing both too dumb and too smart. English girls were not taught the "vulgar" fractions in better schools until the war, because they were just that, vulgar; 11/9 is vulgar, but 9/11 is not. Swiss girls for decades were not introduced to geometry. American males find calculus "manly," and so on, and so on. It is woman's complicity in the process of intimidation that has doomed her heretofore. Insofar as feminist consciousness raising is designed to analyze and eventually exorcize such intimidation, feminism itself will eventually solve the problem for us. But, until then, women and girls need all the help they can get.

REFERENCES

Note. A complete bibliography on the subject of mathematics and anxiety has been prepared by Dr. Lorelei Brush, Department of Psychology, Wesleyan University, and is available from the Math Clinic, Wesleyan University, Middletown, Connecticut 06457.

Aiken, L. Update on attitudes and other affective variables in learning mathematics. *Review of Educational Research,* 1976, **46,** 293–311.

Donady, B., & Tobias, S. Counseling the Math Anxious. *Journal of NAWDC,* 1977, **41,** 13–16. (9)

Donady, B., & Tobias, S. Math anxiety. *Teacher Magazine,* 1977, 95(3), 71–74. (b)

Ernest, J. *Mathematics and sex.* University of California, Santa Barbara, 1976, Ford Foundation reprint.

Horner, M. The motive to avoid success and changing aspirations of college women. In J. Bardwick (Ed.), Readings on the psychology of women. New York: Random House, 1972.

Kogelman, S. Debilitating mathematics anxiety: Its dynamics and etiology. Unpublished master's essay, Smith College School of Social Work, 1975.

Kogelman, S., & Warren, J. *Mind over math.* New York: Dial, 1978.

Sawyer, W. W. *Mathematicians delight.* Harmondsworth, England: Penguin Books, 1949.

Schildkamp-Kündiger, E. *Die Frauenrolle und die Mathematikleistung.* Dusseldorf, Germany: Schwann, 1974.

Sells, L. High school mathematics as the critical filter in the job market. Unpublished, 1973. Available as part of a $3.50 math packet from Wesleyan Math Clinic, Wesleyan University, Middletown, Connecticut.

Skemp, R. *The Psychology of Learning Mathematics.* Harmondsworth, England: Penguin Books, 1971.

Tobias, S. Math Anxity: Why is a smart girl like you counting on your fingers? *Ms. Magazine,* 1976.

Tobias, S. *Overcoming math anxiety.* New York: W. W. Norton, 1978.

IV

Conclusion

Toward the Future—
Liberation and Negotiation

$\mathcal{T}$he recent attention to women's mental health concerns is long overdue. The number of books and articles in this area is multiplying each month. In this book, I have tried to present a wide range of perspectives and new empirical research regarding women's issues in psychotherapy. Many of the chapters, including mine, are reacting to the prejudices against women that have existed within the mental health system. Baker (1978) recently noted that the women's movement in general is in the angry stage. He cites Alinsky (1946), who described the stages of a political movement. The first stage involves making a group of people aware of their oppression. This awareness produces anger, which produces political energy. The angry energy must be directed at an enemy until the movement is recognized as a political force. Once the political movement is acknowledged, the negotiation process involved in politics can begin. Alinsky (1946) adds that anger is no longer necessary and, in fact, can be counterproductive in this last political phase.

Baker (1978) is applying Alinsky's (1946) analysis to the women's movement in general and specifically to the difficulty in passing the Equal Rights Amendment. However, the same analysis can be made of the forces for women's rights within the mental health care delivery system. Early books such as *The Feminine Mystique* (Friedan, 1963) aimed to make women aware of the restrictions on their lives and pointed out that orthodox psychoanalytic theory and therapy supported the status quo. Later books such as *Women and Madness* (Chesler, 1972) and *Psychotherapy: The Hazardous Cure* (Tennov, 1975) generated more anger and directed this anger at "traditional" (psychoanalytic or medical model) psychotherapy and psychotherapists. These angry books were able, in a dramatic fashion, to attract attention to the prejudices within the mental health field. Many resulting articles have attacked these prejudices and therefore directed the justifiable anger at the sexism within psychoanalytic theory and

at the biased views of women held by many psychotherapists.

Perhaps now we can begin the third stage. As Miller
(1973) has noted, penis envy, masochism, innate biological
passivity, and submissiveness should be considered dead
issues. Similarly, the democratic values of freedom, equality, and growth as discussed by the humanists must apply
to both men and women. Instead of continuing to attack
enemies, we must negotiate our demands within the field
of mental health. This requires a more moderate approach, a persistent and data-based demand for specific
goals. Women are in the majority as consumers of psychotherapy and can bring organized pressure to bear on the
different political systems.

As for the specific demands, many of them were discussed in Chapter 1, and reiterated the views of the APA
Task Force. Similar task forces exist in every profession
within the mental health field. In addition to the rights of
women clients discussed in Chapter 1, several other
changes should be negotiated. These concern women
within the mental health professions. They include:

- The allocation of more federal grant money to study the
  problems discussed in Part II, such as childbearing,
  women's work-related problems, and depression.
- Better representation of women within the administration and leadership of professional organizations and
  mental health agencies.
- Monitoring of the quality and availability of graduate
  and postgraduate training in women's issues in psychotherapy.
- Insistence on the implementation of affirmative action
  programs in graduate schools, universities, and agencies. Most women professionals hear comments such as,
  "We need to get around affirmative action, but ...," or
  "We'll interview just to satisfy the requirements." We
  cannot collude in this process.

- Support and role modeling experiences such as discussion groups or seminars for graduate students and new women professionals.

Although women are not in the majority and certainly are not often in decision-making positions with the professional organizations, universities, and mental health agencies, we are a significant number. We can now move beyond anger to these specific changes for the future.

REFERENCES

Alinsky, S. *Reveille for radicals.* Chicago: University of Chicago Press, 1946.

Baker, R. Aunt Ms. needs you. *New York Times,* July 1978.

Chesler, P. *Women and madness.* New York: Doubleday, 1972.

Friedan, B. *The feminine mystique.* New York: W. W. Norton, 1963.

Miller, J. B. *Psychoanalysis and women: Contributions to new theory and therapy.* New York: Brunner/Mazel, 1973.

Tennov, D. *Psychotherapy: The hazardous cure.* New York: Abelard-Shuman, 1975.

Name Index

Subject Index